34,50
77 E

Greece

WORLD BIBLIOGRAPHICAL SERIES
General Editors:
Robert L. Collison (Editor-in-chief)
Sheila R. Herstein
Louis J. Reith
Hans H. Wellisch

OTHER VOLUMES IN THE SERIES
1. *Yugoslavia*, John J. Horton
2. *Lebanon*, Shereen Khairallah
3. *Lesotho*, Shelagh M. Willet and David Ambrose
4. *Rhodesia/Zimbabwe*, Oliver B. Pollak and Karen Pollak
5. *Saudi Arabia*, Frank A. Clements
6. *USSR*, Anthony Thompson
7. *South Africa*, Reuben Musiker
8. *Malawi*, Robert B. Boeder
9. *Guatemala*, Woodman B. Franklin
10. *Pakistan*, S. Aleem Qureishi
11. *Uganda*, Robert L. Collison
12. *Malaysia*, Lim Huck Tee
13. *France*, Frances Chambers
14. *Panama*, Eleanor Langstaff
16. *USA*, Sheila R. Herstein and Naomi Robbins
18. *New Zealand*, R. F. Grover
19. *Algeria*, Richard Lawless
20. *Sri Lanka*, H. A. I. Goonetileke
    Belize, Ralph Lee Woodward, Jr.
22. *Bangladesh*, M. A. Razzaque
23. *Luxembourg*, Carlo Hury

Greece
VOLUME 17

Mary Jo Clogg
Richard Clogg
Compilers

CLIO PRESS
OXFORD, ENGLAND · SANTA BARBARA, CALIFORNIA

© Copyright 1980 by Clio Press Ltd.

All rights reserved. No part of this publication may be reproduced, stored in any retrieval system, or transmitted in any form or by any means, electronic, mechanical, photocopying or otherwise, without the prior permission in writing of the publishers.

British Library Cataloguing in Publication Data

Clogg, Richard
  Greece.—(World bibliographical series; 17)
  1. Greece, Modern—Bibliography
  I. Title II. Clogg, Mary Jo
  III. Series
  016.9495   Z2281

ISBN 0-903450-30-5

Clio Press Ltd.,
Woodside House, Hinksey Hill,
Oxford OX1 5BE, England.
Providing the services of the European
Bibliographical Centre and the American
Bibliographical Center.

American Bibliographical Center-Clio Press,
Riviera Campus, 2040 Alameda Padre Serra,
Santa Barbara, Ca. 93103, U.S.A.

Designed by Bernard Crossland
Computer typeset by Peter Peregrinus Ltd.
Printed in Great Britain
by T. & A. Constable Ltd., Edinburgh

THE WORLD BIBLIOGRAPHICAL SERIES

This series will eventually cover every country in the world, each in a separate volume comprising annotated entries on works dealing with its history, geography, economy and politics; and with its people, their culture, customs, religion and social organization. Attention will also be paid to current living conditions—housing, education, newspapers, clothing etc.—that are all too often ignored in standard bibliographies; and to those particular aspects relevant to individual countries. Each volume seeks to achieve, by use of careful selectivity and critical assessment of the literature, an expression of the country and an appreciation of its nature and national aspirations, to guide the reader towards an understanding of its importance. The keynote of the series is to provide, in a uniform format, an interpretation of each country that will express its culture, its place in the world, and the qualities and background that make it unique.

SERIES EDITORS

Robert L. Collison (Editor-in-chief) is Professor Emeritus, Library and Information Studies, University of California, Los Angeles, and is currently the President of the Society of Indexers. Following the war, he served as Reference Librarian for the City of Westminster and later became Librarian to the BBC. During his fifty years as a professional librarian in England and the USA, he has written more than twenty works on bibliography, librarianship, indexing and related subjects.

Sheila R. Herstein is Reference Librarian and Library Instruction Coordinator at the City College of the City University of New York. She has extensive bibliographic experience and recently described her innovations in the field of bibliographic instruction in 'Team teaching and bibliographic instruction', *The Bookmark*, Autumn 1979. In addition, Professor Herstein co-authored a basic annotated bibliography in history for Funk & Wagnalls *New encyclopedia*, and for several years reviewed books for *Library Journal*.

Louis J. Reith is librarian with the Franciscan Institute, St. Bonaventure University, New York. He received his PhD from Stanford University, California, and later studied at Eberhard-Karls-Universität, Tübingen. In addition to his activities as a librarian, Dr. Reith is a specialist on 16th century German history and the Reformation, and has published many articles and papers in both German and English. He was also editor of the *American Society for Reformation Research Newsletter*.

Hans H. Wellisch is Associate Professor at the College of Library and Information Services, University of Maryland, and a member of the American Society of Indexers and the International Federation for Documentation. He is the author of numerous articles and several books on indexing and abstracting, and has most recently published *Indexing and abstracting: an international bibliography*. He also contributes frequently to *Journal of the American Society for Information Science, Library Quarterly*, and *The Indexer*.

Contents

INTRODUCTION xi
    Acknowledgements xvi

THE COUNTRY AND ITS PEOPLE 1

GEOGRAPHY 4
    General 4   Atlases and gazetteers 9
    Regional 5   Travel 10
    Political 8   Tourism and travel guides 14

PREHISTORY AND ARCHAEOLOGY 19

HISTORY 21
    History of the Balkans 21   History of Greece 22

POPULATION 46
    General 46   Emigration 49
    Internal migration 47

MINORITIES 52

GREEKS OVERSEAS 55

LANGUAGE 64
    General 64   Grammars 68
    Dictionaries 67

RELIGION 71

Contents

SOCIETY 77
    Sociology 77   Anthropology 80

HEALTH AND WELFARE 88

POLITICS 90
    General 90   Communism 94
    The military 91   Politics since the 1950s 95

CONSTITUTION AND LEGAL SYSTEM 102

ADMINISTRATION 104

FOREIGN RELATIONS 105

ECONOMY 111
    General 111   European Economic
    Regional 113   Community 115
    Foreign aid 114

FINANCE AND BANKING 117

INDUSTRY 121

AGRICULTURE 123

TRANSPORT 127

LABOUR MOVEMENT AND TRADE UNIONS 129

STATISTICS 131

ENVIRONMENT 132

EDUCATION 133

SCIENCE 138

Contents

THE ARTS 139
    Visual arts   139
    Individual artists   141
    Architecture   142
    Handicraft and design   143
    Music and dance   145
    Theatre and film   147
    Folklore   148
    Folk customs, costumes, cookery   150

SPORT 152

LITERATURE 153
    General literary history and criticism   153
    Anthologies   155
    Major writers   156

PRINTING AND PUBLISHING 166

MASS MEDIA 168
    General   168
    Newspapers   169
    Weeklies and monthlies   170

PROFESSIONAL PERIODICALS 173

ENCYCLOPAEDIAS 175

BIBLIOGRAPHIES 176
    General   176
    Historical writings and travels   178
    Library catalogues   180
    Specialized   181

INDEX OF AUTHORS, TITLES AND SUBJECTS 185

MAP OF GREECE 225

Introduction

On 1 January 1981 Greece became the tenth member of the European Economic Community. For Greece, entry both constituted one of the most important developments in the 150 years since she gained her independence from the Ottoman Empire and signalled her 'legitimisation' as a European country. For the E.E.C., too, this was a significant step. For not only is Greece, though developing fast, less developed economically than any of the existing members of the Community, but she is the heir to a markedly different historical, religious and cultural tradition. Observers sometimes speak of a north-south divide within the existing Community. But the cultural divide between a broadly Protestant northern Europe and a Catholic south is of relatively little significance in comparison with the cultural divide between Catholic/Protestant western Europe and Orthodox southeastern Europe. The heritage of Orthodox Christianity and four, or more, centuries of Ottoman rule have left their distinctive impress on Greek society and its underlying value system. Greece under the Ottoman Turks was effectively insulated from the great movements such as the Renaissance, the Reformation and Counter-Reformation, the Enlightenment, the French Revolution and the Industrial Revolution that played such a decisive part in shaping the historical evolution of western Europe.

One of the main purposes of this volume is to provide guidance for those, be they academics, diplomats, Eurocrats, businessmen or others with a serious interest in the country, who wish to acquire an informed understanding of the present state of Greece and of the forces that have helped to shape her present society. This bibliography is not intended for the academic specialist in the field of modern Greek studies, a small but growing group, although we would hope that it will prove of value to those embarking on the advanced study of modern Greece. We would, on the other hand, hope that that mythical beast, the 'intelligent general reader', will find this bibliography of use. For, during the past two decades, as

Introduction

the Greek tourist industry has reached the 'take-off' stage, Greece has become the preferred holiday destination of many 'intelligent general readers', attracted as much by the country's antiquities and uniquely attractive ambience as by the lure of sun, sea and sand. A remarkably high percentage of those who take their holidays in Greece return again and again and a considerable number of these take a real interest in the country, its people, its culture and its language. In London alone the number of evening classes required to cater for those wanting to acquire a knowledge of the language is remarkable. We hope that this bibliography will be of use to these informed devotees of Greece and will provide the necessary guidance for those who wish to acquire a more profound knowledge of a society that is as attractive as it is unfamiliar.

In keeping with the other volumes in this series, the overwhelming majority of the titles listed are in English. In only a few cases are titles given in Greek and this only where nothing remotely equivalent is available in English or an accessible Western language, or where the value of a given title inheres more in its illustrations than its text. A few titles are also listed in the major Western languages but again this has been done only when a book is particularly important or where there is nothing comparable in English. Limiting this bibliography to works in English has not proved unduly restrictive, for there exists a substantial and continually growing corpus of writings in English about modern Greece, to join the mountains of literature devoted to ancient Greece and the very considerable body of writing on Byzantine or mediaeval Greece. Much of the most significant work on modern Greece in recent years has come from the pens of Greek Americans and this, in itself, is a testimony to the intellectual coming of age of the 'Greek American community, which has only relatively recently become aware of its economic and indeed, political, power.

The Greek American community traces its roots back to the 1890s, although its growth was severely restricted in the early 1920s by the introduction of stringent quota restrictions. Since 1965, however, these quota restrictions have been relaxed and large-scale immigration has once again resumed. Second and even third generation Greek Americans feel a close identity with Greece. Given the extent to which Greek emigrants and their descendants identify with their country of origin and the extent to which Greece lays claim to the allegiance of Greeks abroad (there is, for instance, a Minister for Overseas Greeks in the Greek government) it seems only logical to devote a section to studies of the Greek communities outside

Introduction

Greece. Much the largest of the communities of this modern Greek *diaspora* is to be found in the United States, where there are well over a million Americans of Greek descent. Greek emigrants have also made their way in large numbers in the post-war period to Canada and Australia. In Australia, for instance, Greek immigrants since the Second World War have been outnumbered only by British and Italian migrants, and there are now something like 400,000 Greek Australians. There are also substantial Greek communities in South Africa, New Zealand and in certain regions of Africa and Latin America.

Another significant demographic development of the post-war period has been the virtual extinction of the once flourishing Greek communities of Turkey (principally concentrated in Istanbul which remains the seat of the Ecumenical Patriarch, the leader of world Orthodoxy) and of Egypt, which in the person of Constantine Cavafy produced one of the greatest poets of modern times. A different category of Greek migrant in recent years has been composed of those who have sought work, on a more or less temporary basis, in western Europe, and particularly West Germany, as 'guest workers'. Whether, now that Greeks will soon enjoy the right freely to seek employment anywhere within the E.E.C., this phenomenon will increase or whether, with growing prosperity within Greece itself, these migrant workers will decide to return home, remains to be seen. One thing is certain, however, *xeniteia*, or sojourning in foreign parts, will form a crucial part of the Greek experience, and it is only right that this dimension of the life of the Greeks in modern times should be reflected in this volume.

Another category of books which figures particularly prominently in this bibliography is anthropological and sociological studies of Greek society. During the last twenty years there has been a remarkable proliferation of such studies, many of high quality. The reasons for this are not far to seek. Greece is a country which since the war has been undergoing a rapid process of modernization, yet enough of traditional society and values remain to afford a fertile field for anthropological research. Moreover, field work is a great deal easier to carry out in Greece than in many other developing countries. We have tried to give an indication of the range of these anthropological and sociological studies, which have added new dimensions to our understanding of the values and mechanisms underpinning Greek society. Greek politics, for instance, cannot begin to be understood without an awareness of the central role of patron-client relationships.

Introduction

Greece is unusual, and probably unique as a country, in the fact that the closer one comes to modern times the less literature is available, in English at least. Over the centuries vast resources have been devoted to the study of the language, literature and society of ancient Greece. Moreover, despite the dramatic decline in the study of ancient Greek that has occurred in the Western world in recent decades, the flow of publications devoted to the ancient world has been scarcely affected. During the last century or so the study of the post-classical Greek world has developed apace and the study of Byzantine Greece is flourishing. It is literally only in the last decade or so that modern Greek studies have reached 'take-off' stage and emerged as an independent discipline rather than a mere appendage to the study of ancient or mediaeval Greece.

Yet if the heavy emphasis in the English-speaking world on the study of ancient Greece has inhibited the development of the serious study of modern Greece, it has not been wholly without benefit to students of post-mediaeval Greece. It was, after all, interest in the physical remains of Greek antiquity that attracted generations of travellers to the Greek lands. We are fortunate in having at our disposal very many more travel accounts, stretching back over a long period of time, than exist for the other countries of the Balkan peninsula. Moreover, many of these accounts, even when their authors' principal preoccupation was with the ancient Greeks rather than their latter-day descendants, contain much valuable information. Some of these travel accounts, indeed, constitute an essential source of information about the Greek lands under Ottoman rule. William Martin Leake, who travelled extensively in mainland Greece and the Peloponnese during the first decades of the 19th century, is in a class of his own as an acute and painstaking observer of the modern Greeks and of the geography of the Greek world. No one interested in Greek society in the decades before the War of Independence, even if they have access to the Greek sources for this period, can afford to neglect Leake's numerous works.

The outbreak of the struggle for Greek independence in 1821 immediately aroused the sympathies of enlightened opinion in Europe and many philhellene volunteers flocked to Greece to offer their services to the insurgent Greeks. The spectacle of the Greeks fighting, seemingly against overwhelming odds, to wrest their independence from their Ottoman overlords provoked a new flurry of writing about Greece. This was of uneven quality. Against the romantic effusions of enthusiastic philhellenes must be set the jaundiced polemics of those who were bitterly disillusioned to find

Introduction

that the modern inhabitants of the Greek lands bore precious little resemblance to the worthies of Periclean Athens. Yet among the philhellenes there were those such as the Scot, George Finlay, who were able to write about the modern Greeks in a manner both shrewd and sympathetic. Finlay lived on in Greece until his death in 1875 and his many writings about Greece are still required reading for the serious student.

The fact that the study of the language, history, and literature of ancient Greece still loomed so large in the intellectual formation of the educated classes of western Europe ensured a steady stream of curious, and frequently perceptive, visitors to Greece during the 19th century, many of whom felt obliged to commit their experiences to print. A new impetus to writing about Greece came again with the First World War, which was to provoke a long-lasting and bitter schism in Greece between those who shared Prime Minister Venizelos's eagerness to align Greece with the Entente Powers and those who preferred the neutralism of King Constantine I. Much of this writing was polemical in tone and was concerned to document the alleged crimes of Venizelists and Constantinists, but the 'National Schism' did serve to focus serious interest on Greece, as did her disastrous entanglement in Asia Minor in the aftermath of the First World War and the huge inflow of refugees that was the consequence of her massive defeat at the hands of the Turkish nationalists in 1922. Throughout the first four decades of the present century, the writings of William Miller stand out for their affectionate yet penetrating appreciation of Greek life and politics.

The complex politics of the wartime occupation and the ensuing civil war, which ranged communists against royalists, acted as a further catalyst to the serious study of Greek history and politics. A number of those who were engaged in liaison with the Greek anti-Axis resistance on behalf of the British military authorities have written accounts of their experiences and the recent opening of the official British and American (but not as yet Greek) records for this period have stimulated a further crop of writings. The fact that in the years immediately after the Second World War Greece became a key battleground of the Cold War provoked further studies, both of the reasons for internecine conflict within Greece and of the effects of growing American political and economic penetration of the country in the aftermath of the enunciation of the Truman Doctrine in 1947.

Somewhat paradoxically it was the establishment of the Colonels' dictatorship in April 1967 that was to give a decisive boost to the

Introduction

serious study of modern Greek history, literature, society and politics. The seven-year dictatorship, whose incompetence was matched only by its brutality, gave rise to a whole literature in a variety of languages. Much of this was polemical in tone, but the international furore aroused by the Colonels and their misdeeds did undoubtedly help stimulate a serious interest in all aspects of modern Greece. Within Greece itself there was much soul-searching in an effort to explain how such a seemingly anachronistic military dictatorship could establish itself in post-war Europe and some of the results of these enquiries are now accessible in English.

Doubtless Greece's acceptance as a full member of the European Economic Community will provoke further research on a country that, uneasily at times, stands poised between East and West. In compiling this bibliography we have been struck both by the abundance of material that now exists in English on many aspects of modern Greece and by the paucity of writing on certain topics. Given the importance of tourism to the Greek balance of payments, for example, there appears to have been little serious research into the impact, economic, social and ecological, of the massive annual inflow of tourists into the country. In 1979, for instance, some 6,000,000 tourists visited Greece, with a population of some 9,500,000.

Acknowledgements
Inevitably a work of this kind is greatly indebted to earlier bibliographical endeavours. In our case we have found three sources of bibliographical information to have been of particular value. These are *Modern Greek society: a social science newsletter*, *Mandatophoros: a bulletin of modern Greek studies* and Evan Vlachos, *Modern Greek society: continuity and change: an annotated classification of selected sources* (Fort Collins, Colorado: Colorado State University, 1969) (q.v.). Although our bibliography makes no pretence to be exhaustive, it is equally inevitable that important works that should have been included will be missing. We offer our apologies in advance to those whose works have been omitted through ignorance, inadvertence or, in one or two cases, sheer inaccessability.

The labour of compilation has been greatly eased by ready access to the unmatched resources of the Burrows Library at King's College, University of London, and of the British Library. The Burrows Library, which is run with exemplary efficiency by Mary Elliott, was created in the 1920s as a memorial to Ronald Burrows, a former principal of the College and a close friend and supporter

Introduction

of Eleftherios Venizelos. It has subsequently been enriched by a number of generous individual benefactions and by gifts from the Greek government. Finally, it is a pleasant duty to thank Adrianne Bradshaw for patiently and efficiently typing the entries, and Victoria Solomonidis for assistance in locating material in Athens.

Richard and Mary Jo Clogg
London, February 1980

The Country and its People

1 **Modern Greece.**
John Campbell, Philip Sherrard.   London: Benn; New York: Praeger, 1968. 426p. map. bibliog.
A comprehensive and rounded introduction to modern Greece, particularly valuable for its emphasis on culture and society.

2 **Greek life in town and country.**
William Miller.   London: George Newnes, 1905. 311p.
One of the most interesting and informative books about Greece ever written. Miller, a distinguished historian and long-time resident in Athens, had a profound and sympathetic knowledge of all aspects of Greek life which is reflected in this book. He wrote of the Greece of his time that 'socially and politically alike, [it] is as good an example of absolute democracy as can be found anywhere'.

3. **The Greeks: how they live and work.**
Brian Dicks.   Newton Abbot, England: David & Charles; New York: Praeger, 1972. 175p.
A comprehensive and easily digested compendium of information about modern Greece, including geography, politics, economy, transport, education and entertainment. Provides a dimension often missing from conventional narrative histories and succeeds in its aim of conveying to the reader 'the main characteristics and problems current in contemporary Greek life'.

4 **Greece: a portrait.**
Athens: Research and Publicity Center (KEDE), 1979. 191p.
A useful compendium of information in summary form about all aspects of present-day Greece, published with an eye to Greece's entry into the E.E.C. Topics covered include the constitution, the political system, the structure of government, the judiciary, defence, international relations, the economy, basic

The Country and its People

statistics, social welfare, religion, culture, the mass media, Greek emigrant communities. Particularly useful is a complete list of museums in Greece. Provided that due allowance is made for the fact the book's purpose is to create a favourable impression of Greece on the eve of entry into the Common Market, a mine of pertinent information, not easily available elsewhere.

5 **Portrait of Greece.**
Nicholas Gage. New York: New York Times, 1971. 300p.

An intelligent and informative account of Greece and the Greeks. The author, an American born in Greece in 1939, provides an interesting and, at times harrowing, account of the tribulations of his native village, Lia, in the 1940s. He records its decline from a prosperous community of some 1,200 before the war to a dying village of some 180, reflecting a decline in village life that has manifested itself throughout Greece. He also has sensible things to say about the Colonels' regime of 1967-74. The book also contains a comprehensive 'special interest guide' giving details on matters of interest to the tourist or business visitor to Greece.

6 **Introducing Greece.**
Edited by Francis King. London: Methuen, 1956. 262p.

A well-written collection of essays on the different regions of Greece, from ancient to modern times, by authors who are either Greek or who have a long acquaintance with the country. Ian Scott-Kilvert writes on Athens, Attica and Delphi; Robert Liddell on the Peloponnese and the Aegean; Peter Sheldon on Crete and Thessaly; Kostas Tachtsis on Epirus; Dorothy Davies on Macedonia and Thrace; and Maria Vassilakis on the Ionian Islands. The Greece they describe has undergone major changes since the book was written.

7 **Passport to Greece.**
Leslie Finer. London: Longman, 1964. 259p.

Although now somewhat out of date, this remains one of the most informative introductions to Greece for the tourist. Charmingly illustrated by Spiros Vasiliou.

8 **Classical landscape with figures.**
Osbert Lancaster. London: John Murray, 1947. Reprinted 1975. 224p.

An affectionate portrait of early post-war Greece by Osbert Lancaster, evocatively illustrated with his own sketches.

9 **The feasts of memory: a journey to a Greek island.**
Elias Kulukundis. New York: Holt, Rinehart & Winston, 1967. 241p.

A story 'of exile, of the *xenitia* of an island and a people'. The author, born in Syros, the son of a ship owner and the grandson of a sea captain of Kasos, and brought up in America, movingly recounts his attempt to rediscover his Greek roots.

10 **The pursuit of Greece: an anthology.**
Philip Sherrard. London: John Murray, 1964. 291p.

An anthology of writings about Greece intended to reflect 'the living fate of Greece, which is not a doom but a destiny, a process rather, in which past and

The Country and its People

present blend and fuse, in which nature and man and something more than man participate...'.

11 **A Greek portfolio.**
Constantine Manos. London: Secker & Warburg, 1972. 118p.

'Each photograph in this portfolio is a personal experience and a particular moment in time for both the photographer and for the subject. The people in these photographs live in small villages and isolated farmhouses scattered over the Greek countryside. They are mostly poor people but extremely proud and strongly defined as individuals'.

12 **Cities of the world: Athens.**
Kevin Andrews. London: Phoenix House, 1967. 102p.

Short, lively, well-written, idiosyncratic but well-informed account of one of the least attractive cities of southern Europe by a long-term resident.

13 **Athens alive, or the practical tourist's companion to the fall of man.**
Kevin Andrews. Athens: Hermes Publications, 1979. 354p.

A fascinating collection of extracts, ranging from Libanius of Antioch to Ernest Hemingway, illustrating the history of Athens. In the words of the author, the book is also a guide 'not to antiquities or streets or entertainments or city life or even history, since it is impossible to quote primary sources for all the main events, but a guide to another area, equally real, in which the Athenian population lives without thinking about it: the dimension of Time'.

14 **Athens.**
William Wyatt Davenport. Amsterdam: Time Life Books, 1978. 200p. bibliog.

Not even the superb photographs (by Constantine Manos and Michael Freeman) that accompany a somewhat uneven text can disguise the city's essential lack of charm.

Geography

General

15 **Greece.**
London: Admiralty, Naval Intelligence Division, 1944-45. 3 vols. maps. (Geographical Handbook Series).

Although by now inevitably somewhat out of date these volumes maintain much of their original value and are a mine of information on the physical and economic geography of the country. The historical chapters form the basis of W. A. Heurtley, H. C. Darby, C. W. Crawley, C. M. Woodhouse, *A short history of Greece from early times to 1964* (Cambridge, England: Cambridge University Press, 1965), 202p. A separate handbook on the Dodecanese islands, under Italian rule between 1912 and 1947, was published in 1943.

16 **Die griechischen Landschaften: eine Landeskunde.** (The Greek landscape: a geographical and historical study.)
Alfred Philippson. Frankfurt am Main, G.F.R.: V. Klostermann, 1950-59. 4 vols. (in 8 pts.). bibliog.

A massively detailed study of the Greek landscape, profusely illustrated with maps, based on the work of the 19th century German geographer Alfred Philippson.

17 **Essays on the historical geography of the Greek world in the Balkans during the Turkokratia.**
B. G. Spiridonakis. Thessaloniki, Greece: Institute for Balkan Studies, 1977. 171p. maps. bibliog.

Contains chapters on the Greek geographic environment; main thoroughfares and cities; Hellenism and the Balkans; Greek demographic dynamics in the Balkans; and Greek population movements during the *Tourkokratia* or period of Ottoman rule.

Geography. Regional

18 **An historical geography of the Balkans.**
Edited by Francis W. Carter. London: Academic Press, 1977. 599p.

Despite its title this is not a systematic historical geography of the countries of the Balkan peninsula but a disparate collection of essays on aspects of Balkan historical geography. Of particular interest to those concerned with Greece are the contributions of J. L. Bintliff, 'New approaches to human geography: prehistoric Greece, a case study'; J. M. Wagstaff, 'Settlements in the South-Central Peloponissos, c.1618'; M. Sivignon, 'The demographic and economic evolution of Thessaly (1881-1940)'; and Richard I. Lawless, 'The economy and landscapes of Thessaly during Ottoman rule'.

Regional

19 **Greek regional development.**
Benjamin Ward. Athens: Center of Economic Research, 1963. 160p. bibliog. (Research Monograph Series, 4).

A study of regional development in a country notorious for its centralizing tendencies. Recent efforts to encourage regional decentralization and regional economic development have not met with any conspicuous success.

20 **The study of Greek rural settlement: a review of the literature.**
J. M. Wagstaff. *Erdkunde. Archiv für wissenschaftliche Geographie*, vol. 23 (1969), p. 306-17.

A survey of some thirty-five studies of rural settlement patterns in Greece. Most of these are in western languages.

21 **Come over into Macedonia: the story of a ten-year adventure in uplifting a war-torn people.**
Harold B. Allen. New Brunswick, New Jersey: Rutgers University Press, 1943. 313p.

An account by the Director of Education for the (American) Near East Foundation (formerly Near East Relief) of attempts to encourage modern farming techniques and improve living conditions among the predominantly refugee populations of Macedonia between 1928 and 1938. Contains much of interest on the problems posed by rural underdevelopment and on peasant attitudes to modernization.

22 **Thessaloniki: the impact of a changing hinterland.**
George W. Hoffman. *East European Quarterly*, vol. 2, no. 1 (March 1968), p. 1-27.

A study of the relationship of Thessaloniki, the principal town and port of northern Greece and long an important commercial centre, with its hinterland, viewed in historical perspective.

Geography. Regional

23 **La Thessalie: analyse géographique d'une province grecque.**
(Thessaly: geographical analysis of a Greek province.)
Michel Sivignon. Lyons, France: Institut des Études
Rhodaniennes des Universités de Lyons, 1975. 572p. bibliog.
(Mémoires et Documents 17).
A detailed geographical analysis of the province of Thessaly. One of the few up-to-date studies devoted to Greek regional geography.

24 **Western Thessaly in transition.**
A. C. de Vooys. *Tijdschrift van het Koninklijk Nederlandsch Aardrijkskundig Genootschap*, vol. 76 (1959), p. 31-54.
A study of the changes that have occurred in the agriculture of the plain of Thessaly, for many years the granary of Greece, in the post-war period.

25 **The land of Nestor: a physical geography of the southwest Peloponnese.**
William G. Loy. Washington, D.C.: Foreign Field Research Program, National Academy of Sciences. 163p. bibliog.
A detailed study of the geography of southwest Peloponnese in its historical context.

26 **A geographical analysis of two villages in the Peloponnesos.**
A. C. de Vooys, J. J. C. Piket. *Tijdschrift van het Koninklijk Nederlandsch Aardrijkskundig Genootschap*, vol. 75 (1958), p. 30-55.
The authors conclude that the Greek peasant 'is far less conservative in his farming system than one might be inclined to think.... In those parts of Greece that have been "opened up" to modern ideas, a strong dynamism is discernible'. This prognosis has been proved to be correct.

27 **War and settlement desertion in the Morea, 1685-1830.**
J. M. Wagstaff. *Transactions of the Institute of British Geographers*, n.s. vol. 3, no. 3 (1977), p. 295-308.
This article examines the effects of two major wars, the Venetian conquest of the Peloponnese (1684-87) and the Greek War of Independence (1821-27), on settlement patterns and concludes that warfare merely accelerated a pattern of settlement desertion in the Peloponnese that was primarily caused by long term social and economic factors.

28 **Vendetta, war and society in the morphogenesis of rural settlements in the Mani, Greece.**
J. M. Wagstaff. *Atti del convegno 'I paesaggi rurali Europei'*. Perugia, Italy (1975), p. 517-29.
An interesting study of the influence of internal violence on the morphogenesis of the predominantly rural settlements of the Mani.

Geography. Regional

29 **House types as an index in settlement study: a case study from Greece.**
J. M. Wagstaff. *Transactions and Papers of the Institute of British Geographers*, no. 7 (1965), p. 65-79.
An article testing the hypothesis that 'by analysing the rural house, the social organization of its inhabitants should be discoverable'.

30 **A small coastal town in southern Greece: its evolution and present condition.**
J. M. Wagstaff. *Town Planning Review*, vol. 37, no. 4 (Jan. 1967), p. 255-70.
An historical and geographical study of Yithion, a town in the remote Mani peninsula of the southern Peloponnese.

31 **La population des îles de la Grèce: essai de geographie insulaire en Mediterranée orientale.** (The people of the Greek islands: an essay in the insular geography of the eastern Mediterranean.)
Emile Y. Kolodny. Aix-en-Provence, France: Edisud, 1974. 3 vols. bibliog.
A massively detailed study, rich in historical as well as current data of the population of the Greek islands, which number almost 1,000. The third volume is entirely devoted to maps and tables.

32 **Crete: a case study of an underdeveloped area.**
Leland G. Allbaugh. Princeton, New Jersey: Princeton University Press, 1953. 572p.
Results of a survey into living conditions in Crete begun in 1948 by the Rockefeller Foundation at the invitation of the Greek government. Much detailed information on the island during the period of post-war reconstruction.

33 **Pobia: étude géographique d'un village crétois.** (Pobia: a geographical study of a Cretan village.)
Guy Burgel. Athens: Centre des Sciences Sociales d'Athènes, 1965. 141p. bibliog.
An in-depth geographical study of the village of Pobia (1,700 inhabitants) in the plain of Mesara in Crete. Full weight is given to sociological, demographic and economic factors. Copiously illustrated with maps, diagrams and photographs.

34 **The Cyclades or life among the insular Greeks.**
J. Theodore Bent. London: Longman, 1885. 501p.
A useful insight into life in the Aegean islands in the later 19th century, with many observations about folk customs then current.

Geography. Political

35 **Kalymnos: island of the sponge fishermen.**
H. Russell Bernard. In: *Technology and social change.* Edited by H. R. Bernard, P. J. Pelto. New York: Macmillan; London: Collier-Macmillan, 1972. p. 278-316.

A study of the sponge fishing industry of Kalymnos which, despite the competition posed by synthetic sponge, still makes a considerable contribution to the island economy, although the traditional practice of diving for sponges is virtually extinct on the other Aegean islands. Particularly interesting is the author's account of the somewhat crude diving techniques employed in the past by the islanders and of the economics of the trade.

36 **Kalymnian sponge diving.**
H. Russell Bernard. *Human Biology*, vol. 39, no. 2 (May 1967), p. 103-30.

A study of the life-style and diving techniques of the sponge divers of the island of Kalymnos. The author concludes that 'the hallmark of manhood among Kalymnian divers is intrepidity to the point of defying death. They pay no attention to the standard rules of diving, especially the rules of stage ascent. In 1965 the casualty rate was over 7%. The Kalymnian case demonstrates in dramatic terms the interaction of cultural norms on physical as well as mental health'.

Political

37 **The Dodecanese: diversity and unity in island politics.**
R. E. Kasperson. Chicago: University of Chicago, 1966. 184p. 2 maps. bibliog. (Department of Geography Research Paper no. 108).

A study in political geography aimed at exploring 'the effects of selected economic, social, and political experiences upon political diversity and unity in the Dodecanese Islands', which became a part of the Greek state as recently as 1947. The author remarks on 'the Dodecanesian's overwhelming sense of identity and self-awareness which continues to resist the inroads of modern technology'.

38 **Maps and politics: a review of the ethnographic cartography of Macedonia.**
H. R. Wilkinson. Liverpool, England: Liverpool University Press, 1951. 366p. bibliog.

A fascinating study of the conflicting pretensions of the various ethnic groups who have laid claim to Macedonia, copiously illustrated with cartographical illustrations. The author's approach to this complex problem is notably fairminded.

Geography. Atlases and gazetteers

39 **Géographie humaine de la Grèce: éléments pour l'étude de l'urbanisation.** (A human geography of Greece: materials for the study of urbanization.)
Bernard Kayser. Paris: Presses Universitaires de France, 1964. 147p. bibliog.
A study based on the 1961 census, covering topics such as the demographic development of Greece, its present population structure, migration and urbanization.

Atlases and gazetteers

40 **Oikonomikos kai koinonikos atlas tis Ellados: Economic and social atlas of Greece: Atlas économique et sociale de Grèce.**
Bernard Kayser, Kenneth Thompson, Roger Vaternelle, Basil P. Coukis. Athens: National Statistical Service of Greece, Center of Economic Research and Social Sciences Centre, 1964. 508p.
There are relatively few serious geographical studies of Greece. This represents a very useful attempt to express statistical data, mainly from the year 1961 (when there was a General Census of Population and a Census of Agriculture) in map form. These tabulated maps cover headings such as rainfall, communications, administrative districts, population distribution and density, birth, death and marriage rates, internal and external migration, education, health, cultivated area and crops, animal husbandry, forests, mineral resources, industry, hotels, archaeological sites and foreign trade. Although much of the statistical information needs up-dating, this is an invaluable and well produced book.

41 **Viomikhanikos atlas tis Ellados: apographia 1963. Industrial atlas of Greece: census of 1963. Atlas industriel de la Grèce: recensement de 1963.**
Athens: National Statistical Service of Greece, 1966. Unpaginated.
An atlas indicating the distribution of industrial units in Greece.

Geography. Travel

42 **Greece: official standard names approved by the United States Board on Geographic Names.**
Washington, D.C.: Office of Geography, Department of the Interior, 1955. 404p. (Gazetteer no. 11).

43 **A gazetteer of Greece.**
Permanent Committee on Geographical Names for British Official Use. London: Royal Geographical Society for the Admiralty and War Office, 1942. 161p.
Contains a useful list of the maps on which this gazetteer was based.

44 **Place names of southwest Peloponnesus: register and indexes.**
Demetrius J. Georgacas, William A. McDonald. Minneapolis, Minnesota: University of Minnesota Press, 1967. 403p.
A comprehensive listing of some 10,000 toponyms in the southwest Peloponnese, the most comprehensive collection so far published of the place names of a Greek region. Italian, Slavic, Albanian and Turkish influences are apparent. A source of considerable confusion with regard to Greek place names generally is the practice of renaming place names clearly of non-Greek origin or of rendering popular names in a more puristic form.

Travel

45 **Chapters on mediaeval and renaissance visitors to Greek lands.**
James Morton Paton. Princeton, New Jersey: American School of Classical Studies at Athens, 1951. 212p. (Gennadeion Monographs no. 3).
Studies of the travels of various early visitors to the Greek lands.

46 **Travels in northern Greece.**
William Martin Leake. London: John Murray, 1835. Reprinted, Amsterdam: Adolf Hakkert 1967. 4 vols.
A classic among the many books of travels in Greece in English. Leake's zeal and powers of observation are unmatched.

47 **Travels in the Morea.**
William Martin Leake. London: John Murray, 1830. 3 vols.
A companion, devoted to the Peloponnese, to the same author's *Travels in northern Greece.*

Geography. Travel

48 Liberated Greece and the Morea scientific expedition: the Paytier album in the Stephen Vagliano collection.
Edited by Stelios A. Papadopoulos, with notes on the plates by Agapi A. Karakatsani. Athens: National Bank of Greece, 1971. 107p.

At the conclusion of the Greek war of independence a French expeditionary force was despatched in 1828 to the Morea, or Peloponnese, on behalf of the three protecting powers, Britain, France and Russia, to maintain the peace. This force was accompanied by the Morea Scientific Expedition, which included naturalists, architects, archaeologists and geographers. One of the team, Captain Eugène Peytier, who was responsible for much of the expedition's geographical work, painted some superb watercolours which are reproduced in this excellently printed and helpfully annotated book.

49 Edward Lear in Greece: journals of a landscape painter in Greece and Albania.
London: William Kimber, 1965. 222p. 2 maps.

A reprint of the *Journals of a landscape painter in Albania, Illyria etc.* (London, 1851), written by Edward Lear, noted both for his talents as a watercolour painter and as a writer of nonsense verse. The twenty lithographs included in the original edition are reprinted.

50 In the mountains of Greece.
H. D. F. Kitto. London: Methuen, 1933. 150p.

An intelligent and entertaining account of travel in rural Greece in the early 1930s by a distinguished classical scholar. Throws much incidental light on the Greek rural scene.

51 Roumeli: travels in northern Greece.
Patrick Leigh Fermor. London: John Murray, 1966. 248p.

A well-, if sometimes over-written account, with historical digressions, of the author's travels in mainland Greece. Chapter 3 contains an entertaining account of the meaning of Romiosyni or 'Modern Greekness' with a well-known tabulation on p. 107-13 of the characteristics of the 'Romios' and of the 'Hellene'. The author's intoxication with language occasionally gets the better of him as in 'Tyrnavos is the Priapic song of a phallophore, Mavrolevfi the ululation of icon-bearing firewalkers'.

52 Mainland Greece.
Robert Liddell. London: Longman, Green, 1965. 225p.

A well-written travelogue which largely excludes Thrace, Macedonia and Thessaly, together with Athens and Attica. An appendix covers the Monastic Republic of Athos.

53 An affair of the heart.
Dilys Powell. London: Hodder & Stoughton, 1957. 280p.

An excellently written and often moving account of the author's travels in Greece in the 1940s and 1950s. Particularly focussed on her association with the village of Perachora in the Gulf of Corinth, which her first husband Humfry Payne, Director of the British School at Athens, excavated in the early 1930s until his

Geography. Travel

premature death. Much incidental information about social and political conditions in a Greece recovering from the ravages of foreign occupation and civil war.

54 The traveller's journey is done.
Dilys Powell. London: Hodder & Stoughton, 1943. 131p.

A moving and strangely compelling account of Dilys Powell's relationship with her first husband, Humfry Payne, and of his relationship with Greece. Payne, a distinguished archaeologist and director of the British School at Athens, died at the tragically early age of thirty-four.

55 Epirus.
Arthur Foss. London, Boston: Faber & Faber, 1978. 224p. bibliog.

An account of Epirus past and present, illuminated by the author's own experiences in the region at the end of the wartime occupation. Epirus is one of the most rugged and beautiful but least known regions of Greece.

56 Views of Attica.
Rex Warner. London: John Lehmann, 1950. 174p.

Although the author disclaims 'the knowledge of a Baedeker' or 'the precision of a statistician', he has written a lively and well-written guide to Athens and the places easily visited from Athens in a day. He writes interestingly of his experiences as Director of the British Institute in Athens, which he ran for the British Council between 1945 and 1947, when Greece moved from liberation towards civil war.

57 The colossus of Maroussi.
Henry Miller. London: Heinemann, 1960. 248p.

A somewhat overblown account of the novelist's experiences in Greece just before the Second World War. The central figure is the poet Katsimbalis.

58 A fringe of blue: an autobiography.
Joice Nankivell Loch. London: John Murray, 1968. 245p.

A chronicle of the eventful life of an Australian engaged first in relief work in Poland in the aftermath of the First World War, and then among the refugees who flooded into Greece from Asia Minor in the 1920s. She subsequently settled in Ouranopolis on the frontier between the monastic republic of Athos and mainland Greece.

59 Mani: travels in the southern Peloponnese.
Patrick Leigh Fermor. London: John Murray, 1958. 320p. map.

Travels in the Mani peninsula, the central of the three prongs that point southwards from the Peloponnese. A rugged people, geographically isolated from the rest of the Peloponnese, the Maniots were traditionally noted for piracy and the blood feud. This latter propensity is reflected in the region's architecture, with village houses taking the form of defensible towers.

Geography. Travel

60 The flight of Ikaros: a journey into Greece.
Kevin Andrews. London: Weidenfeld & Nicolson; Boston: Houghton Mifflin, 1959. 255p.

An account of the author's travels in the Peloponnese while undertaking a study of the castles of Frankish Greece. These travels between 1947 and 1951 largely coincided with the 'Third Round' of the Greek Civil War: the tragic repercussions of the fighting on the villagers he met are a persistent theme of the book. Andrews' excellent command of the language gives a particular quality to this book.

61 The Morea.
Robert Liddell. London: Jonathan Cape, 1958. 255p.

An account of travels in the Peloponnese by a perceptive observer of the Greek scene.

62 Prospero's cell: a guide to the landscape and manners of the island of Corcyra.
Lawrence Durrell. London: Faber & Faber, 1945. 142p.

A delightful personal account of life in pre-war Corfu, long before the age of mass tourism inflicted serious environmental damage to the island, together with a short appendix for travellers.

63 Aegean Greece.
Robert Liddell. London: Jonathan Cape, 1954. 284p.

A well-written account of travels in the Aegean, written by a long-time resident in Greece.

64 Reflections on a marine Venus: a companion to the landscape of Rhodes.
Lawrence Durrell. London: Faber & Faber, 1953. 198p. bibliog.

A delightful and beautifully written account of Rhodes immediately after the Second World War, with a calendar of flowers and saints for the island, together with an appendix on peasant remedies.

65 Night sky at Rhodes.
Stephen Toulmin. London: Methuen, 1963. 221p. map.

An account of the making of a documentary film about the origins of Greek science. Intelligent, informative and well-written, providing many insights into contemporary Greece.

66 The Great Island: a study of Crete.
Michael Llewellyn Smith. London: Longman, 1965. 182p.

A highly readable travel account-cum-history of Crete or the 'Great Island', the only part of Greece occasionally to manifest autonomist tendencies. The book is a clear guide to the history and culture of an island that fell to the Ottoman Turks only in 1669. From the early 13th century it developed a flourishing popular literature much inspired by Italian models. The island, which was the birthplace

Geography. Tourism and travel guides

of Greece's most famous statesman, Eleftherios Venizelos, was reunited with the kingdom of Greece in 1912.

67 **The stronghold: an account of the four seasons in the White Mountains of Crete.**
Xan Fielding. London: Secker & Warburg, 1953. 316p. map.

An account 'of a more or less carefree year spent among people who seem to fit so perfectly into their startling surroundings that at times I imagined it was not the landscape that had conditioned their lives but their personalities that had conditioned the landscape'. The author had, some ten years earlier, spent three years on the island as a British liaison officer during the occupation.

68 **The villa Ariadne.**
Dilys Powell. London: Hodder & Stoughton, 1973. 252p.

A beautifully written account, impressionistic and atmospheric, of the involvement of British archaeologists in Cretan excavations, named after Sir Arthur Evans' villa at Knossos, which subsequently passed into the hands of the British School at Athens. A large part of the book is taken up with a fascinating and moving reconstruction of how one such archaeologist, J. D. S. Pendlebury, met his death during the German airborne invasion of Crete in May 1941.

69 **The winds of Crete.**
David McNeil Doren. London: John Murray, 1974.

An account by an American of his six years living on Crete; provides a useful insight into rural life on the Greek islands.

Tourism and travel guides

70 **Greece 1978.**
Athens: National Tourist Organization of Greece, 1977. 255p.

Handsomely produced yearbook for intending tourists to Greece. Beautifully illustrated, with useful maps and up-to-date information on internal travel and hotel accommodation.

71 **Tourism policy and international tourism in OECD member countries.**
Paris: Organization for Economic Co-operation and Development. Annual.

Scattered information on the development of tourism in Greece may be found in these annual volumes.

Geography. Tourism and travel guides

72 The Blue Guides: Greece.
Stuart Rossiter. London: Ernest Benn; New York: Rand McNally, 1977. 3rd ed. 768p. maps.

Probably the best and most comprehensive single volume guide to Greece.

73 Pausanias' guide to Greece.
Translated from the Greek and with an introduction by Peter Levi. Harmondsworth, England: Penguin Books, 1971. 2 vols. maps. bibliog.

Pausanias, a doctor from Asia Minor, travelled extensively in mainland Greece during the 2nd century A.D. and recorded what he saw in painstaking detail. Peter Levi has produced an admirable edition of this fundamental work.

74 Hellenic traveller: a guide to the ancient sites of Greece and the Aegean.
Guy Pentreath. London: Faber & Faber; New York: Crowell, 1964. 338p. map.

A guide to the sites of ancient Greece prompted by the author's long years of experience as a lecturer for Swan's Hellenic Cruises.

75 The living past of Greece: a time-traveller's tour of historic and prehistoric places.
A. R. Burn, Mary Burn, with a foreword by Lawrence Durrell. London: Herbert Press, 1980. 288p. bibliog.

A scholarly but lively guide to the physical remains of Greek antiquity.

76 Greece.
Robin Mead. London: Batsford, 1976. 168p. maps.

A useful, basic and up-to-date introduction to Greece.

77 Villes et paysages de Grèce: Athènes et ses monuments du xviie siècle à nos jours. (Towns and landscapes of Greece: Athens and its monuments from the 17th century to the present.)
Lya Matton, Raymond Matton. Athens: Institut Français d'Athènes, 1963. 342p. bibliog. maps.

A comprehensive and well-illustrated guide to Athens and its monuments, accompanied by excellent maps and illustrations.

78 The companion guide to southern Greece: Athens, the Peloponnese, Delphi.
Brian de Jongh. London: Collins, 1972. 415p. bibliog.

A comprehensive guide to southern Greece, mainly focussed on antiquity but with some attention to more recent times.

Geography. Tourism and travel guides

79 Monemvasia: the Gibraltar of Greece.
W. R. Elliot. London: Denis Dobson, 1971. 128p. bibliog.

A description, larded with quotations from historical sources, of one of the most beautiful towns of Greece.

80 The Blue Guides: Crete.
Stuart Rossiter. London: Ernest Benn; Chicago: Rand McNally, 1974. 117p. maps.

As carefully written and as useful as its companion volume on Greece (q.v.). Notable for its outstandingly clear maps.

81 Travellers' guide: Crete.
John Bowman. London: Jonathan Cape, 1970. 280p.

A detailed, well-written and informed guide to the antiquities of the 'Great Island' of Crete, with particular emphasis on the remains of Minoan civilization. It also contains useful practical information for the intending tourist.

82 The traveller's guide to Corfu and the other Ionian islands.
Martin Young. London: Jonathan Cape, 1971. 344p. bibliog. maps.

A comprehensive guide, with much practical information, to the Ionian Islands whose several centuries of Venetian rule, while the rest of Greece was subject to the Ottoman Turks, have left a distinctive impression on the society and architecture of the islands.

83 The Ionian Islands: Zakynthos to Corfu.
Arthur Foss. London: Faber & Faber, 1969. 272p. bibliog. maps.

A well-written account of the Ionian islands, with many historical asides. A less practical guide than Martin Young's *Travellers' guide* (see preceding item).

84 Corfu.
Margaret Hopkins. London: Batsford, 1977. 176p. map.

An introductory guide to Corfu, the largest of the Ionian islands.

85 The companion guide to the Greek islands.
Ernle Bradford. London: Collins; New York: Harper & Row, 1975. 320p. maps.

A detailed and well-illustrated guide to the Greek islands.

86 The Greek islands.
Lawrence Durrell. London: Faber & Faber, 1978. 287p. map.

A guide to the islands of Greece, accompanied by a useful appendix listing the flowers and festivals of the islands month by month.

Geography. Tourism and travel guides

87 Greek island hopping: a handbook for the independent traveller.
Dana Facaros.   London: Gentry Books; New York: Hippocrene Books, 1979. 352p.

A comprehensive and up-to-date guide to the Greek islands aimed at the non-package tourist, with maps, lists of hotels, etc.

88 The Aegean: a sea guide to its coasts and islands.
H. M. Denham.   London: John Murray, 1970. 2nd ed. 247p.

An invaluable guide for those fortunate enough to be able to navigate their own craft around the Aegean. It is replete with useful tips, maps and historical information for intrepid navigators. The author's love for the waters of the eastern Mediterranean survived an initiation as a seventeen-year-old midshipman atop the crow's nest of a battleship during the Dardanelles campaign of 1915.

89 The Ionian islands to Rhodes: a sea guide.
H. M. Denham.   London: John Murray, 1972. 130p. maps.

A guide to the Aegean for the yachtsman, profusely illustrated with sketch maps and photographs.

90 The traveller's guide to Rhodes.
Jean Currie.   London: Jonathan Cape, 1975. Rev. ed. 272p. maps. bibliog.

A comprehensive and practical guide to the largest of the Dodecanese islands, Rhodes, which is largely overrun by Scandinavian tourists during the summer months.

91 Motoring and camping in Greece.
Andrew Christie.   London: Faber & Faber, 1965. 280p.

A guide for the motorist and camper. The author rightly claims that 'motorists with a few years experience of stock car racing feel quite at home on the streets of Athens' and that 'no motorist is ever quite the same after driving through Athens'.

92 Die Bergwelt Griechenlands: ein Führer für Wanderer und Bergsteiger. (The mountain world of Greece: a guide for hikers and climbers.)
Orestis M. Colettis.   Stuttgart, G.F.R.: J. Fink Verlag, 1963. 134p. maps. bibliog.

A guide for the hiker and mountaineer in Greece, accompanied by useful maps.

93 Flowers of Greece and the Aegean.
Anthony Huxley, William Taylor.   London: Chatto & Windus, 1977. 180p. map.

A profusely illustrated guide to the flora of Greece and the eastern Mediterranean.

Geography. Tourism and travel guides

94 **Flowers of the Mediterranean.**
Oleg Polunin, Anthony Huxley. London: Chatto & Windus, 1965. Reprinted, 1978. 260p. maps. bibliog.
A profusely illustrated guide to the wild flowers of the Mediterranean lands.

Prehistory and Archaeology

95 **The Mycenaeans.**
William Taylor. London: Thames & Hudson, 1961. 243p. bibliog.

A popular but scholarly interpretation of the Mycenaean age, copiously illustrated. Contains a useful summary of the 'Linear B' controversy.

96 **Greece in the Bronze Age.**
Emily Vermeule. Chicago, London: University of Chicago Press, 1964. 406p. bibliog.

A thorough yet readable account of the Bronze Age in Greece. Well-illustrated.

97 **Ancient Greece from the air.**
R. V. Schoeder. London: Thames & Hudson, 1974. 256p. bibliog.

The results of an imaginative scheme to photograph the most significant sites of ancient Greece from the air. The spectacular photographs and helpful maps add a new dimension to the study of the topography of ancient Greece.

98 **The Minnesota Messenia expedition: reconstructing a Bronze Age regional environment.**
Edited by William A. McDonald, George R. Rapp. Minneapolis, Minnesota: University of Minnesota Press, 1972. 338p. maps.

Starting with an anthropological study of a contemporary farming community in Messenia, successive chapters gradually work backwards in an effort to reconstruct, on an interdisciplinary basis, the regional environment of Bronze Age Messenia. A good example of the 'new' archaeology in action.

Prehistory and Archaeology

99 Greek architecture.
A. W. Lawrence. Harmondsworth, England: Penguin Books, 1957. 327p. maps. bibliog. (The Pelican History of Art Z11).

A comprehensive, clearly written and well-illustrated history of the architecture of Greece from neolithic until Roman times.

100 A handbook of Greek art.
G. M. A. Richter. London: Phaidon, 1959. 421p. bibliog.

A massively illustrated study covering architecture, sculpture, gems, coins, jewellery, metalwork, pottery and vase painting, glass, furniture, textiles, paintings and mosaics.

101 Greece and its myths.
Michael Senior. London: Gollancz, 1978. 286p. maps. bibliog.

A popular account of the 'myths of Greece viewed in the context of the places to which they are related'. Its value to the tourist is enhanced by illustrations.

102 Lord Elgin and the marbles.
William St. Clair. London: Oxford University Press, 1967. 309p. bibliog.

The story of how the Elgin marbles, the most impressive of the surviving sculptures of the Parthenon, ended up in the British Museum in the early 19th century. Although a convincing case can be made that Lord Elgin effectively saved many of the sculptures from inevitable destruction, it is not surprising that the Greeks resent the fact that such an important element in their cultural heritage is to be found abroad. St. Clair tells an intriguing story with verve and skill.

History

History of the Balkans

103 Southeastern Europe under Ottoman rule 1354-1804.
Peter F. Sugar. Seattle, Washington; London: University of Washington Press, 1977. 365p. bibliog. (A History of East Central Europe, vol. 5).

A scholarly history of the Balkans under Ottoman rule providing the indispensable overall context in which the Greek national movement developed. Particularly useful for the Ottoman background. Contains a detailed bibliographical essay and appendices listing the reigns of the Ottoman sultans, major military campaigns, Phanariot princes of Moldavia and Wallachia, a glossary of geographical names, etc.

104 The establishment of the Balkan national states, 1804-1920.
Charles Jelavich, Barbara Jelavich. Seattle, Washington; London: University of Washington Press, 1977. 358p. maps. bibliog. (A History of East Central Europe, vol. 8).

The 19th and early 20th centuries witnessed the emergence of the states that now comprise the Balkans. This study provides a useful overview of this process and enables the Greek national movement to be studied in its overall Balkan context.

105 The eastern question 1774-1923: a study in international relations.
M. S. Anderson. London: Macmillan; New York: St. Martin's Press, 1966. 436p. bibliog.

Given that the independence which Greece secured in the 1830s was heavily qualified and dependent on the goodwill of the Great Powers, and that the new state laid claim to large areas inhabited predominantly by Greeks but under Ottoman rule, a knowledge of Great Power rivalries in the Balkans and Near East in modern times is essential for an understanding of modern Greek history.

History of Greece

Ancient Greece

106 **The world of Odysseus.**
Moses Finley. Harmondsworth, England: Penguin Books, 1972. 191p. bibliog.
A penetrating insight into Greek society in Homeric times; that is, in the centuries after the end of the Mycenaean age, but before the rise of the city-states.

107 **The ancient Greeks.**
M. I. Finley. London: Chatto & Windus, 1963. 207p. bibliog. maps.
A lucid short account of the world of the ancient Greeks, with chapters on archaic Greece, the classical city-state, literature, science, philosophy and popular morals, the visual arts and the Hellenistic age.

108 **A history of Greece to the death of Alexander the Great.**
J. B. Bury, revised by Russell Meiggs. London: Macmillan, 1951. 3rd ed. 925p.
A classic history of Greece up to and including the age of Alexander the Great.

109 **A traveller's history of Greece.**
A. R. Burn. London: Hodder & Stoughton, 1965. 332p. bibliog. map.
A history of Greece up until the Roman occupation 'including literature, art, philosophy, science, religion, etc. suitable for a bright science graduate to read from cover to cover in the train from Ostend to Athens'. Although few now make the arduous three-day train journey to Greece, this book admirably fills its intended purpose.

110 **The Greek experience.**
Maurice Bowra. London: Weidenfeld & Nicolson; Cleveland, Ohio: World Publishing, 1957. 211p.
A highly successful attempt by a distinguished classical scholar to form 'some general picture of what the Greeks were', covering roughly the period from Homer to the fall of Athens in 404 B.C.

111 **The Greeks overseas.**
John Boardman. Harmondsworth, England: Penguin Books, 1964. 288p.
A study of the way in which the Greeks left the imprint of their civilization on both East and West in ancient times.

History. History of Greece. Byzantium

112 **Ancient Greek literature.**
Maurice Bowra. London: Oxford University Press, 1967. 137p. bibliog.

A lucid and concise account of the literature of ancient Greece, among European literatures 'the earliest of which anything has survived, and it has had the widest influence on posterity'.

113 **The heritage of Hellenism.**
John Ferguson. London: Thames & Hudson, 1973. 180p. bibliog. maps.

A well-illustrated short account of the Hellenistic age in the eastern Mediterranean between the death of Alexander the Great in 323 B.C. and the battle of Actium in 31 B.C.

Byzantium

114 **History of the Byzantine state.**
George Ostrogorsky, translated from the German by Joan Hussey. Oxford, England: Blackwell, 1968; New Brunswick, New Jersey: Rutgers University Press, 1957. 616p.

An authoritative history of the Byzantine Empire.

115 **The Cambridge mediaeval history, vol. 4. The Byzantine Empire. Pt. 1: Byzantium and its neighbours. Pt. 2: Government, church and civilization.**
Edited by J. M. Hussey, with the assistance of D. M. Nicol, G. Cowan. Cambridge, England: Cambridge University Press, 1966-67.

A comprehensive survey of the thousand year Empire of Byzantium, giving due weight to both political and cultural factors.

116 **The history of the decline and fall of the Roman Empire.**
Edward Gibbon, edited by J. B. Bury. London: Methuen, 1909. 5th ed. 7 vols.

The definitive edition of Gibbon's immortal account of 'the triumph of barbarism' and of 'the extinction of a degenerate race of princes'. Bury also provided an introduction, appendices and an index.

History. History of Greece. General histories of modern Greece

117 **Byzantium and Byzantinism.**
Romilly Jenkins. Cincinnati, Ohio: University of Cincinnati, 1963. 42p. (Lectures in Memory of Louise Taft Semple).

An amusing and learned, if not altogether convincing, attempt to revive the thesis of the early 19th century German historian J. Ph. Fallmerayer that the modern Greeks are not the lineal descendants of the ancient Greeks.

General histories of modern Greece

118 **A history of Greece from its conquest by the Romans to the present time, B.C. 146 to A.D. 1864.**
George Finlay, revised by H. F. Tozer. Oxford, England: Clarendon Press, 1877. 7 vols.

Finlay first went to Greece as a philhellene volunteer during the War of Independence and lived in Athens until his death in 1875. A trenchant observer of the politics of the fledgling Greek state, his history is still required reading.

119 **Modern Greece: a short history.**
C. M. Woodhouse. London: Faber & Faber, 1977. 2nd ed. 332p. bibliog. maps.

A concise and well-written account of the history of the Greeks from the rise of Constantinople in 320 A.D. to the downfall of the Colonels' regime in 1974.

120 **A short history of modern Greece.**
Richard Clogg. Cambridge, England: Cambridge University Press, 1979. 242p. bibliog. map.

A short history of Greece from 1204 until 1978, with the principal emphasis on the 20th century.

121 **Greece without columns: the making of the modern Greeks.**
David Holden. London: Faber & Faber, 1972. 336p. bibliog.

A jaundiced but at times perceptive view of the Greeks and their history. The author takes a relatively sympathetic view of the Colonels' regime.

122 **The unification of Greece 1770-1923.**
Douglas Dakin. London: Ernest Benn; New York: St. Martin's Press, 1972. 344p. bibliog. maps.

A large-scale study of the process of the unification of the Greek state. The author distinguishes four wars of independence: the first between 1821 and 1832; the second the struggle of the Cretans for *enosis*, or union, with the motherland between 1866 and 1908; the third, the Macedonian struggle between 1897 and the First and Second Balkan wars in 1912-13; the fourth, the struggle in Thrace and Asia Minor between 1919 and 1922. Useful appendices provide a dynastic

History. History of Greece. 1453-1821

table of the Greek monarchy and a comprehensive listing of the governments of Greece between 1833 and 1924.

123 **The Greek tragedy.**
Constantine Tsoucalas. Harmondsworth, England: Penguin, 1969. 208p.

An impressively argued attempt to explain the historical origins of the Colonels' dictatorship of April 1967 and to analyse the 'constellation of social, political and international forces' that made this and earlier interruptions to orderly political development possible.

124 **Greece in transition: essays in the history of modern Greece, 1821-1974.**
Edited by John T. A. Koumoulides, with the assistance of Domna Visvizi-Dontas. London: Zeno, 1977. 334p.

A collection of essays on various aspects of modern Greece, with chapters covering history, politics, foreign relations, the church, the monarchy, the press and the army.

125 **Modern Greek nationalism.**
Stephen G. Xydis. In: *Nationalism in Eastern Europe.* Edited by Peter F. Sugar, Ivo J. Lederer. Seattle, Washington; London: University of Washington Press, 1969. p. 207-58.

A study of the development in recent centuries of Greek nationalism, an understanding of which is essential for an understanding of the historical evolution of the modern Greek state.

126 **Greece: past and present.**
Edited by John T. A. Koumoulides. Muncie, Indiana: Ball State University, 1979. 156p.

The proceedings of a conference on Greece past and present, a number of the articles of which are of value to those interested in modern Greece.

1453-1821

127 **The fall of Constantinople.**
Steven Runciman. Cambridge, England: Cambridge University Press, 1965. 256p. bibliog.

A superbly written, exciting yet scholarly account of the conquest of Constantinople in 1453 by the Ottoman Turks, an event that was to send shockwaves through Christian Europe.

History. History of Greece. 1453-1821

128 The Greek nation, 1453-1669: the cultural and economic background of modern Greek society.
Apostolos E. Vacalopoulos, translated from the Greek by Ian Moles, Phania Moles. New Brunswick, New Jersey: Rutgers University Press, 1976. 457p. maps.

A massively documented history of one of the least known periods of modern Greek history by one of the country's leading historians.

129 The making of modern Greece: from Byzantium to independence.
D. A. Zakythinos, translated from the Greek and introduced by K. R. Johnstone. Oxford, England: Blackwell; Totowa, New Jersey: Rowman & Littlefield, 1976. 235p. bibliog.

A somewhat old-fashioned and unsystematic, but scholarly survey of the 'Dark Ages' of Greek history, the period of Turkish rule. Well translated.

130 Aegean quest: a search for Venetian Greece.
Eric Forbes-Boyd. London: Dent, 1970. 203p.

A popular account of Venetian rule in Euboea and a number of the islands of the Aegean.

131 Studies in Latin Greece, A.D. 1205-1715.
P. W. Topping. London: Variorum, 1977. 394p.

A collection of reprinted articles on various aspects of the history and society of Frankish Greece. Affords interesting insight into the sometimes uneasy accommodation that existed between Latin Catholic overlord and Greek Christian subject.

132 The 'past' in medieval and modern Greek culture.
Edited by Speros Vryonis. Malibu, California: Undena Publications, 1978. 256p.

Progonoplexia, or obsession with the ancestral past, has long been one of the most characteristic features of Greek culture ever since the first stirrings of the Greek national movement in the 18th century. A number of articles in this collection of symposium papers throw light on the burden of the past on modern Greece, e.g., John A. Petropulos, 'The modern Greek state and the Greek past'; Evangelos Petrounias, 'The modern Greek language and diglossia'; Margaret Alexiou, 'Modern Greek folklore and its relation to the past: the evolution of Charos in Greek tradition'; Speros Vryonis, 'Recent scholarship on continuity and discontinuity of culture: classical Greeks, Byzantines, modern Greeks'.

133 The revival of Greek thought 1620-1830.
G. P. Henderson. Edinburgh, London: Scottish Academic Press; Albany, New York: State University of New York Press, 1971. 216p.

A competent survey, which incorporates the findings of recent Greek research on the subject, of the intellectual awakening that was such a significant feature of the decades before the outbreak of the Greek War of Independence in 1821.

History. History of Greece. 1453-1821

134 Greek ethnic survival under Ottoman domination.
Perry A. Bialor. In: *The limits of integration: ethnicity and nationalism in modern Europe*. Edited by Oriol Pi-Sunyer. Amherst, Massachusetts: Department of Anthropology, University of Massachusetts, 1971. p. 43-76. (Research Report 9).

An analysis of 'some of the structural factors determining the character of interaction between the dominant Muslim-Turkish society and the subject Balkan Greek population which militated against assimilation and encouraged the maintenance of ethnic boundaries of the subject group'.

135 Travel literature and the rise of neo-Hellenism in England.
James M. Osborn. *Bulletin of the New York Public Library*, vol. 67, no. 5 (May 1963), p. 229-300.

A study of the manner in which the accounts of travellers in the Greek land contributed to the revival of interest in ancient Greek civilization in England.

136 The klephtic ballads in relation to Greek history (1715-1821).
John W. Baggally. Oxford, England: Blackwell, 1936. 109p.

A useful attempt to place the ballads of the klephts or bandits, who in the popular imagination symbolized resistance to Ottoman oppression, within their historical context. With many examples of the ballads, in admirable translation.

137 Adamantios Korais: a study in Greek nationalism.
Stephen George Chaconas. New York: Columbia University Press, 1942. 181p. bibliog.

Adamantios Korais (1748-1833), a Greek born in Smyrna but living in Paris from 1788 until his death, is traditionally regarded as the intellectual mentor of the movement for Greek independence. The author of this scholarly study sets himself the task of analysing the factors that influenced Korais' national consciousness, the nature of Korais' nationalism and the practical effect of his incessant labours to inculcate a sense of national feeling among his fellow Greeks. Chaconas provides an excellent analysis of the evolution of Korais' thought but surely exaggerates Korais' importance in arguing that 'in reality [his] work laid the foundation and supplied the philosophy for the uprising of 1821'. One of the most remarkable texts of this remarkable nationalist prophet and classical scholar, his *Mémoire sur l'état actuel de la civilization dans la Grèce* (1803), has been translated by Elie Kedourie in his *Nationalism in Asia and Africa* (London: Weidenfeld & Nicolson, 1970), p. 153-88.

History. History of Greece. 1821-1913

138 **The movement for Greek independence 1770-1821: a collection of documents.**
Edited and translated with an introduction by Richard Clogg. London: Macmillan, for the School of Slavonic and East European Studies; New York: Barnes & Noble, 1976. 232p. bibliog.

A collection of documents, mostly translated from the Greek, illustrating the development of the Greek national movement, the first developed national movement to emerge in the context of the multi-national Ottoman Empire.

139 **The struggle for Greek independence: essays to mark the 150th anniversary of the Greek War of Independence.**
Edited by Richard Clogg. London: Macmillan; Hamden, Connecticut: Archon Press, 1973. 259p.

A collection of essays mainly concentrating on the antecedents to the Greek War of Independence.

1821-1913

140 **The Greek struggle for independence, 1821-1833.**
Douglas Dakin. London: Batsford; Berkeley: University of California Press, 1973. 344p. bibliog.

A comprehensive history of the Greeks' protracted struggle for independence from the Turks. Deals fully with the internecine strife among the Greeks that accompanied much of the fighting.

141 **The question of Greek independence: a study of British policy in the Near East, 1821-1833.**
C. W. Crawley. Cambridge, England: Cambridge University Press, 1930. 271p. bibliog. map.

A detailed study of the international context within which the Greek War of Independence was fought. Essential to an understanding of the process by which the Greeks ultimately gained their independence.

142 **The Greek War of Independence: its historical setting.**
C. M. Woodhouse. London: Hutchinson, 1952. 167p. bibliog.

A clear and concise account of the Greek War of Independence which makes sense of a period of Greek history that can be baffling in its complexity.

History. History of Greece. 1821-1913

143 Hellenism and the first Greek war of liberation, 1821-1830: continuity and change.
Nikiforos P. Diamandouros, John P. Anton, John A. Petropulos, Peter Topping. Thessaloniki, Greece: Institute for Balkan Studies, 1976. 237p.

A collection of papers originally delivered at a symposium held in 1971 at Harvard University, under the auspices of the Modern Greek Studies Association, to mark the 150th anniversary of the Greek War of Independence. The essays throw much new light on Greece under the Ottomans and on the struggle for emancipation. Contains a valuable bibliographical essay by Nikiforos Diamandouros.

144 The memoirs of general Makriyannis 1797-1864.
Edited and translated by H. A. Lidderdale. London: Oxford University Press, 1966. 234p.

Translation of the memoirs of General Ioannis Makriyannis, one of the most interesting of the protagonists of the Greek War of Independence. The translator captures the flavour of Makriyannis' remarkable Greek, but unfortunately omits 'much of the unworthy quarrellings and intrigues of chieftains and politicians whose misdeeds are best left forgotten'.

145 Kolokotrones, the klepht and the warrior: sixty years of peril and daring: an autobiography.
Translated from the Greek with an introduction and notes by Mrs. Edmonds. London: T. Fisher Unwin, 1892. 317p.

A translation of the memoirs of the leading military figure of the Greek War of Independence, Theodore Kolokotronis, a former klepht or brigand. Rich in anecdote and historical detail.

146 That Greece might still be free: the philhellenes in the War of Independence.
William St. Clair. London: Oxford University Press, 1972. 412p. bibliog. maps.

The cause of the insurgent Greeks in the 1820s attracted the sympathy of enlightened opinion throughout the civilized world. Philhellene volunteers, the most famous of whom was Lord Byron, flocked to Greece. Some fought bravely alongside the embattled Greeks; others saw in a free Greece a testing ground for their utilitarian schemes of social reform; others were disillusioned to find that the modern Greeks seemed to have little in common with the worthies of Periclean Athens. St. Clair provides a well-written, if somewhat jaundiced, account of the philhellenic movement. His book complements two earlier studies: Douglas Dakin, *British and American philhellenes* (Thessaloniki, Greece: Institute of Balkan Studies, 1955) and C. M. Woodhouse, *The philhellenes* (London: Hodder & Stoughton, 1969).

History. History of Greece. 1821-1913

147 **Hellas observed: the American experience of Greece 1775-1865.**
Stephen A. Larrabee. New York: New York University Press, 1957. 357p. bibliog.

A fascinating study of the American discovery of Greece during the crucial period of the struggle for Greek independence.

148 **The battle of Navarino.**
C. M. Woodhouse. London: Hodder & Stoughton, 1965. 191p. bibliog.

Scholarly and well-written account of what the Duke of Wellington referred to as 'the untoward event'. This was the destruction, by a combined British, French and Russian fleet, in the Bay of Navarino in the western Peloponnese on 20 October 1827 of a Turkish-Egyptian fleet. This manifestation of 'peaceful interference' by the Great Powers ensured the successful outcome of the Greek War of Independence.

149 **Cyprus and the war of Greek independence 1821-1829.**
John T. A. Koumoulides. London: Zeno, 1974. 117p. bibliog. map.

A study of the impact on Cyprus of the struggle for Greek independence.

150 **Capodistria: the founder of Greek independence.**
C. M. Woodhouse. London: Oxford University Press, 1973. 544p. bibliog.

A large scale, scholarly study of Count Ioannis Kapodistrias who, after many years as a diplomat in the service of Tsar Alexander I of Russia, was elected as the first president of Greece in 1828 and assassinated in 1831. A somewhat dessicated figure, Kapodistrias' familiarity with the world of Great Power diplomacy stood Greece in good stead during the crucial period in which the frontiers of the new state were being negotiated. Schooled in the tradition of Russian autocracy, Kapodistrias' authoritarian ways did not endear him to substantial sections of his people. No one could deny, however, his genuine commitment to the cause of resurgent Greece.

151 **Otho I, king of Greece: a biography.**
Leonard Bower, Gordon Bolitho. London: Selwyn & Blount, 1939. 263p.

A biography of Otto, the first king of Greece, who, after a thirty year reign, was driven from the throne in 1862. Despite a genuine love for his adopted country, Otto never managed to establish any permanent hold on the affection of his subjects.

152 **Politics and statecraft in the kingdom of Greece 1833-1843.**
John Anthony Petropulos. Princeton, New Jersey: Princeton University Press, 1968. 646p. bibliog.

A massively documented study of the politics of the first part of the reign of Otto I, when he governed without a constitution. This was imposed on him by the

History. History of Greece. 1821-1913

'revolution' of 1843, the first, but certainly not the last, instance of military intervention in the Greek political system. A sure guide to the politics of the new state at a time when political alignments tended to revolve around the question of allegiance to one or other of the three protecting powers, hence the appellation 'British', 'French' and 'Russian' parties.

153 The Greeks of to-day.
Charles K. Tuckerman. New York: Putnam, 1878. 2nd ed. 369p.

A sympathetic but shrewd account of mid-19th century Greece by the first American minister to Greece.

154 Britain's Greek empire: reflections on the history of the Ionian Islands from the fall of Byzantium.
Michael Pratt. London: Rex Collings, 1978. 206p. bibliog.

In 1815 the Ionian Islands (Corfu, Cephalonia, Levkas, Cythera, Paxos, Ithaca and Zante) became 'a single, free, and independent state under the exclusive protection of His Britannic Majesty'. Pratt's book is focussed mainly on the history of the islands during the British protectorate, which ended with the cession of the islands to Greece in 1864, on the accession to the Greek throne of the Danish Prince William of Glücksburg as King George I of the Hellenes. All that remains of a legacy of fifty years of British rule are an idiosyncratic form of cricket, *tsin tsin birra* (ginger beer) and a good road system. The photographs by Philip Boucas are excellent.

155 The Dilessi murders.
Romilly Jenkins. London: Longman, 1961. 190p. bibliog.

Scholarly and highly entertaining account of the kidnapping and subsequent murder in 1870 of a group of British aristocrats returning to Athens from an excursion to Marathon. Throws interesting light on the interconnection of politics and brigandage in 19th century Greece. Chapter six on 'Truth and "Ethnic" Truth' is particularly thought-provoking. One of the few good books in English on later 19th century Greek history.

156 Greece and the Great Powers 1863-1875.
Domna N. Dontas. Thessaloniki, Greece: Institute for Balkan Studies, 1966. 223p. bibliog.

A study of the policy of the European powers towards Greece in the decade before the outbreak of the great crisis which convulsed the Balkans between 1875 and 1878 and which has been studied from the Greek perspective by Evangelos Kofos (see following item).

157 Greece and the eastern crisis 1875-1878.
Evangelos Kofos. Thessaloniki, Greece: Institute for Balkan Studies, 1975. 283p. bibliog.

Greece was only peripherally involved in the great crisis that convulsed European Turkey between 1875 and the Congress of Berlin in 1878. An indirect outcome of the crisis was the cession to Greece by the Ottoman Empire in 1881 of the province of Thessaly and a part of Epirus. This careful study examines the impact of the crisis on Greece.

History. History of Greece. 1821-1913

158 **Die politischen Parteien Griechenlands: ein neuer Staat auf dem Weg zur Demokratie 1821-1910.** (The political parties of Greece: a new state on the road to democracy 1821-1910.)
Hariton Korisis. Hersbruck, Nürnberg, G.F.R.: Karl Pfeiffer, 1966. 230p.

A history of the development of political parties in Greece, which contains much material of value on the somewhat idiosyncratic political system of 19th century Greece.

159 **Greece under King George.**
R. A. H. Bickford-Smith. London: Richard Bentley, 1893. 350p. map.

A comprehensive account of late 19th century Greece, giving particular weight to the economy.

160 **Consciousness and history: nationalist critics of Greek society 1897-1914.**
Gerasimos Augustinos. Boulder, Colorado: East European Quarterly; New York: Columbia University Press, 1977. 182p. bibliog.

Greece's rapid and shattering defeat in the Greco-Turkish war of 1897 gave rise to a great deal of introspective soul-searching in Greece. This useful book reviews the criticisms of nationalists, seeking an explanation of the impasse which Greece had seemingly reached.

161 **Greece: a political essay.**
P. J. Vatikiotis. Beverly Hills, California; London: Sage Publications, 1974. 87p.

A stimulating and provocative analysis of the political problems of the independent Greek state, with particular emphasis on 'the paradox of a modern state in a traditional society', patronage and civil-military relations. Paints an unattractive view of the Greek character: 'family solidarity, scrambling for scarce resources, and widespread insecurity breed servility, bureaucratic inefficiency, intrigue, and unconscionable pursuit of self-interest'.

162 **The royal house of Greece.**
Arthur S. Gould Lee. London: Ward Lock, 1948. 296p.

Sympathetic account of the trials and tribulations of the Greek royal family, and its Balkan ramifications. The reader is left with little understanding of the reasons for the unpopularity of the Glücksberg dynasty in the eyes of many Greeks.

History. History of Greece. 1913-1940

163 **Venizelos: patriot, statesman, revolutionary.**
Doros Alastos. London: Lund Humphries, 1942. 304p. bibliog.
The great Greek statesman, Eleftherios Venizelos, is ripe for a major historical biography. In the interim Doros Alastos' account remains a serviceable guide to the career of a politician of extraordinary ability and charm.

1913-1940

164 **Greece and the Great Powers, 1914-1917.**
George B. Leon. Thessaloniki, Greece: Institute for Balkan Studies, 1974. 521p. bibliog.
The First World War had a particular significance for Greece as it saw the genesis of the 'National Schism', the division of Greece into two antagonistic and at times warring camps. The basic precipitant of this disastrous split, which was to distort the whole course of Greece's political development during the inter-war years, was the argument as to whether Greece should align herself with the Entente Powers (Britain, France and Russia) or whether she should remain neutral. Eleftherios Venizelos was the principal protagonist of alignment with the Entente, King Constantine I the main proponent of neutralism. With both the Entente and Central (Germany and Austro-Hungary) Powers bidding for support in the country, their intrigues culminated in outright and flagrant intervention in Greece's internal affairs by the Entente. This resulted in the ousting by Britain and France in 1917 of King Constantine and the replacement of a royalist, neutralist government by the pro-Entente Venizelos. In this excellent study, Professor Leon examines in detail the way in which Great Power rivalries determined the course of events in Greece between 1914 and 1917.

165 **The gardeners of Salonika: the Macedonian campaign 1915-1918.**
Alan Palmer. London: André Deutsch, 1965. 286p. bibliog.
One of the least-known operational areas in the First World War was the Salonica front. Here, from October 1915 onwards, British, French, Serbian, Italian and, later, Greek troops confronted Austro-Hungarian, German and Bulgarian forces. Long intervals of stalemate were punctuated by extremely fierce fighting, while malaria and other diseases took a heavy toll. The highly successful offensive, launched in September 1918 under the command of General Louis Franchet d'Espérey, helped to precipitate the 11 November armistice on the western front.

166 **Gallipoli memories.**
Compton Mackenzie. London: Cassell, 1929. 406p.
This first volume of the distinguished novelist's memoirs of his experiences in Greece during the First World War. Covers roughly the period of the Gallipoli campaign and deals also with Mackenzie's intelligence activities in the Aegean islands. In Mackenzie's own view it 'adds nothing of the least historical value to the literature of the war', although like the other volumes it is replete with anecdote and verbatim conversation.

History. History of Greece. 1913-1940

167 First Athenian memories.
Compton Mackenzie. London: Cassell, 1931. 402p.

Covers in considerable detail Mackenzie's activities as an intelligence officer in Athens in 1915 at a time when Prime Minister Venizelos and King Constantine were embroiled in increasingly bitter conflict as to whether Greece should side with the Entente powers or remain neutral. Many entertaining anecdotes about rivalry between the German and Anglo-French intelligence services. Mackenzie regards Britain's treatment of Greece at this period as 'one of the most disreputable examples of muddling through in our history'.

168 Greek memories.
Compton Mackenzie. London: Cassell, 1932. 455p.

Carries the story of Mackenzie's activities in Athens on behalf of British intelligence through 1916 when the *dikhasmos* or schism between the pro-Entente statesman Venizelos and the neutralist King Constantine became irrevocable. Written in part to counter Sir Basil Thomson's *The allied secret service in Greece* (London: Hutchinson, 1931). Thomson's description as Director of Intelligence (1919-21) 'suggested a more intimate knowledge of Greek affairs than he possessed'. As a result of action by the British Foreign Office, *Greek memories* was withdrawn on publication day. Charged under the Official Secrets Act with revealing details of his wartime service in Greece, Mackenzie was fined £100 - the sales of his book benefitted considerably from the attendant publicity.

169 Aegean memories.
Compton Mackenzie. London: Chatto & Windus, 1940. 419p.

The fourth and final volume of the distinguished novelist's memoirs of his experiences in Greece during the First World War. Carries the story through the summer of 1917, when King Constantine was forced into exile and Venizelos' Provisional Government based in Thessaloniki was recognized by Britain and France as the legal government of Greece. Regarded by Mackenzie himself as the 'most entertaining volume of the series', it contains the generous measure of anecdotage that characterize the other volumes of the quartet. Enlivened, as are the other volumes, by the author's enthusiastic championing of the Venizelist cause.

170 Ionian vision: Greece in Asia Minor, 1919-1922.
Michael Llewellyn Smith. London: Allen Lane, 1973. 401p. bibliog. maps.

An account of Greece's disastrous attempt to annexe part of western Asia Minor in the aftermath of the First World War. This provided the catalyst for the Turkish national revival led by Mustafa Kemal (Atatürk), the eventual expulsion of the Greek army, and the sacking of Izmir (Smyrna) in September 1922. The 'catastrophe', as it is called in Greece, in turn sparked off domestic political upheaval, the judicial murder of a number of politicians, and was followed by a compulsory exchange of populations between Greece and Turkey. The definitive study of a traumatic episode in Greek history.

History. History of Greece. 1913-1940

171 **The western question in Greece and Turkey: a study in the contact of civilisations.**
Arnold J. Toynbee. London: Constable, 1922. 420p. map.
An informed study of the Greek entanglement in Asia Minor in the aftermath of the First World War.

172 **Smyrna 1922: the destruction of a city.**
Marjorie Housepian. New York: Harcourt, Brace & World, 1968; London: Faber & Faber, 1972. 275p. bibliog. map.
The rout of the Greek army of occupation in western Asia Minor at the hands of the nationalist forces of Mustafa Kemal (Atatürk) in September 1922 was followed by the destruction of 'Gavur Izmir' (Infidel Izmir), as the Turks called it, and the massacre of many of its inhabitants. Marjorie Housepian's book is a salutary reminder that this was as much an Armenian as a Greek tragedy. Perhaps the best eye-witness account of these tragic events is that of the U.S. consul in the city, George Horton, *The blight of Asia* (Indianapolis, Indiana: Bobbs-Merrill, 1926).

173 **The eastern question, the last phase: a study in Greek-Turkish diplomacy.**
Harry J. Psomiades. Thessaloniki, Greece: Institute for Balkan Studies, 1968. 145p. bibliog.
A scholarly study of the background to the treaty of Lausanne of 1923, which ended the Greco-Turkish war of 1919-22, and of the concomitant convention governing the exchange of populations between Greece and Turkey, and of their immediate aftermath.

174 **The Balkan exchange of minorities and its impact upon Greece.**
Dimitri Pentzopoulos. Paris, The Hague: Mouton, 1962. 293p. bibliog. (Publications of the Social Sciences Center, Athens, no. 1).
A study of the various population exchanges of the early 1920s which resulted in a massive influx of frequently destitute refugees into an already impoverished country. The principal exchange was with Turkey and some 380,000 Muslims were exchanged for some 1,100,000 orthodox Christians. The most valuable chapters of this excellent book focus on the impact, ethnological, economic, political, social and cultural of this forced migration. One consequence, for instance, was the virtual doubling of the population of Athens between 1920 and 1928.

175 **Greece and the Greek refugees.**
Charles B. Eddy. London: George Allen & Unwin, 1931. 280p. bibliog.
A detailed account by the American chairman of the Refugee Settlement Commission of the remarkably successful settlement in Greece in the 1920s of some 1,200,000 Greek refugees, most of them from Asia Minor, but some also from Russia and Bulgaria.

History. History of Greece. 1913-1940

176 **Greece today: the aftermath of the refugee impact.**
Eliot Grinnell Mears. Stanford, California: Stanford University Press, 1929. 336p. bibliog.

A comprehensive and useful anatomy of Greece in the wake of the Exchange of Populations, covering topics such as rural occupations, natural resources, urban industries, communications, international trade, business technique, public finance, education, politics and foreign affairs. Three appendices contain statistical information about the resettlement of the refugees exchanged in the aftermath of the 'catastrophe' of 1922. Considering the numbers involved, and the proportion in which they stood to the overall population of Greece, the refugees were resettled with a remarkable degree of success and the social dislocation consequent on their arrival minimized. A companion volume to the same author's volume on Turkey.

177 **Greece.**
William Miller. London: Benn, 1928. 351p.

A richly informative panorama of Greece in the 1920s.

178 **The second reign of George II: his role in politics.**
Everett J. Marder. *Southeastern Europe*, vol. 2, pt. 1 (1975), p. 53-69.

George II briefly ruled Greece in 1922-23. This was followed by a twelve-year exile spent mainly in London. In 1935, after a rigged plebiscite, he returned to Greece where he remained upon the throne until the German conquest in May 1941. In September 1946, after yet another plebiscite, he returned to the throne, dying some six months later in April 1947. This study, based mainly on the reports of the U.S. ambassador in Greece, considers George's second period on the throne, during which he came to be identified in the popular mind with the dictatorship of General Metaxas.

179 **Greece and the British connection 1935-1941.**
John S. Koliopoulos. Oxford, England: Clarendon Press, 1977. 315p. bibliog.

From the first years of the independent Greek state Britain exercised a major influence on the affairs of Greece. The British involvement in Greece was never greater than during the years before 1947, when the United States assumed the hegemony traditionally exercised by Britain. This book examines in considerable detail Anglo-Greek relations between the restoration of King George II to his throne in 1935 and the German invasion of Greece in 1941, i.e. approximately the period of the quasi-fascist dictatorship of General Ioannis Metaxas. Koliopoulos demolishes the view still met with in Greece that the British actually installed the Metaxas dictatorship, but demonstrates that the Foreign Office in many respects found the dictator easier to deal with than his elected predecessors. He demonstrates, too, the extent to which King George was regarded by the Foreign Office as the best guarantor of British interests in Greece. Particularly useful is the account of the dramatic events between the Italian invasion of October 1940 and the German invasion of April 1941. King George's courageous behaviour during this critical period explains, at least in part, the strong British official support he enjoyed during the Second World War, when his stock within Greece itself was at a low ebb.

1940-1949

180 **Greece: a political and economic survey 1939-1953.**
Bickham Sweet-Escott. London, New York: Royal Institute of International Affairs, 1954. 207p. bibliog. maps. tables.

A survey of Greece during a crucial fifteen year period that included the Axis occupation and ensuing civil war. Particularly valuable for its chapters on economic developments.

181 **The struggle for Greece 1941-1949.**
C. M. Woodhouse. London: Hart-Davis, MacGibbon, 1976; Brooklyn Heights, New York: Beekman/Esanu, 1979. 324p. bibliog.

Careful analysis, based on a wide range of sources, of the three 'rounds' in the communist bid for power in Greece in the 1940s; the attempt to monopolize resistance to the Germans in 1943-44; the communist insurgency of December 1944 which was suppressed by British forces; and the fully fledged civil war between 1946 and 1949. This book explains why, alone of the countries of the Balkans, Greece emerged from the chaos of the Second World War without a communist government. The author barely alludes to his own role as commander of the Allied Military Mission to the Greek resistance during the Second World War.

182 **Apple of discord: a survey of recent Greek politics in their international setting.**
C. M. Woodhouse. London: Hutchinson, 1948. 320p.

A penetrating analysis of the politics of war-time occupation and of the profound political crisis that erupted in Greece after the liberation by the second commander of the British (Allied) military mission to the Greek resistance.

183 **War and post-war Greece: an analysis based on Greek writings.**
Floyd A. Spencer. Washington, D.C.: Library of Congress, 1952. 175p.

A careful analysis of Greek writings on the occupation and civil war periods published before the early 1950s. Inevitably there has been an enormous amount published on this period in Greece since this book was compiled. The Colonels' regime in particular stimulated a great interest in the decade of the 1940s, as Greeks sought an understanding of their post-war political crises.

184 **The hollow legions: Mussolini's blunder, 1940-1941.**
Mario Cervi, translated from the Italian by Eric Mossbacher. London: Chatto & Windus, 1972. 336p.

A highly readable account of the debacle of Mussolini's invasion of Greece in October, launched in an attempt to demonstrate to Hitler that the Italians, too, were capable of lightning military victories and out of pique at Hitler's failure to consult his principal ally. After a series of deliberate Italian provocations in the summer of 1940, Mussolini's minister in Athens woke the Greek dictator at 3 A.M. on 28 October with a harsh ultimatum due to expire at 6 A.M. Metaxas'

History. History of Greece. 1940-1949

famous reply, 'Alors c'est la guerre', is commemorated by the annual 'Ochi' (No) Day holiday in Greece. Mussolini's invasion launched from Albania, which Italy had occupied in April 1939, was soon rebuffed and Greek forces occupied Korcë (Korytsa) and Gjirokastër (Argyrokastro) in Southern Albania and were only prevented by atrocious weather conditions from capturing the important supply port of Vlorë. The military stalemate on the Albanian front was ended only with the blitzkrieg German invasion of Greece in April 1941. In the winter of 1940-41 Greece was Britain's only active ally against the Axis and the imagination of the world was caught by the spectacle of the Greek David worsting the Italian Goliath. The Greek forces certainly fought heroically but, as Cervi demonstrates, the disparity in men and equipment of the Greek forces vis-à-vis the Italian was not as great as was thought at the time. In some respects the Greek forces were superior to the Italians in numbers and equipment and certainly in morale.

185 **Greece 1940-1941.**
Charles Cruickshank. London: Davis-Poynter, 1976. 206p. bibliog.

A concise account of the Italian and German invasions of Greece in October 1940 and April 1941, particularly critical of Anthony Eden, the British foreign secretary, for allowing a disastrous misunderstanding to develop between the Greek and British military authorities over contingency plans to meet the expected German invasion.

186 **Greece and Crete 1941.**
Christopher Buckley. London: H.M. Stationery Office, 1952. 311p.

A volume in the official popular military histories of the Second World War. Churchill's decision to commit British and Dominion troops to Greece early in 1941 was due more to a sense of 'noblesse oblige' and a desire to bolster Yugoslav and Turkish resistance to the Axis than to any real hope of military success although some historians have argued that Hitler's excursus occasioned an ultimately fatal delay in his invasion of the Soviet Union.

187 **The struggle for Crete 20 May-1 June 1941: a story of lost opportunity.**
I. McD. G. Stewart. London: Oxford University Press, 1966. 518p. bibliog.

After the fall of the Greek mainland to the German invasion forces at the end of April 1941, Greek and British forces withdrew to the island of Crete, intending to hold it as an impregnable fortress. In fact, it was rapidly overrun in a lightning German airborne attack, code-named *Merkur*. German losses were, however, substantial and Hitler never again launched an airborne attack on such a scale. The author, who served as a medical officer during the battle, believes, as do many other observers, that Crete should not have been lost.

188 **The kapetanios: partisans and civil war in Greece, 1943-1949.**
Dominique Eudes, translated from the French by John Howe. London: New Left Books, 1972. 381p. bibliog.

A lively account of the fate of the left in Greece in the 1940s, marred by a tendency to overstate a supposed antithesis between the 'Stalinist' bureaucrats of the Greek communist party (K.K.E.), who thought that the struggle to resist the Axis occupation and to establish a post-war communist regime should be con-

History. History of Greece. 1940-1949

ducted mainly in the towns, and the 'Titoists', such as Ares Veloukhiotis, who were eager to exploit the potential of peasant-based resistance in the mountains. Eudes has had access to the recollections of some prominent members of the communist dominated National Liberation Front (E.A.M.), but the book's value as a historical source is weakened by the absence of references and the author's tendency to reconstruct at a distance of thirty years verbatim conversations of various protagonists in the resistance and subsequent civil war.

189 **British policy in south-east Europe in the Second World War.**
Elizabeth Barker. London: Macmillan, 1976. 320p.

Although it intentionally devotes less attention to Greece than to the other countries of south-east Europe, this first-rate book, based on the relevant British archives for the period, is indispensable for an understanding of the general Balkan context of British policy towards Greece during the Second World War. It throws particularly valuable light on the famous 'percentages' agreement between Churchill and Stalin of October 1944. This developed from an earlier understanding over Russian preponderance in Romania and British preponderance in Greece.

190 **British policy towards wartime resistance in Yugoslavia and Greece.**
Edited by Phyllis Auty, Richard Clogg. London: Macmillan for the School of Slavonic and East European Studies; New York: Barnes & Noble, 1975. 308p. bibliog.

The proceedings of a conference held in 1973, the purpose of which was to reconsider British policy towards the wartime resistance movements in Yugoslavia and Greece in the light of the official British records which were released in 1972 and of the recollections of a number of those responsible for the formulation and execution of British policy. The principal factors to emerge were that there were several, often conflicting, strands to British policy, which cannot be considered monolithic, and that the policy making process was frequently disturbed by inter-service rivalries, confusion, ignorance and prejudice.

191 **Case study in guerilla war.**
D. M. Condit. Washington, D.C.: Warfare Research Division. Special Operations Research Office. The American University, 1961. 337p. bibliog.

Sought to derive lessons in counter-guerilla warfare from the experience of Greece at a time when U.S. involvement in Vietnam was beginning, e.g. 'The Germans in Greece were not able to destroy the guerillas entirely; but they were able, with forces approximating only three times the strength of the guerilas, to contain them, and prevent their becoming a crucial military factor'. The successful containment of communist insurgency in Greece, however, was due in part to factors that were not present in the Vietnam situation.

192 **Greek entanglement.**
E. C. W. Myers. London: Hart-Davis, 1955. 290p. map.

An account of his experiences in Greece by the first commander of the British military mission to the Greek resistance. Parachuted into Greece in September 1942, Myers commanded the highly successful operation to destroy the Gorgopotamos viaduct which carried the Athens-Thessaloniki railway, a vital German

History. History of Greece. 1940-1949

supply line. He subsequently acted as liaison between the British military authorites in Cairo and the Greek guerillas, but after accompanying a high-level guerila delegation to Cairo in August 1943, the Foreign Office vetoed his return to Greece.

193 **We fell among Greeks.**
Denys Hamson.   London: Jonathan Cape, 1946. 221p.

One of the first 'war' books published by a British participant in the Greek resistance. A jaundiced account of his ten months in Greece by a disillusioned member of the original 'Harling' party parachuted into Greece, under the command of Brigadier E. C. W. Myers, in September 1942, to sever the Athens-Thessaloniki railway line.

194 **Ill met by moonlight.**
W. Stanley Moss.   London: Harrap, 1950. 192p.

An account of the kidnapping in April 1944 by British officers and members of the Cretan resistance of General Kreipe, the German commandant in Crete, and his spiriting out of the island.

195 **The Cretan runner: his story of the German occupation.**
George Psychoundakis, translated with an introduction by Patrick Leigh Fermor, annotated by the translator and Xan Fielding.   London: John Murray, 1955. 242p. map.

An account by a Cretan shepherd of his experiences in helping British officers sent to Crete during the Second World War to coordinate resistance to the German occupation forces on the island. Affords a rare insight into the mentality of one of the many thousands of humble Greeks who were ready to make any sacrifice to manifest their detestation of the foreign occupiers of their country.

196 **Baker Street Irregular.**
Bickham Sweet-Escott.   London: Methuen, 1965. 278p.

Fascinating and excellently written account of the wartime Special Operations Executive by an insider. The manuscript was completed in 1954 but was not cleared for publication under the Official Secrets Act until ten years later. Although the author's ambition of being parachuted into Greece was not fulfilled, his interest in Greek affairs is apparent throughout. Invaluable for an understanding of the activities in Greece of the much maligned S.O.E., caught in the crossfire between the Foreign Office, with its concern for the long-term political implications of British policy in Greece, and the military authorities with their primary objective of inflicting the maximum damage against the Axis occupiers, irrespective of the political consequences.

197 **When Greek meets Greek.**
Reginald Leeper.   London: Chatto & Windus, 1950. 244p.

Intelligent apologia of the British ambassador to the Greek government between 1943 and 1946 (from March 1943 to October 1944 in Cairo and Italy, from October 1944 in Athens). Affords a useful insight into official British policies and attitudes at a time when Britain exercised a preponderant influence in Greek affairs.

History. History of Greece. 1940-1949

198 **War in the Aegean.**
Peter Smith, Edwin Walker. London: William Kimber, 1974. 304p. bibliog.

A study of the ill-fated British attempt to capture the Dodecanese islands in the wake of the Italian armistice of September 1943. A massive German counter-attack rapidly put an end to the brief British occupation of the islands. The failure of the Dodecanese campaign earned for the Commander-in-Chief, Middle East, General 'Jumbo' Wilson, the Churchillian epithet 'The wizard of Cos'.

199 **The economy and finance of Greece under occupation.**
Stephen G. Xydis. New York: Greek Government Office of Information, 1945(?). 48p.

A succinct account of the devastation occasioned to the Greek economy by four years of Axis occupation. During this period Greece suffered one of the highest rates of inflation in recorded history.

200 **Revolt in Athens: the Greek communist 'second round', 1944-1945.**
John O. Iatrides. Princeton, New Jersey: Princeton University Press, 1972. 340p. bibliog.

A level-headed and convincing account of the communist insurgency of December 1944. This resulted in bitter street fighting in Athens between the communist-led resistance army (E.L.A.S.) and British forces seeking to prop up the authority of the beleaguered national government of George Papandreou. Iatrides sees all parties to the dispute, the British, the left and the national government, as sharing responsiblity for a tragic conflict that fatally polarized Greek politics.

201 **The Greek trilogy: resistance-liberation-revolution.**
W. Byford-Jones. London: Hutchinson, 1945. 270p.

Vivid eye-witness account, with much incidental detail, of the liberation of Greece, with a particularly valuable description of the crucial demonstration by E.A.M., the communist-backed National Liberation Front, on 3 December 1944. This resulted in shooting by the police, thus precipitating the so-called 'second round', the communist insurgency which some have interpreted as an outright bid for power by the Greek communist party, others as an attempt to oust the fiercely anti-communist Greek prime minister of the day, George Papandreou.

202 **The Greek dilemma: war and aftermath.**
William Hardy McNeill. London: Gollancz, 1947. 240p.

A penetrating and even-handed analysis of the slide towards civil war in Greece by the then assistant military attaché at the U.S. embassy in Athens, who has since become one of America's foremost historians and a stimulating observer of the Greek scene (see index for his other works listed here).

203 **The divided land: an Anglo-Greek tragedy.**
Geoffrey Chandler. London: Macmillan, 1959. 214p.

Well-written and intelligent eye-witness account of the period between 1944 and 1946 during which Greece drifted from the euphoria of liberation to outright civil war, with the left making a determined bid to seize power by force. An epilogue takes the story to 1949 when the communists conceded defeat. For a time a press

History. History of Greece. 1940-1949

officer for the British Embassy in Volos and Thessaloniki, the author enlivens his text with contemporary cartoons from the Greek press. He believes that Britain's 'lack of policy meant that we forfeited our reputation for those virtues of constancy, of impartiality and justice with which the Greeks credited us and for which we were most respected'.

204 The Greek Civil War 1944-1949.
Edgar O'Ballance. London: Faber & Faber; New York: Praeger, 1966. 237p. bibliog. map.

An analysis, from a military perspective, of the three 'rounds' of the communist attempt to win power in Greece between 1943 and 1949.

205 Memories of a mountain war: Greece, 1944-1949.
Kenneth Matthews. London: Longman, 1972. 284p.

The shrewd, elegantly written and frequently entertaining recollections of the B.B.C.'s correspondent in Greece during the troubled period of the liberation and subsequent civil war.

206 Report on the Greeks: findings of a Twentieth Century Fund team which surveyed conditions in Greece in 1947.
Frank Smothers, William Hardy McNeill, Elizabeth Darbishire McNeill. New York: Twentieth Century Fund, 1948. 226p.

In early 1947, with the Greek Civil War in full swing and the 'Cold War' developing rapidly, the Twentieth Century Fund sent three observers to Greece. Their mission, at this crucial juncture in Greece's history, was to give the reader 'a personal feeling of acquaintance with the Greeks - who they are, what they are like, how they make their living, their conditions of life and, most especially, their attitudes and opinions'. By and large, the authors succeeded in this objective.

207 The Greek Civil War.
John Campbell. In: *The international regulation of civil wars.* Edited by Evan Luard. London: Thames & Hudson, 1972. p. 37-64.

During the Greek Civil War the United Nations proved more effective in mitigating its potential for international conflict than in many other post-war crises. The author concludes that the U.N. 'was not able to prevent the civil war breaking out, a war whose domestic origin was almost immediately and inextricably bound to the aims of conflicting foreign states. It could not materially stem its course, nor fundamentally alter the outcome. Yet the war ended without the fighting passing beyond the borders of Greece or involving the troops of other nations. For this not inconsiderable blessing the UN shares a measure of credit'.

208 Greece: American dilemma and opportunity.
L. S. Stavrianos. Chicago: Henry Regnery, 1952. 246p.

A perceptive account of the troubled decade of the 1940s, which is critical of British policy towards Greece and argued, unsuccessfully as it turned out, for American support of the forces of moderation in the country.

History. History of Greece. 1940-1949

209 **No ordinary crown: a biography of King Paul of the Hellenes.**
Stelio Hourmouzios. London: Weidenfeld & Nicolson, 1972. 375p.

The history of the monarchy in Greece has been a stormy one. King Paul, who reigned between 1947 and 1964, was the only monarch to have ascended the throne in orthodox circumstances and to have died peacefully while in possession of it, without previously having been driven into exile. This is a biography by the former secretary to Paul's brother, King George II.

210 **A measure of understanding.**
Frederica. Queen of the Hellenes. London: Macmillan, 1971. 270p.

An autobiography of the controversial but undoubtedly courageous German-born queen of Greece between 1947 and 1964, the mother of the last king, Constantine II.

211 **The metamorphosis of Greece since World War II.**
William H. McNeill. Chicago: University of Chicago Press; Oxford, England: Blackwell, 1978. 264p.

A stimulating and provocative analysis of social change and modernization in post-war Greece, a period during which the country has been transformed from a predominantly rural to a predominantly urban society. The author argues that the traditional values of the Greek peasant and, in particular, 'the centrality of exchange and the critical importance of the skills of the market place' have eased the transition from village to city and have contributed to the rapid pace of economic and social change. He sees antagonism between food-deficit mountain villages and the food-surplus villages of the plains as having been one of the main determinants of political and social unrest in modern Greece. He regards, for instance, the wartime resistance to the Germans and Italians as having been primarily motivated not by ideology, but by the need for mountain villagers to find food. Indeed he argues that the absence of mass-based resistance to the Colonels' dictatorship is explained by the fact that population pressure and consequent need for food in the mountain villages was by the late 1960s very much reduced. Parts of his analysis, which is based on a long acquaintance with Greece and first-hand observation in six villages, widely scattered geographically and reflecting the particular characteristics of both the mountains and the plains, have aroused controversy, particularly among anthropologists and sociologists. But the book is essential reading for anyone who would understand the nature of post-war Greek society. It is difficult to dissent from his overall conclusion that in terms of satisfying 'human wants and aspirations' the development of Greece during the last thirty years represents 'an extraordinary success story'.

History. History of Greece. Regional history

Regional history

212 History of Macedonia 1354-1833.
A. E. Vacalopoulos, translated from the Greek by Peter Megann. Thessaloniki, Greece: Institute of Balkan Studies, 1973. 758p. bibliog. maps.

A massively documented, scholarly history of Macedonia. Sets the scene for the bitter disputes over the region that were waged by Greek, Bulgarian and Serbian nationalists at the end of the 19th and the beginning of the 20th centuries.

213 The Greek struggle in Macedonia, 1897-1913.
Douglas Dakin. Thessaloniki, Greece: Institute for Balkan Studies, 1966. 538p. bibliog. maps.

A detailed and scholarly study of the Greek effort, principally against the Bulgarians, to secure as large a share as possible of Macedonia when the Turks' hold on their European provinces crumbled at the end of the 19th and the beginning of the 20th centuries.

214 Turkey in Europe.
Odysseus, *pseud. for* C. N. E. Eliot. London: Edward Arnold, 1900. 475p.

Brilliant analysis, published anonymously by a British diplomat, of the European provinces of the Ottoman Empire as it sank into irreversible decline. The chapters on the Turks, Greeks, Bulgarians, Serbs, Albanians and Vlachs and on Islam and Eastern Orthodoxy are full of penetrating insights about a region where to this day the burden of the past is of great significance.

215 Macedonia: its races and their future.
H. N. Brailsford. London: Methuen, 1906. 336p.

An intelligent, informed analysis, based on personal observation of the highly complicated Macedonian question in the years after the great Bulgarian-inspired uprising of Ilinden (St. Ilias' day) 1903. Graphically portrays the misery caused by the competing nationalisms of Greece, Bulgaria, Serbia and Romania to the complex ethnological mix of Macedonia during the last years of Ottoman rule. There are chapters on the nature of Ottoman rule in the area, on the Bulgarians, Vlachs, Greeks and Albanians of the region, together with an assessment of the impact of the various reform proposals imposed by the Great Powers on the region. The author has a noticeable anti-Greek bias.

216 The occupation of Chios by the Germans and their administration of the island: described in contemporary documents.
Philip P. Argenti. Cambridge, England: Cambridge University Press, 1966. 375p.

A scholarly and detailed account of the island during the German occupation between 1941 and 1944, the penultimate in a long series of studies of the island by a prominent native son, Philip Argenti. One of the few scholarly monographs on the impact of occupation on a specific area of Greece, although one rather on

History. History of Greece. Regional history

the periphery of the dramatic events taking place on the mainland. Much of the book is taken up with documents of varying value. Well produced and indexed.

217 **Thasos, son histoire, son administration de 1453 à 1912.**
(Thasos, its history and administration from 1453 to 1912.)
A. E. Bakalopoulos. Paris: de Boccard, 1953. 200p. (École Français d'Athènes. Études Thasiennes no. 2).
A history of the island of Thasos under Ottoman rule, supplemented by many original documents of the period.

218 **Mykonos: chronique d'une île de l'Égee.** (Mykonos: chronicle of an Aegean island.)
Jean Baelen. Paris: Les Belles Lettres, 1964. 99p.
A short, popular account of the history of an island that has in recent years become a popular playground of the international jet set.

219 **A history of Thessaloniki.**
Apostolos E. Vacalopoulos, translated from the Greek by T. F. Carney. Thessaloniki, Greece: Institute for Balkan Studies, 1972. 153p.
A history of Greece's second city, which until 1912 formed part of the Ottoman Empire, and whose atmosphere is markedly different from that of Athens.

220 **La ville convoitée: Salonique.** (The coveted town: Thessaloniki.)
P. Risal. Paris: Perrin, 1914. 368p.
A detailed history of Thessaloniki as one of the leading cities of the Ottoman Empire. Since its acquisition by Greece in 1912 the city has lost much of its picturesque charm.

221 **Old and new Athens.**
Dimitrios Sicilianos, translated from the Greek by Robert Liddell. London: Putnam, 1960. 379p.
Shortened version of the Greek original. Imparts much information on the history of the city in a somewhat discursive and ill-organized fashion.

Population

General

222 A reconstruction of the demographic history of modern Greece.
Vasilios G. Valaoras. *Milbank Memorial Fund Quarterly*, vol. 38, no. 2 (April 1960), p. 115-39.

A useful insight into Greek demographic history, based on a mass of statistics. A significant fact to emerge from this study is that by 1950 'the population was short by about ten per cent of the expected total, or, in actual numbers, by more than eight-tenths of a million (600,000 missing persons and 240,000 never born)'. The birth rate and death rate have both decreased sharply since the Second World War, the rate of population increase in the 1960s being about one per cent annually.

223 Dimographikai exelixeis en Elladi 1950-1980: demographic trends in Greece 1950-1980.
George S. Siampos. Athens: Ministry of Coordination, 1969. 2nd ed. 295p. bibliog.

Text in Greek with a substantial English summary. A detailed analysis of demographic trends in Greece. The population of Greece which stood at 7,554,000 in 1950 was expected to rise to 9,340,000 by 1980. This represents a very low rate of increase, caused in part by a low fertility rate and large scale emigration.

224 Some effects of famine on the population of Greece.
V. G. Valaoras. *Milbank Memorial Fund Quarterly*, vol. 24, no. 3 (July 1946), p. 215-34.

A careful analysis of the effects of the wartime famine, particularly acute during the winter of 1941-1942, in Greece. Valaoras estimates that Greece lost about 450,000 people from the effects of the famine during the early months of the occupation. Food deprivation affected adult males more than it did women and children.

Population. Internal migration

225 **Control of family size in Greece: the results of a field survey.**
V. G. Valaoras, Antonia Polychronopoulou, Dimitri
Trichopoulos. *Population Studies*, vol. 18, no. 3 (March
1965), p. 265-78.
The birth rate in Greece has been declining since the 1930s and the authors
conclude that 'the present low fertility rates of Greece stem from a strong desire
of married couples, all over the country, to keep the sizes of their families to a
manageable level of about two or three children per family'.

226 **The determinants of birth rate in developing countries: an
econometric study of Greece.**
Constantine G. Drakatos. *Economic Development and
Cultural Change*, vol. 17, no. 2 (July 1969), p. 596-603.
The author finds that the percentage of rural population and/or the percentage of
literates affords a more accurate indicator of birth rate than does per capita
income. 'It was also found that another important determinant of the birth rate is
the ratio of reproductive to total population, which in Greece is seriously affected
by emigration'.

Internal migration

227 **Exode rurale et attraction urbaine en Grèce.** (Rural
migration and urbanization in Greece.)
Bernard Kayser, Pierre-Yves Pechoux, Michael
Sivignon. Athens: National Centre of Social Research,
1971. 223p.
A detailed case study of rural migration and urbanization during the 1960s, based
on a study of four groups of communities in Paros, one of the islands of the
Cyclades, in the plain of Messenia in the Peloponnese, in the plain of Thessaly
and in eastern Macedonia.

228 **Population, internal migration and urbanization in Greece.**
J. J. Baxevanis. *Balkan Studies*, vol. 6, no. 1 (1965), p.
83-98.
An analysis of the reasons for the very rapid process of urbanization in Greece
during recent decades. Government efforts to stem internal migration from the
rural areas to the cities and, in particular, Athens, either through legislation or
other means, have been of little effect.

229 **The internal migrant.**
Calliope Moustaka. Athens: Social Sciences Centre, 1964.
105p.
An examination of internal migration and the urbanization of rural migrants
involving a case study of migrants from Zagori to Yannina and Athens and

Population. Internal migration

migrants from Paros to Athens. Among the reasons prompting such internal migration (amounting, between 1951 and 1962, to some twenty-six per cent of the population), according to Dr. Moustaka's informants, were a desire to give children a better education and the attractions of urban life contrasted with the deprivations of village life. Economic considerations, however, predominated.

230 **Kinship, class and selective migration.**
Ernestine Friedl. In: *Mediterranean family structures*. Edited by J. G. Peristiany. Cambridge, England: Cambridge University Press, 1976. p. 363-87.

A study of the factors, 'local, social, and cultural', determining migration from a Boeotian village to Athens between 1930 and 1965. It throws important light on the causes of the massive process of urbanization that has characterized post-war Greece. Professor Friedl found that the greater the family's economic resources the more likely it was to migrate from the village.

231 **Regional employment in Greece.**
C. L. Papageorgiou. Athens: National Centre of Social Research, 1973. vol. 1, 277p. bibliog.; vol. 2, 155p. bibliog.

A technical study of 'prevailing regional differences and their effect as an inducement towards interregional and international migration'. This is an important question in Greece, given the propensity to 'astyphilia', or migration towards the cities, and to emigration abroad. No post-war Greek government has shown much capacity to deal with the problem of rural depopulation.

232 **Economy and population movements in the Peloponnesos of Greece.**
John J. Baxevanis. Athens: National Centre of Social Research, 1972. 86p. bibliog.

A study of internal migration in the Peloponnese during the post-war period. The author estimates that outward migration from the Peloponnese amounts to some 15,000 persons annually, while some 30,000 persons change residence annually. This explains the fact that for the last thirty-five years the region has registered a net annual population loss. At the time of Baxevanis' study the population of the Peloponnese was 985,620.

233 **A study of Greek regional migration.**
Constantin Papageorgiou. *Oxford Agrarian Studies*, new series, vol. 1, no. 1 (1972), p. 3-19.

Between 1959 and 1965 outward migration in Greece rose from 24,000 to 117,000 annually. The author analyses the reasons for this outward flow. He notes, *inter alia*, that 'for as long as employment opportunities as attractive as in Germany exist it is difficult to halt migration. The money wages offered in Germany were three times higher than in Athens and four times the agricultural wages. A level of money wages as high as that allows any deductions to be made for the higher cost of living. Even if only one third could be saved and sent back home this might be equivalent to twice the annual income at home if the seasonal characteristics of agricultural labour are taken into account'.

Population. Emigration

234 **Refugees and economic migrants in great Athens: a social survey.**
Eva E. Sandis. Athens: National Centre of Social Research, 1973. 195p. bibliog. maps.
A sociological analysis of the Athens suburb of Nea Ionia, focussing particularly on its refugee population (mainly from Asia Minor) and on internal migrants from the villages. Topics considered include occupational patterns and aspirations, neighbourhood ties and community utilization.

Emigration

235 **International labor migration and economic development with special reference to Greece.**
X. Zolotas. Athens: Bank of Greece, 1966. 62p. (Bank of Greece Papers and Lectures, no. 21).
A consideration of the effects, economic and demographic, of large-scale intra-European migration by Greek workers.

236 **Capital-labor substitution in a developing country: the case of Greece.**
T. P. Lianos. *European Economic Review*, vol. 6, no. 2 (April 1975), p. 129-41.
Whereas in the past outwards migration has been viewed as a safety valve, defusing the potential for social unrest represented by chronic un- and under-employment, the reverse is now the case. Growing labour shortages are seen as posing a threat to future industrial growth.

237 **Some economic aspects of short-run Greek labor emigration to Germany.**
Eleutherios N. Botsas. *Weltwirtschaftliches Archiv*, vol. 105, no. 1 (1970), p. 163-73.
A consideration of some of the factors underlying short-term emigration by Greek migrant workers to West Germany.

238 **Some social aspects of the return movement of Greek migrant workers from West Germany to rural Greece.**
Joanna Manganara. *Epitheorisi Koinonikon Erevnon. The Greek Review of Social Research*, no. 29 (Jan.-April 1977), p. 65-75.
A study of the 'social effects of intra-European emigration and the return movement on traditional rural Greece and on returners themselves', based on research in Rhodes and Corfu. The author argues that, unlike permanent emigration overseas and internal migration, the phenomenon of intra-European migration on a

Population. Emigration

temporary basis cannot be considered as a safety valve and may be a precipitant of social unrest.

239 Enquêtes sociologiques sur les emigrants grecs. (Sociological investigations of Greek emigrants.)
Elie Dimitras. Athens: Centre national de recherches sociales, 1971. 3 vols.

A three-part study of Greek migrant workers in Western Europe. The first volume concentrates on Greeks about to emigrate to France or West Germany; the second on Greek migrant workers in France, Belgium and Germany; and the third (written in English in collaboration with Evan Vlachos) on migrant workers who have returned to Greece.

240 Essai sur l'émigration grecque: étude démographique, économique et sociale. (An essay on Greek emigration: a demographic, economic and social study.)
N. J. Polyzos. Paris: Recueil Sirey, 1974. 247p. bibliog.

A study of emigration from Greece in historical perspective, together with a consideration of the economic conditions that have given rise to it.

241 Emigration from Greece.
Sotirios Agapitidis. *Migration*, vol. 1, no. 1 (Jan.-March 1961), p. 53-61.

The author concludes that 'the future course of Greek migration depends mainly on the rate of economic development and on the type of association of Greece with the wider economic groupings of developed countries. The first will tend to diminish emigration while the second will encourage it'.

242 Flows of Greek out-migration and return migration.
Theodore P. Lianos. *International Migration*, vol. 13 (1975), p. 119-33.

The purposes of this article are: '(i) to describe briefly the flows of migration from and to Greece, (ii) to examine the extent to which the process of migration from and return to Greece has any effect on the allocation of labor, the occupational structure of migrants and their age distribution, and (iii) to provide an econometric investigation of out-migration to and return migration from West Germany'.

243 Greece.
George Coutsoumaris. In:*The brain drain*. Edited by Walter Adams. New York: Macmillan; London: Collier-Macmillan, 1968. p. 166-82.

Greece has traditionally exported talent and entrepreneurial skill rather than goods and it is not surprising to find that the country has one of the highest incidences of 'brain drain'. The author estimates that Greece in the late 1960s was losing about 1,000 graduates a year.

Population. Emigration

244 **Brain drain: the case of Greece.**
Isaac D. Sabetai. *Epitheorisis Koinonikon Erevnon. The Greek Review of Social Research*, no. 26-27 (Jan.-Sept. 1976), p. 76-83.

The author isolates three main factors in explaining the high rate of emigration of skilled manpower from Greece, '(a) the state of demand for a supply of highly-skilled manpower; (b) the state of the educational system; and (c) the political situation'.

Minorities

245 The religious minorities of Chios: Jews and Roman Catholics.
Philip P. Argenti. Cambridge, England: Cambridge University Press, 1970. 581p. bibliog.

Right up until modern times there have been significant Roman Catholic and Jewish minorities on the island of Chios. This detailed study offers a fascinating insight into a little-known aspect of religious life in Greece.

246 The Moslem minority in western Thrace.
K. G. Andreades. Thessaloniki, Greece: Institute for Balkan Studies, 1956. 84p.

A study of the Turkish minority of western Thrace, which was exempted from the 1923 Exchange of Populations between Greece and Turkey as were the Greeks of Istanbul, Imvros and Tenedos. Published shortly after the anti-Greek riots of September 1955 in Istanbul, the purpose of this book is to demonstrate that Greece treats its Muslim (predominantly Turkish) minority well and that its members regard themselves as loyal citizens of the Greek state.

247 The nomads of the Balkans: an account of life and customs among the Vlachs of northern Pindus.
A. J. B. Wace, M. S. Thompson. London: Methuen, 1914. Reprinted 1972. 332p.

An invaluable scholarly account of the transhumant Vlach communities of northern Pindus, principally Samarina, on the eve of the Balkan Wars; at the time the Romanian government was taking an active interest in the Vlachs, whose language has a close connection with Romanian. Contains a wealth of fascinating material on the history, architecture, customs, folklore and language of the Vlachs who remain a significant minority in present day Greece.

Minorities

248 **Les pasteurs du Pinde septentrional.** (The shepherds of the northern Pindus.)
M. Sivignon. *Revue de géographie de Lyon,* vol. 43, no. 1 (1968), p. 5-43.
An account of life in the villages of northern Pindus, inhabited mainly by communities of transhumant Vlach shepherds.

249 **The nomadic peoples of northern Greece: ethnic puzzle and cultural survival.**
Irwin T. Sanders. *Social Forces,* vol. 33, no. 2 (Dec. 1954), p. 122-29.
A study of three groups of nomadic people in Greece, the Koutzovlachs (Vlachs), the Karagouni (or Arvanito-Vlachs) and the Sarakatsanoi, whose ethnic origins are still a matter for debate in the Balkans.

250 **What is an ethnic group?: ecology and class structure in northern Greece.**
Muriel D. Schein. *Ethnology: an international journal of cultural and social anthropology,* vol. 14, no. 1 (Jan. 1975), p. 83-97.
A consideration of the ethnicity of the two groups of transhumant shepherds in Greece, the Vlachs or Aroumanians, who speak a form of Romanian, and the Sarakatsanoi, who are Greek-speaking.

251 **Histoire des israelites de Salonique.** (History of the Jews in Salonika.)
Joseph Nehama. Thessaloniki, Greece: Molho, 1935-36, Jewish Community of Thessaloniki, 1978; Buenos Aires: Fédération Sephardite Mondiale, 1959. 7 vols.
When Thessaloniki was incorporated into the Greek kingdom in 1912 the largest single element in its population was not Greek but Jewish. This large and flourishing community of Sephardic Jews were the descendants of Jews expelled from Spain in 1492 who had found a greater tolerance in the Ottoman Empire than in Christian Europe. Among themselves the Jews of Thessaloniki spoke an archaic form of Spanish which they wrote with Hebrew characters (Ladino). The community was decimated by the Nazis during the Second World War and the present Jewish population is very small. Nehama's seven volume history chronicles the fortunes of the community over five centuries.

252 **The social structure of the Jewish community of Salonica at the end of the nineteenth century.**
Paul Dumont. *Southeastern Europe,* vol. 5, pt. 2 (1978), p. 33-72.
An important study of the Jewish community of Thessaloniki at its apogee, before it was threatened by Greek competition after the city was incorporated into the Greek state in 1912. At the turn of the century, of some fifty large firms established with local capital, thirty-eight were owned by Sephardic Jews, eight by *deunmehs* (nominally Muslim crypto-Jews) and eight by Greeks.

Minorities

253 **Usos y costumbres de los Sefardies de Salonica.** (Uses and customs of the Sephardic Jews of Thessaloniki.)
Michael Molho, translated from the French by F. Perez Castro.   Madrid, Barcelona: Instituto Arias Montano, 1950. 341p.

Affords an insight into a way of life that has now largely disappeared, with many examples of the lore and customs of the Sephardic Jews of the city.

254 **Farewell to Salonica: portrait of an era.**
Leon Sciaky.   London: W. H. Allen, 1946. 213p.

A nostalgic glimpse of the Sephardic Jewish community of Thessaloniki in its prime.

255 **In memoriam: hommage aux victimes juives des Nazis en Grèce.** (In rememberance: a tribute to the Jewish victims of the Nazis in Greece.)
Michael Molho.   Thessaloniki, Greece: Nicolaides, 1948, 1949; Buenos Aires, 1953. 3 vols.

A moving account of the destruction by the Nazis of the once flourishing Jewish communities of Greece. Some 60,000 Greek Jews, out of a total of 70,000, died during the occupation, with the great Sephardic community of Thessaloniki being virtually wiped out. The Italian occupation authorities were far less brutal in their treatment of the Jews than were the Germans. The third volume is devoted to the vast Jewish cemetery of Thessaloniki, now the site of the university, and was published in Buenos Aires where there is a considerable community of Jews of Thessalonikan origin.

256 **The Jews of Greece.**
L. S. Stavrianos. *Journal of Central European Affairs*, vol. 8 (1948), p. 256-69.

A brief survey of the history of Greek Jewry, with particular reference to its virtual destruction during the Second World War.

Greeks Overseas

257 **Apodimoi Ellines.** (Greeks abroad.)
Athens: Ethnikon Kentron Koinonikon Erevnon, 1972. 158p.
Detailed facts and figures about all aspects of the modern Greek *diaspora*.

258 **The Greeks in the United States.**
Theodore Saloutos. Cambridge, Massachusetts; London: Harvard University Press, 1964. 445p. bibliog.
The definitive history of the Greeks in the United States up until the mid-1960s when, with the lifting of quota restrictions, the latest wave of large-scale Greek immigration began. Provides a lucid guide to the processes of acculturation and assimilation of an ethnic group of growing influence in its adopted country and to the often stormy internal politics of a community that has tended to re-live the political quarrels of the mother country in the New World.

259 **Greek Americans: struggle and success.**
Charles C. Moskos. Englewood Cliffs, New Jersey: Prentice-Hall, 1980. 162p. bibliog.
A perceptive, wide-ranging and up-to-date analysis of the development of the Greek American community, which now numbers over a million and is something of an economic and political power in the land. The Greeks have found in the United States fertile ground for the deployment of their entrepreneurial talents, and they now constitute one of the best educated, most prosperous and most articulate ethnic groups.

260 **The Greeks in America: a student's guide to localized history.**
Theodore Saloutos. New York: Teachers College Press, Columbia University, 1967. 36p.
A useful summary of the author's *The Greeks in the United States* (q.v.). With suggestions for further reading.

Greeks Overseas

261 They remember America: the story of the repatriated Greek-Americans.
Theodore Saloutos. Berkeley, Los Angeles: University of California Press, 1956. 153p. bibliog.

A study of Greek emigrants to the United States who returned to Greece, concentrating particularly on the period 1908 to 1924. The author concludes that these returning migrants 'could not help but bring to Greece some of both the material and the intangible qualities of American life'.

262 Causes and patterns of Greek emigration to the United States.
Theodore Saloutos. *Perspectives in American History*, vol. 7 (1973), p. 381-437.

Between 1820 and 1971 over half a million Greek emigrants arrived in the United States. This study analyses the causes of this massive (in the context of the small Greek state) migration and examines its patterns. 'The big waves of Greek immigration came from 1900 to 1914, in the immediate wake of the First World War, and after 1965.'.

263 The Greek Orthodox Church in the United States and assimilation.
Theodore Saloutos. *International Migration Review*, vol. 7, no. 4 (1973), p. 395-408.

The author concludes that the Greek Orthodox Church in the United States 'faced the inevitable and finally conceded that it was unable to resist the forces of assimilation and preserve the Greek national identity as she once thought. And she conceded this very slowly and reluctantly, primarily in the years since World War II and especially since 1960'.

264 From Mars Hill to Manhattan: the Greek Orthodox in America under Athenagoras I.
George Papaioannou. Minneapolis, Minnesota: Light and Life, 1976. 288p. bibliog.

A study of the Orthodox Church in the United States between 1931 and 1948, during the tenure of Athenagoras (Spyrou) of the Archbishopric of North and South America. Athenagoras subsequently became Ecumenical Patriarch. As archbishop he did much to heal the factionalism of the Greek-American community and to reorganize the administrative structure of the archdiocese.

265 New Smyrna: an eighteenth century Greek odyssey.
E. P. Panagopoulos. Gainesville, Florida: University of Florida Press, 1966. 207p. bibliog.

A clearly written, well-researched and altogether fascinating account of the first mass migration from Greece to the New World in the 1760s. The author vividly describes the vicissitudes and collapse of the short-lived colony at New Smyrna in Florida.

Greeks Overseas

266 **A study of the Greeks in Chicago.**
Grace A. Abbot. *American Journal of Sociology*, vol. 15 (1910), p. 379-93.

A pioneering study of the nascent Greek community of Chicago at a time of massive Greek emigration to the United States. In 1907 alone 46,283 Greeks entered the United States. The author, director of the League for the Protection of Immigrants, noted that the Greek migrants she encountered were 'bright, industrious, and capable men and women. Better than some and not so well as others they are meeting the dangerous temptations which come with long hours and unwholesome living conditions'.

267 **Detroit's Greek community.**
Marios Stephanides. In: *Ethnic groups in the city. Culture, institutions and power.* Edited by Otto Feinstein. Lexington, Massachusetts; London: Heath Lexington Books, 1971. p. 115-28.

A study of the Greek-American community of Detroit, which by the end of the 1960s was some 35,000 strong and mostly engaged in the restaurant business.

268 **The Greeks of Carbon County.**
Helen Zeese Papanikolas. *Utah Historical Quarterly*, vol. 22 (1954), p. 143-64.

At the turn of the century a sizeable community of Greek emigrants established itself in Carbon County, Utah. They were mainly involved in coalmining and were the victims of ethnic prejudice and of the unbridled capitalism of the early 20th century United States.

269 **Faith, hard work, and family: the story of the Wyoming Hellenes.**
Dean P. Talagan. In: *Peopling the high plains: Wyoming's European heritage.* Edited by Gordon Olaf Hendrickson. Cheyenne: Wyoming State Archives and Historical Department, p. 149-68.

A study of the Greek community of Wyoming.

270 **Greek sponge boats in Florida.**
H. Russell Bernard. *Anthropological Quarterly*, vol. 38, no. 2 (April 1965), p. 41-55.

A study of the Greek community of Tarpon Springs, Florida, which dates from the early years of the present century and is engaged primarily in sponge fishing, using skills imported from islands such as Symi and Kalymnos in the Dodecanese where fishing is a traditional occupation. In recent years the sponge fishing industry has been severely threatened by the use of synthetic substitutes.

Greeks Overseas

271 **The Greek American family.**
George A. Kourvetaris. In: *Ethnic families in America: patterns and variations*. Edited by Charles H. Mindel, Robert W. Habenstein. New York: Elsevier, 1976. p. 168-91.
A study of the Greek-American family over three generations.

272 **Greek-American professionals: 1820's-1970's.**
George A. Kourvetaris. *Balkan Studies*, vol. 18, no. 2 (1977), p. 285-315.
The author finds that a genuine Greek-American professional class was rather slow to emerge in the years after the Second World War. He contends that 'as an ethnic group Greek-Americans have not kept up with their share in the more established and prestigious professions and institutions in the U.S. vis-à-vis their numbers and compared to other ethnic groups'. Yet there is now plenty of evidence that they are making up for lost time. The child of a Greek-American family, for instance, is now twice as likely to receive a college education as the national average.

273 **The assimilation of Greeks in the United States, with special reference to the Greek community of Anderson, Indiana.**
Evangelos C. Vlachos. Athens: National Centre of Social Research, 1968. 200p. bibliog.
An examination of 'what assimilation means for the members of the ethnic group, whether it is destructive of any roots with the past and therefore leaves the individual with no base on which successfully to make the transition from one cultural perspective to another, or if it is constructive by providing in addition to the American national consciousness the realization of an ethnic tradition'.

274 **Cultural change among three generations of Greeks.**
Helen Capanidou Lauquier. *The American Catholic Sociological Review*, vol. 12, no. 3 (1961), p. 223-32.
A study of the nature and degree of cultural change among three generations of Greeks in San Antonio, Texas.

275 **Naming patterns and kinship among Greeks.**
Nicholas Tavuchis. *Ethnos*, vol. 26, nos. 1-4 (1971), p. 152-62.
The author considers the 'extent to which two generations of Greek-Americans have actually followed norms pertaining to the personal names of children and found no evidence that would indicate a weakening of commitment to naming norms among the families surveyed'.

Greeks Overseas

276 **Family and mobility among Greek Americans.**
Nicholas Tavuchis. Athens: National Center of Social Research, 1972. 191p. bibliog.
A study of kinship and social mobility patterns among a sample of second generation Greek-Americans, with some consideration of aspects of the acculturation process.

277 **First and second generation Greeks in Chicago.**
G. A. Kourvetaris. Athens: National Centre of Social Research, 1971. 111p. bibliog.
A study of the development and social stratification of the large Greek-American community of Chicago. One interesting statistic to emerge is that whereas the author's sample was predominantly Democratic in its politics, significantly more second than first generation Greeks supported the Republican party.

278 **The unassimilated Greeks of Denver.**
G. James Patterson. *Anthropological Quarterly*, vol. 43, no. 4 (Oct. 1970), p. 243-53.
A study of the, by the time of this study, elderly group of unassimilated Greek immigrants of Denver, Colorado. They clustered around the last surviving *kapheneion*, or coffee houses, in the old Greek town and were a source of some embarrassment to the predominantly middle class and assimiliated members of the Denver Greek community.

279 **Formal organization and the Americanization process with special reference to the Greeks of Boston.**
Mary Bosworth Treudley. *American Sociological Review*, vol. 14, no. 1 (Feb. 1949), p. 44-52.
A study of the Americanization process among Greek immigrants to the United States. 'Greek Americans have proved to be as great "joiners" as any of the older American stocks. They have set up a bewildering array of associations'.

280 **Assimilation and voting behavior: a study of Greek-Americans.**
Craig R. Humphrey, Helen Brock Louis. *International Migration Review*, vol. 7, no. 1 (1973), p. 34-45.
The authors' findings suggest that 'over three generations of residence in the United States, Greek-Americans have not reached full assimilation into American society, based on the concept of assimilation. It is true that upward mobility has been achieved, both as consequence of and resulting in, a change in fashions, language patterns, and rates of intermarriage. In addition, Greek-Americans by the third generation evidence a significant decrease in ethnic identification. Yet the assimilation process remains incomplete insofar as Greek-Americans retain vestiges of ethnic social behavior and remain influenced in their voting behavior by the appearance of a fellow ethnic's name on the ballot'.

Greeks Overseas

281 The history of the Order of AHEPA (The American Hellenic Educational Progressive Association) 1922-1972, including the Greeks in the New World, and immigration to the United States.
George J. Leber. Washington. D.C.: Order of AHEPA, 1972. 588p.

A mine of information on the history of AHEPA, the most influential Greek-American ethnic organization, which has tended to favour a more assimilationist policy than its principal rival GAPA (the Greek American Progressive Association).

282 The Greek press in America.
S. Victor Papacosma. *Journal of the Hellenic Diaspora*, vol. 5, no. 4 (Winter 1979), p. 45-61.

A study of the Greek-American press since the first newspaper *Neos Kosmos* (New World) was published in 1892.

283 Greeks in Australia.
Edited by Charles Price. Canberra: Australian National University Press, 1975. 228p.

Greece is par excellence a country of emigration. In the post-war period Australia has been a favoured destination of Greek migrants. Between 1947 and 1970 some 200,000 Greeks settled in Australia, a number exceeded only by migrants from Great Britain and Italy. These essays consider various aspects of the community and include a valuable general essay by M. P. Tsounis on the Greek communities in Australia.

284 After the Odyssey: a study of Greek Australians.
Gillian Bottomley. St. Lucia, Australia: University of Queensland Press, 1979. 208p. bibliog.

As a consequence of massive immigration in the post-war period, the Greek community in Australia now constitutes (after the Italians) the second-largest group whose native language is not English. The Greeks are also the most concentrated ethnic group, living almost exclusively in towns. As Greek migrants have largely come from rural areas they have had to make a double adjustment, to urban living as well as to an alien culture. Gillian Bottomley provides a comprehensive analysis of this process.

285 Greek children in Sydney.
Eva Isaacs. Canberra: Australian National University, 1976. 128p.

A study of Greek immigrant schoolchildren in Australia and of the problems they and their parents have experienced in adapting to Australian life. In certain classes in certain areas of Sydney as many as eighty-six per cent of children are Greek.

Greeks Overseas

286 **Migrants, unionism and society.**
Petro Georgiou. *Australian and New Zealand Journal of Sociology*, vol. 9, no. 1 (Feb. 1973), p. 32-51.
A study, based on the Greek community, of immigrant attitudes towards trade unionism in Australia.

287 **From southern Europe to New Zealand: Greeks and Italians in New Zealand.**
I. H. Burnley. Sydney, Australia: University of New South Wales Press, 1972. 165p. bibliog.
Greek emigration to New Zealand has been on a small scale compared to emigration to the United States, Canada and Australia. By 1968 there were some 3,000 first generation Greeks in New Zealand, predominantly of peasant origin.

288 **The church and the coffeehouse: alternative strategies of urban adaptation among Greek migrants to Auckland.**
Josephine Baddeley. *Urban Anthropology*, vol. 6, no. 3 (1977), p. 217-36.
The author finds that among the 400-strong Greek community of Auckland there are two main centres of association: the church and the coffeehouse. The first is the focus of those who have migrated to New Zealand directly from established Greek communities; the second that of those who have lived outside established Greek communities. The church attracts a higher concentration of those in manual occupations than does the coffeehouse, while the coffeehouse Greeks are more likely to intermarry with New Zealanders.

289 **The Greeks in Canada.**
G. D. Vlassis. Ottawa, Canada, 1953. 364p.
A pioneering account of the Greek community in Canada. Contains a wealth of disparate information, much of it biographical.

290 **The Greeks of Vancouver: a study of the preservation of ethnicity.**
G. James Patterson. Ottawa, Canada: National Museums of Canada, 1976. 162p. (National Museum of Man: Mercury Series, Canadian Centre for Folk Culture Studies. Paper no. 18).
A study of the 10,000-strong Greek community of British Columbia which has 'preserved its ethnic characteristics to a degree no longer found among Greek communities in the United States or among some other ethnic groups in Canada'.

Greeks Overseas

291 Adaptation and integration of Greek working class immigrants in the city of Toronto, Canada: a situational approach.
Judith A. Nagata. *International Migration Review*, vol. 4, no. 1 (1969), p. 44-69.

'The position of the recently arrived, working class Greek immigrant may be conceptualized as one of precarious marginality in which two social networks must be managed and a narrow course steered between the demands of two cultures.'.

292 L'hellénisme et l'Égypte moderne. (Hellenism and Modern Egypt.)
Athanase G. Politis. Paris: Félix Alcan, 1928, 1930. 2 vols.

From the time of Mehmet Ali until the establishment of Nasser's nationalist regime in the 1950s there existed a large and flourishing Greek community in Egypt, concentrated mainly in Alexandria and Cairo. The Greeks of Egypt were one of the wealthiest and most influential of the communities of the Greek diaspora in modern times. Politis' history deals with the community up until the end of the 1920s.

293 Les hellènes dans l'intérieur de l'Égypte: leur apport au relèvement économique et social du pays. (The Greeks of the interior of Egypt: their role in the economic and social development of the country.)
Cl. Tsourkas. Thessaloniki, Greece: Institute of Balkan Studies, 1957. 24p.

A brief analysis of the contribution of the substantial Greek community of Egypt to the economic development of their adopted country. President Nasser's decision to nationalize foreign firms forced the great bulk of the community into emigration.

294 The Hellenic presence in Ethiopia: a study of a European minority in Africa (1740-1936).
Theodore Natsoulas. *Abba Salama. A Review of the Association of Ethio-Hellenic Studies*, vol. 8 (1977), p. 8-218.

A full-length scholarly study, with bibliography, of the development of the Greek mercantile community of Ethiopia, which played a significant role in the economic life of the country. The author concludes that, overall, the Greek contribution to Ethiopia has been salutary.

Greeks Overseas

295 **Demetros and Giyorgis: two Greeks in early eighteenth century Ethiopia.**
Richard Pankhurst. *Abba Salama. A Review of the Association of Ethio-Hellenic Studies*, vol. 8 (1977), p. 233-39.

The 18th century saw a remarkable expansion of the Greek diaspora, with Greek colonies being established in America and in Bengal. This article throws light on a lesser known aspect of the Greek diaspora, the Greeks of Ethiopia.

296 **Hellenism in England: a short history of the Greek people in this country from the earliest times to the present day.**
Theodore E. Dowling, Edwin W. Fletcher. London: Faith Press; Milwaukee, Wisconsin: Young Churchman Company, 1915. 159p.

A short history of the Greek community in Britain. This dates from the 17th century, when a Greek church was built in Soho Square, near Greek Street in London, and an unsuccessful attempt made to turn Gloucester Hall, Oxford, into a centre for the education of young Greeks. A Greek of Chios, Constantine Rhodocanakis, became one of King Charles II's 'chymists'. In the 19th century a flourishing Greek mercantile community came into existence, based mainly in Manchester and Liverpool, and dominated by Greeks of Chios. Not the least of the contributions of the Greeks to life in England was the opening in 1652 of the first coffee house.

Language

General

297 Medieval and modern Greek.
Robert Browning. London: Hutchinson University Library, 1969. 151p. bibliog.

The Greek language has had a continuous tradition extending over almost three millenia. Written in the conviction that 'if one wants to learn Greek, it does not really matter whether one begins with Homer, with Plato, with the New Testament, with the Romance of Digenis Akritas, or with Kazantzakis' this book affords a scholarly, succinct and clearly written account of the development of the Greek language from Hellenistic times to the present day.

298 The generative interpretation of dialect: a study of modern Greek phonology.
Brian Newton. Cambridge, England: Cambridge University Press, 1972. 236p. bibliog.

The central aim of this book is the establishment of a descriptive framework for the study of modern Greek dialects. The author classifies Greek dialects into five basic groups: Peloponnesian-Ionian; northern Greek; old Athenian; Cretan; and south-eastern (Chios, the Dodecanese and Cyprus).

299 Cypriot Greek: its phonology and inflections.
Brian Newton. The Hague: Mouton, 1972. 186p. bibliog.

Although the Greek of Cyprus is 'quite closely related to that spoken on the Greek mainland' it has a number of distinctive features which are comprehensively analysed in this book.

Language. General

300 **On the verb in modern Greek.**
Irene P. Warburton. Bloomington, Indiana: Indiana University, in association with Mouton, The Hague, 1970. 169. bibliog. (Indiana University Publications. Language Science Monographs, vol. 4).
A linguistic description of the verb forms in modern Greek, in accordance with Chomskyan linguistic theory.

301 **Noun morphology of modern demotic Greek: a descriptive analysis.**
Dimitri Sotiropoulos. The Hague: Mouton, 1972. 133p. bibliog.
The author has undertaken a descriptive analysis of the noun in modern demotic Greek.

302 **Mediterranean bibliography I: Italian loan words in modern Greek.**
Henry Kahane, Renée Kahane. *Annuaire de l'Institut de Philologie et d'Histoire orientales et slaves*, vol. 7 (1939-44), p. 187-228.
With its very extensive seaboard and long maritime tradition Greece has always been much more open to Mediterranean influences than her Balkan neighbours. This article lists references documenting the influence of Italian on the vocabulary of modern Greek.

303 **English loan words in modern Greek.**
D. C. Swanson. *Word. Journal of the Linguistic Circle of New York*, vol. 14, no. 1 (April 1959), p. 26-46.
An entertaining and instructive study of the ever increasing influence of English on the vocabulary of modern Greek. The author holds 'the excesses of Hollywood' to be responsible for several popular borrowings.

304 **L'influence du français sur le grec. Emprunts lexicaux et calques phraseologiques.** (The influence of French on Greek: loan words and grammatical borrowings.)
Nicolas G. Contossopoulos. Athens, 1978. 210p. bibliog.
A scholarly study of the influence of French on modern Greek, an influence which, particularly during the 19th and early 20th centuries, has been very considerable. In recent years, however, English has had a greater impact on Greek than has French.

Language. General

305 **Der Vokalismus der griechischen Lehnwörter im Türkischen.**
(The vowel system of the Greek loan words in Turkish.)
Charalambos Symeonidis. Thessaloniki, Greece: Institute
for Balkan Studies, 1976. 143p.

Modern Greek contains many loan words from Turkish. Yet Greek also had some influence on Turkish, particulary in terms of vocabulary, as this study demonstrates.

306 **Modern Greek and American English in contact.**
P. David Seaman. The Hague: Mouton, 1972. 312p.
bibliog.

A socio-linguistic study of the interaction of the Greek of immigrants in the U.S.A. with American English. Inevitably American Greek is heavily penetrated by English both in terms of syntax and vocabulary, e.g. 'grocery' - 'grosaritsa'. The author writes that 'it seems safe to conclude that for most Greek-Americans modern Greek is a secondary language rapidly diminishing in linguistic importance, that it is practically extinct already in the third generation, and will be totally extinct in the fourth generation unless some new linguistic and/or extra-linguistic factors occur to drastically change the present trend'.

307 **Essai sur la phonétique des parlers de Rhodes: contribution à l'étude des dialectes néogrecs.** (A phonetic study of the dialect of Rhodes: a contribution to the study of modern Greek dialects.)
Agapitos G. Tsopanakis. Athens: Verlag der
Byzantinisch-Neugriechischen Jahrbücher, 1940. 199p.
(Texte und Forschungen zur Byzantinisch-Neugriechischen
Philologie, no. 40).

A study of the dialect of Rhodes, with texts.

308 **Modern Greek in Asia Minor: a study of the dialects of Silli, Cappadocia and Pharasa, with grammar, texts, translations and glossary.**
R. M. Dawkins, with a chapter on the subject-matter of the folk-tales by W. R. Halliday. Cambridge, England:
Cambridge University Press, 1916. 695p. maps.

Given the vast geographical areas over which the Greek language has been spoken in modern times, the language has retained a remarkable unity. Before the Greek populations were uprooted after 1922, however, some of the Greek dialects of Asia Minor had begun to deviate significantly from the norm. They had, for example, been heavily influenced by Turkish. 'The body', as Dawkins wrote in this definitive study, 'has remained Greek, but the soul has become Turkish'.

Language. Dictionaries

309 **Babel balkanique: histoire politique des alphabets utilisés dans les Balkans.** (The Balkan Babel: a political history of the alphabets used in the Balkans.)
E. Zakhos-Papazahariou. *Cahiers du Monde Russe et Soviétique*, vol. 13, no. 2 (April-June 1972), p. 145-79.
A fascinating article discussing the political and cultural implications of the use of the Greek alphabet for the printing of texts in Turkish, Armenian, Serbo-Croat, Vlach, Romanian, Bulgarian, Hebrew, Italian and French. Graphically illustrates the extraordinary mixture of nationalities that constituted the Ottoman Empire.

Dictionaries

310 **Mega Ellino-Anglikon lexikon.** (Large Greek-English dictionary.)
William Crighton. Athens, 1960.
A most useful Greek-English dictionary covering both the demotic and *katharevousa* (purified) forms of the language.

311 **The Oxford dictionary of modern Greek (Greek-English).**
J. T. Pring. Oxford, England: Clarendon Press, 1965. 219p.
A most useful dictionary of modern (demotic) Greek. An English-Greek volume is in preparation.

312 **Oxford English picture dictionary: Anglo-elliniko eikonographimeno lexiko.**
E. C. Parnwell. London: Oxford University Press, 1977. 97p.
A useful illustrated compendium of some of the most common everyday words in use in Greek and English.

313 **Vocabulary of modern spoken Greek (English-Greek and Greek-English).**
Donald C. Swanson, with the assistance of Sophia P. Djaferis. Minneapolis, Minnesota: University of Minnesota Press, 1959. 408p.
Intended 'as a practical guide for English speakers wishing to acquire a working knowledge of standard spoken modern Greek', this vocabulary is prefaced by a useful short account of the history of the language, and of its structure, orthography and pronunciation.

Language. Grammars

314 **Oxford English-Greek learner's dictionary.**
D. N. Stavropoulos, A. S. Hornby. London: Oxford University Press, 1977. 839p.
An up-to-date and clearly printed English-Greek dictionary.

315 **Penguin-Hellenews Anglo-Ellinikon lexikon.**
(Penguin-Hellenews English-Greek dictionary.)
Athens: Hellenews-Paideia, 1975. 926p.
A comprehensive and clearly printed English-Greek dictionary, based on G. N. Garmonsway, *The Penguin English dictionary*.

Grammars

316 **Reference grammar of literary dhimotiki.**
Fred W. Householder, Kostas Kazazis, Andreas Koutsoudas. Bloomington, Indiana: University of Indiana; The Hague: Mouton, 1964. 188p. (Indiana University Research Center in Anthropology, Folklore, and Linguistics, Publication no. 31).
A useful reference grammar for those embarking on the study of the demotic form of modern Greek.

317 **A grammar of modern Greek on a phonetic basis.**
Julian T. Pring. London: University of London Press, 1950. 127p. bibliog.
The author's purpose is 'to present the essentials of accidence and syntax in a practical form suitable for the beginner who wishes to acquire rapidly a simple, educated style of conversational Greek'.

318 **Grammaire du Grec moderne.** (A grammar of modern Greek.)
André Mirambel. Paris: Klincksieck, 1949. 243p.
A grammar of the demotic form of modern Greek.

319 **Demotic Greek.**
Peter A. Bien, John Rassias, Chrysanthi Bien, revised and augmented in collaboration with Christos Alexiou. Hanover, New Hampshire: University Press of New England, 1972. 3rd ed. 286p.
A workmanlike course in demotic Greek, for which tapes and a workbook are also available.

Language. Grammars

320 Modern spoken Greek for English-speaking students.
Ann Arpajolu. New York: Hadrian Press, 1964. 443p.
A course based on the one in use at the U.S. Army Language School in Monterey, California.

321 Handbook of the modern Greek vernacular: grammar, texts, glossary.
Albert Thumb, translated from the German by S. Angus. Edinburgh: T. & T. Clark, 1912. 371p. bibliog.
Somewhat dated but still useful guide to the popular language.

322 A manual of modern Greek.
George Thomson. London; Wellingborough, England: Collet's, 1967. 112p.
An introduction to the study of modern Greek consisting of grammar, texts with explanatory notes, and a vocabulary. 'The student who visits Greece equipped with what he has learnt from this book will not know how to order a meal or cash a cheque. But he will know something about the Language Question and will have read some of the finest and most popular examples of contemporary poetry.'.

323 The Greek language.
George Thomson. Cambridge, England: Heffer, 1966. 101p. bibliog.
A guide to the Greek language from Homeric to modern times, based on parts of the innovative Greek course in use at Birmingham University. This offers students the opportunity of studying the Greek language over a period of nearly 3,000 years. 'There is no other language, with the single exception of Chinese, that offers so long a historical perspective.'.

324 Greek diglossia.
Fred W. Householder. *Georgetown University Monograph Series on Languages and Linguistics*, no. 15 (1962), p. 109-32.
'The purpose of the present study is not to recount the history of the "language question" in Greece, a fascinating story which could not be adequately told in any reasonable compass, full of the most remarkable human passions and incredibly illogical behavior; it is to specify as accurately as possible the linguistic marks of katharevousa and dhimotiki, the various degrees and shades of each and the typical situations in which each is used.'.

325 Neugriechisch für Humanisten. (Modern Greek for classicists.)
Hans Eideneier. Munich, G.F.R.: Ernst Heimeran Verlag, 1965. 119p. bibliog.
A 'conversion course' for those with a knowledge of ancient Greek wishing to acquire a working knowledge of the modern language. Given an unbroken continuity of over 3,000 years, modern Greek is remarkably close to the ancient form of the language.

Language. Grammars

326 **Colloquial Greek.**
Katerina Harris. London: Routledge & Kegan Paul, 1976. 248p. bibliog.
'A simple and uncomplicated guide to colloquial (Demotic) Greek.'.

327 **Modern Greek translation.**
L. G. Ftyaras. London: Longman, Green, 1964. 103p.
A useful selection of passages in modern Greek, with annotations, for translation into English. Principally intended for Greek students learning English, it is also useful for non-Greeks learning Greek.

Religion

328 **The Orthodox Church.**
Timothy Ware. Harmondsworth, England: Penguin Books, 1963. 352p. bibliog.
Concise, clearly written and scholarly account of the history, theology and discipline of the Orthodox Church. The author is an English convert to Orthodoxy.

329 **Anatomy of a church: Greek orthodoxy today.**
Mario Rinvolucri. London: Burns & Oates, 1966. 192p. bibliog.
A sympathetic but not uncritical account by a Roman Catholic of the state of the Orthodox Church in Greece in the mid-1960s. Most of what he has to say still holds good today.

330 **Church and state in Greece.**
Charles A. Frazee. In: *Greece in transition: essays in the history of modern Greece, 1821-1974*. Edited by J. T. A. Koumoulides. London: Zeno, 1977. p. 128-53.
A concise survey of church-state relations in independent Greece. The author argues that if the Orthodox Church is to be enabled to 'come to grips with the spiritual problems demanding solutions in contemporary times' it must be free of its dependence on the state.

331 **Handbuch der Ostkirchenkunde.** (A handbook to the Eastern Churches.)
Edited by Endre von Ivanka, Julius Tyciak, Paul Wiertz. Düsseldorf, G.F.R.: Patmos-Verlag, 1971. 839p. bibliog.
Comprehensive surveys of the beliefs, practices and history of the various churches of the East. Contains a very comprehensive bibliography.

Religion

332 Le patriarcat oecumenique dans l'église orthodoxe: étude historique et canonique. (The Ecumenical Patriarchate in the Orthodox church: a historical and canonical study.)
Maximos. Metropolitan of Sardis, translated from the Greek by Jacques Touraille. Paris: Beauchesne, 1975. 422p. bibliog.

A scholarly study of the historical position of the Ecumenical Patriarchate in Constantinople (Istanbul), the senior patriarchate of Orthodox Christendom, by a present member of the Holy Synod.

333 The Great Church in captivity: a study of the patriarchate of Constantinople from the eve of the Turkish conquest to the Greek War of Independence.
Steven Runciman. Cambridge, England: Cambridge University Press, 1968. 455p. bibliog.

A history of the Ecumenical Patriarchate, the senior patriarchate of the Orthodox Church, under Ottoman rule, a period when, on account of the Ottoman *millet* system, the fortunes of the patriarchate were closely linked with those of the Greek people as a whole. Much material on the late Byzantine Church and Orthodox relations with the Western churches during the Turkish period.

334 Protestant patriarch: the life of Cyril Lucaris (1572-1638), Patriarch of Constantinople.
George A. Hadjiantoniou. London: Epworth Press; Richmond, Virginia: John Knox Press, 1961. 160p.

A life of Kyrillos Loukaris, a 17th century Ecumenical Patriarch, strongly attracted by Calvinist doctrines, who was executed by the Turks as a result of Catholic intrigue.

335 Eustratios Argenti: a study of the Greek church under Turkish rule.
Timothy Ware. Oxford, England: Clarendon Press, 1964. 196p. bibliog.

Scholarly and well-written study of Eustratios Argenti of Chios 'the most eminent Greek theologian of the 18th century'. Largely focussed on the somewhat arid theological disputes of the period, e.g. whether Latin Catholic converts to Orthodoxy should be baptized, the book contains much incidental information on the state of the Orthodox Church in the Greek lands at a time when the fate of their church was closely bound up with that of the Greek people themselves.

336 Studies and documents relating to the history of the Greek church and people under Turkish domination.
Theodore H. Papadopoullos. Brussels, 1952. 507p. (Bibliotheca Graeca Aevi Posterioris vol. I).

An edition of the *Planosparaktis (Scourge of error)*, a mid-18th century diatribe against the Patriarch Cyril V composed in political verses. The carefully annotated text is preceded by a very lengthy and informative introduction which throws a great deal of light on the history of the Ecumenical Patriarchate in the

Religion

18th century, when, riddled with corruption and intrigue, its fortunes were at a low ebb.

337 **The Orthodox Church and independent Greece 1821-1852.**
Charles A. Frazee. Cambridge, England: Cambridge University Press, 1969. 220p. bibliog.

A study of the impact of the Greek War of Independence on the Orthodox Church. In an effort to curtail the jurisdiction of the Ecumenical Patriarchate in Constantinople, an autocephalous Greek church was created in 1833, during the regency period of King Otto's reign. This settlement determined the general pattern of church-state relations in Greece that has continued until the present day.

338 **The waters of Marah: the present state of the Greek church.**
Peter Hammond. London: Rockliff, 1956. 186p.

A sympathetic and intelligent account of the Orthodox Church in Greece at a time when Greece was in the throes of civil war in the 1940s. Particularly valuable for its non-metropolitan perspective.

339 **Sociology de l'Orthodoxie grecque: sociology of Greek Orthodoxy.**
Social Compass, vol. 22, no. 1 (1975), 147p.

An issue devoted exclusively to articles on various aspects of the contemporary Orthodox Church in Greece.

340 **Religious brotherhoods: a sociological view.**
Basil Jioultsis. *Social Compass*, vol. 22, no. 1 (1975), p. 67-83.

A study of the religious brotherhoods, such as *Zoi* (Life) and *Sotir* (Saviour) which have played, and continue to play, an important role in the life of the church in Greece.

341 **Theology in present-day Greece.**
Christos Yannaras. *St. Vladimir's Theological Quarterly*, vol. 16, no. 4 (1972), p. 195-214.

A survey of current theological trends in the Orthodox Church in Greece.

342 **The Orthodox Church of Greece: the last fifteen years.**
Charles A. Frazee. *Indiana Social Studies Quarterly*, vol. 32, no. 1 (Spring 1979), p. 89-110.

A sympathetic and well-informed account of the Orthodox Church in Greece during the fifteen years or so since 1965. This period, which included the years of the Colonels' dictatorship, was a stormy one for the church and witnessed, after the return of democracy in 1974, some tentative moves towards a greater separation of church and state.

Religion

343 **Zwischen Konstantinopel und Moskau: orthodoxe Kirchenpolitik im Nahen Osten 1967-1975.** (Between Constantinople and Moscow: the policy of the Orthodox Church in the Near East 1965-1975.)
Friedrich-Wilhelm Fernau. Opladen, G.F.R.: Leske Verlag & Budrich, 1976. 160p.

The second part of this book contains a useful summary of the politics of the Orthodox Church in Greece during the Colonels' dictatorship.

344 **Between partnership and separation: relations between church and state in Greece under the constitution of 9 June 1975.**
A. Basdekis. *Ecumenical Review*, vol. 29, no. 1 (Jan. 1977), p. 52-61.

An analysis of the effects on the traditionally close relationship of church and state in Greece of the country's most recent constitution. The relevant provisions signal a distinct attempt by the civil power to reduce some of the traditional constitutional privileges of the Orthodox Church.

345 **Meteora: the rock monasteries of Thessaly.**
Donald M. Nicol. London: Chapman & Hall, 1963. 210p.

The Meteora monasteries of Thessaly, suspended hundreds of feet in the air atop massive rock formations, are one of the most extraordinary and impressive sights in Greece. This book provides 'an introduction to their history and a general description of the monasteries as they exist today, set against the background of Byzantine monasticism whose ideals they expressed and of the Byzantine world against which they came into being'.

346 **Mount Athos: the garden of the Panaghia.**
Emmanuel Amand de Mendieta. Berlin: Akademie Verlag, with Adolf M. Hakkert, Amsterdam, 1972. 360p. (Berliner Byzantinistische Arbeiten, vol. 41). bibliog.

A scholarly and very thorough study of the history and present state of the Holy Mountain of Athos, whose foundation is dated to 963 A.D. Consisting of twenty ruling monasteries, divided into the coenobitic or 'common life' monasteries, where the monks live as a community, and the less rigorous idiorrythmic, in which property ownership is permitted, together with the various skites, kellia, kalyvia and hermitages, the Monastic Republic has since 1912 been under Greek sovereignty, although still enjoying a notional degree of independence. All monks, however, are Greek citizens. Nowadays the numbers of monks on the peninsula are much diminished, and Greek monks predominate. The total number of monks in the twenty ruling monasteries fell from 7,432 in 1903 to 1,491 in 1965. There are still communities, however, of Russian, Bulgarian, Serbian and Romanian monks. An essential source for the history and organization of this last surviving great centre of Byzantine Orthodox monasticism.

347 **Athos and its monasteries.**
F. W. Hasluck. London: Kegan Paul, 1924. 214p. bibliog.

Although now dated, still of value as a scholarly guide to the history of the extraordinary monastic republic of Mount Athos. Since Hasluck wrote c.1912 the number of monks on the Holy Mountain has declined very considerably.

Religion

348 **The monks of Athos.**
R. M. Dawkins. London: George Allen & Unwin, 1936. 408p.+14p. of additions and corrections.
A scholarly but lively account of the extraordinary monastic republic of Mount Athos, which continues to survive, if not exactly to flourish, against all the odds. Enlivened by accounts of the author's own experiences in visiting the Holy Mountain.

349 **Athos, the Holy Mountain.**
Sidney Loch. London: Lutterworth Press, 1957. 264p. map.
A useful guide to the Holy Mountain, which treats each of the major monasteries chapter by chapter.

350 **Anchored in God: an account of life, art, and thought on the Holy Mountain of Athos.**
Constantine Cavarnos. Athens: Astir, 1959. 230p.
An account by a Greek Orthodox Christian of life on the Holy Mountain more or less as it is today.

351 **Mount Athos.**
John Julius Norwich, Reresby Sitwell. London: Hutchinson, 1966. 191p.
A beautifully illustrated account of a journey to the Holy Mountain in the mid-1960s, when an apparently irreversible decline had set in.

352 **Athos: the mountain of silence.**
Philip Sherrard. London: Oxford University Press, 1960. 110p. bibliog.
A finely illustrated presentation of 'certain aspects of the life of Athos and of its monks'.

353 **New statistical data concerning the monks of Mount Athos.**
George Mantzaridis. *Social Compass*, vol. 22, no. 1 (1975), p. 97-106.
The author notes that in recent years there has been an increase in the number of monks on Mount Athos, a decrease in their average age and an improvement in their level of education. These data provide some hope for the future continuity of this monastic republic.

354 **Le millénaire du Mont Athos, 963-1963: études et mélanges.**
(The millenium of Mount Athos, 963-1963: studies and miscellanea.)
Chevetogne, Belgium: Editions de Chevetogne, 1963; Venice: Fondazione Giorgio Cini, Chevetogne, 1964. 2 vols.
A collection of scholarly articles on art, theology and history to commemorate the millenium of the foundation of the monastic republic of Athos. Vol. 2 contains an enormous bibliography of almost 2,000 items.

Religion

355 **Greek Orthodox-Jewish relations in historic perspective.**
Demetrios J. Constantelos. *Journal of Ecumenical Studies*, vol. 13, no. 4 (Fall 1976), p. 6(522)-16(532).

Takes a more optimistic view than Professor Zvi Ankori (see following item) of the often bitter antagonisms that have traditionally existed between Christian and Jew in the Orthodox world.

356 **Greek Orthodox-Jewish relations in historic perspective: the Jewish view.**
Zvi Ankori. *Journal of Ecumenical Studies*, vol. 13, no. 4 (Fall 1976), p. 17(533)-57(573).

An article by the Professor of the History and Culture of the Jewry of Salonica and Greece at the University of Tel Aviv, Israel, on the often antagonistic relations between Orthodox Christians and Jews in the eastern Mediterranean world.

357 **Eastern churches review.**
Oxford, England: 1966-. Biannual.

Contains useful surveys of current developments within the Orthodox Church in Greece, together with articles of an historical and theological character.

Society

Sociology

358 **Rainbow in the rock: the people of rural Greece.**
Irwin T. Sanders. Cambridge, Massachusetts: Harvard University Press, 1962. 363p.

A detailed sociological analysis of rural Greece during the early 1950s, when Greece was beginning its slow recovery from the devastation of a decade of foreign occupation, resistance and civil war. Although much of the fabric of Greek traditional society was already under threat when Sanders carried out his research, it had not yet undergone the radical transformation of the last twenty-five years. The book presents a composite picture based on a number of different communities; the author assembled a wealth of detail on the social structure and economy of rural Greece before in-depth study of peasant life had become fashionable. Provides revealing insights into the devastation suffered by Greece in the 1940s.

359 **Modern Greece: facets of underdevelopment.**
Nicos P. Mouzelis. London: Macmillan; New York: Holmes & Meier, 1978. 222p.

A penetrating collection of essays, written from a neo-Marxist standpoint, on topics such as the development of Greek capitalism; the relevance of the concept of class to the study of modern Greek society; the comparative study of Greek and Bulgarian peasants between the wars; class structure and the role of the military; capitalism and dictatorship in post-war Greece; and Greek formalism.

360 **Greece.**
Nikos P. Mouzelis, Michael A. Attalides. In: *Contemporary Europe: class, status and power.* Edited by Margaret Scotford Archer, Salvador Giner. London: Weidenfeld & Nicolson, 1971. p. 162-97.

The authors argue that the reasons why Greece differs 'in striking and fundamental ways from the highly developed societies of western Europe' are not linked

Society. Sociology

only to the relatively low level of industrialization. Some of the main features of the Greek class structure 'can only be understood by analysing their formation and persistence, i.e. by examining class struggles and developments during the Ottoman rule and the Greek War of Independence at the beginning of the 19th century'.

361 Greece.
John Koty. In: *The institutions of advanced societies.* Edited by Arnold M. Rose. Minneapolis, Minnesota: University of Minnesota Press, 1958. p. 330-83.

A brief guide to the basic institutions of Greece, e.g. political system, religion, economy, family, education etc., written from the perspective of a sociologist.

362 Some economic and social problems in Greece.
C. Evelpidis. *International Labour Review*, vol. 68 (July-Dec. 1953), p. 151-65.

A useful analysis of the economic and social problems of Greece in the immediate aftermath of the Civil War and as the country was poised for the economic 'take-off' that has characterized the past three decades.

363 The economic and social transformation of modern Greece.
H. J. Psomiades. *Journal of International Affairs*, vol. 19, no. 2 (Feb. 1965), p. 194-205.

The author, writing in the mid-1960s, concluded that more had been done 'in the last decade to bring the people of Greece into the mainstream of national life and into Europe than in any comparable period since 1821'.

364 Political conflict and the diffusion of innovations.
Constantine A. Yeracaris. *Rural Sociology*, vol. 35, no. 4 (Dec. 1970), p. 488-99.

A study which finds a correlation between left-wing political views and a willingness to embrace agricultural innovation.

365 La condition industrielle à Athènes. Études sociogéographique.
(The industrial situation of Athens. A sociogeographical study.)
Guy Burgel. Athens: Centre National de Recherches Sociales, 1970. 4 vols. tables. maps.

A detailed study, more sociological than geographical, of the world of the industrial worker in Athens, replete with statistical tables and maps.

366 Greek society in transition.
Irwin T. Sanders. *Balkan Studies*, vol. 8, no. 1 (1967), p. 317-32.

In analysing the changes that have occurred in Greek society during the post-war period the author concludes that while many Greek values are consonant with modernization, some run counter to the needs of industrialization. 'Will', he asks,

Society. Sociology

'the rugged individualism of the Greek decline or will it put its own stamp on the industrialization process? Will the civilized, almost lackadaisical approach to time and its use give way to the clock-run schedule demanded of efficient producers? Will cooperation in community and economic matters become accepted, offsetting divisiveness and mistrust?'.

367 **Social change in a Greek country town: the impact of factory work on the position of women.**
Ioanna Lambiri. Athens: Centre of Planning and Economic Research, 1965. 163p. (Research Monograph Series, no. 13).

A study of the impact of work in the Piraiki-Patraiki cotton factory on women recruited in the nearby country town of Megara. The author analyses the manner in which established societal values and ways of life are transformed by industrialization and urbanization. A useful case study which throws important light on the wider processes of modernization.

368 **Social stratification in a Greek village.**
Muriel Dimen Schein. *Annals of the New York Academy of Sciences*, vol. 220, no. 6 (1974), p. 488-95.

During a field study in 1967-68 of the pseudonymous village of Kriovrisi in northwestern Greece, the author observed 'a high degree of uniformity in economic level and equality in daily social interaction. However, on formal and ceremonial and political occasions, two distinct social groups would separate out. These two groups do not coincide with occupational groups, migration patterns, or wealth differences. I hypothesize that the two groups have their origins in a two-class structure that once existed in the village. The local economic foundations of this traditional structure have been transformed, but the structure continues to affect access to extravillage kin and nonkin ties, particularly ties to the urban stratification system, and these in turn condition social relations within the village'.

369 **Only on Sundays.**
Muriel Dimen Schein. *Natural History*, vol. 80 (April 1971), p. 52-61.

A study of the everyday life of women in Greek villages.

370 **Margariti: village d'Epire.**
Bernard Kayser. Athens: Centre des Sciences Sociales, 1964. 39p.

A detailed sociological analysis of the Epirot village of Margariti, threatened, as has been the case with many mountain communities during the post-war period, by large-scale outward migration.

Society. Anthropology

371 **Sociology in Greece.**
J. G. Peristiany. In: *Contemporary sociology in western Europe and in America.* Edited by Charles C. Moskos. Rome: Instituto Luigi Sturzo, 1968. p. 263-314.

A history of sociology in Greece, together with an account of research institutions in the social sciences, a survey of current research projects and a checklist of sociological research by Greeks or about Greece.

372 **Present status of sociology in Greece.**
George A. Kourvetaris, Betty A. Dobratz. In: *Handbook of contemporary developments in world sociology.* Edited by Raj. P. Mohan, Don Martindale. Westport, Connecticut; London: Greenwood Press, 1975. p. 307-27.

A survey of the present state of sociology in Greece.

Anthropology

373 **Vasilika: a village in modern Greece.**
Ernestine Friedl. New York: Holt, Rinehart & Winston, 1963. 110p. bibliog. map.

A pioneering anthropological study of a village in Boeotia with chapters on matters such as the economic activities, consumption habits, the system of dowry and inheritance and the human relations of the family and of the village.

374 **Portrait of a Greek mountain village.**
Juliet Du Boulay. Oxford, England: Clarendon Press, 1974. 296p. (Oxford Monographs on Social Anthropology).

A valuable anthropological study of a small mountain village in Euboea, recording the final stages of the community's transition from 'social solidarity to fragmentation', largely the result of large scale migration. Affords a useful insight into the traditional values and beliefs of rural Greece at a time when these are challenged by rapid social change. The author regrets the passing of a whole way of life which, perhaps, she over-idealizes.

375 **Honour, family and patronage: a study of institutions and morals in a Greek mountain community.**
J. K. Campbell. Oxford, England: Clarendon Press, 1964. 393p.

A pioneering anthropological study of the Sarakatsanoi community of transhumant shepherds. The author analyses the social relations of the Sarakatsanoi in considerable detail and the picture he draws of mutual competition and distrust between families that are not connected by marriage or kinship throws important light on the nature of Greek society at large. His stress on the importance of

Society. Anthropology

political and social patronage is particularly illuminating and helps to explain much in Greek society that is puzzling to the outsider.

376 **The dangerous hour: the lore of crisis and mystery in rural Greece.**
Richard H. Blum, Eva M. Blum, assisted by Anna Amera, Sophie Kallifatidou. London: Chatto & Windus; New York: Scribner's, 1970. 410p. bibliog.

An interesting attempt to analyse the way in which Greek peasants and shepherds regard the nature of life and of death, of crisis and of mystery. The authors also seek to draw parallels with the ancient world.

377 **Greek peasants, ancient and modern: a comparison of social and moral values.**
P. Walcot. Manchester, England: Manchester University Press, 1970. 136p. bibliog.

An interesting attempt to compare the value systems of peasants in ancient and modern times, prompted by the author's realization 'that a study of the [modern] Greek peasant was of immense help when it came to the interpretation of Hesiod and Homer'.

378 **The Greek peasant.**
Scott G. McNall. Washington, D.C.: American Sociological Association, 1974. 112p. bibliog. (Arnold and Caroline Rose Monograph Series).

A study of 'the strategies of response and adaptation of Greek peasants subjected to major crises such as industrialization, emigration from the villages to Athens and abroad, political instability, military occupation and war; both civil and international'.

379 **Regional variation in modern Greece and Cyprus: toward a perspective of the ethnography of Greece.**
Edited by Muriel Dimen, Ernestine Friedl. New York: New York Academy of Sciences, 1976. 465p. (Annals of the New York Academy of Sciences, vol. 268).

A compendium of some thirty-five papers on the anthropology and sociology of Greece and Cyprus, with particular emphasis on regional variation. A valuable indication of the range and sophistication of the anthropological and sociological research that has taken place in Greece in recent years.

380 **Pasteurs-nomades méditerranéens: les saracatsans de Grèce.**
(Mediterranean transhumant shepherds: the Sarakatsanoi of Greece.)
G. B. Kavadias. Paris: Gauthier-Villars, 1965. 444p. bibliog.

A detailed study of the way of life, beliefs and value system of the Sarakatsanoi, a community of transhumant shepherds not to be confused with the Vlachs (see

Society. Anthropology

The nomads of the Balkans: an account of life and customs among the Vlachs of northern Pindus).

381 **Greece.**
Dorothy Demetracopoulou Lee. In: *Cultural patterns and technical change. A manual prepared for the World Federation for Mental Health.* Edited by Margaret Mead. New York: New American Library, 1955, p. 57-96.
Part of a study commissioned by UNESCO, this pioneering anthropological study of Greek society is well worth reading. Individuals in Greece, the author reminds us, 'work not collectively but within an intricate web of interdependencies and mutual aid'.

382 **Contributions to Mediterranean sociology: Mediterranean rural communities and social change.**
Edited by J. G. Peristiany. Paris: Mouton, 1968. 349p.
Contains a number of contributions relating specifically to the anthropology of Greece, grouped under the headings: 1) social values, 2) village structure, 3) patron-client relations-marketing, 4) internal and external migration, 5) social change, 6) social prerequisites to economic development. Includes a fascinating article by Georges Condominas on Greek migration to Madagascar, which began in the early 19th century.

383 **Some aspects of dowry and inheritance in Boeotia.**
Ernestine Friedl. In: *Mediterranean countrymen: essays in the social anthropology of the Mediterranean.* Edited by Julian Pitt-Rivers. Paris: Mouton, 1963, p. 113-15.
A study in which 'the dowry and inheritance system of the Boeotian farmers serves as a focus for a more detailed investigation of the circulation of property and persons both among the country villages themselves and between the villages and towns'.

384 **Dowry and inheritance in modern Greece.**
Ernestine Friedl. *Transactions of the New York Academy of Sciences*, vol. 22 (1959), p. 49-54.
A study of the dowry system in Greece, based on the author's researches in the village of Vasilika (*Vasilika: a village in modern Greece*, q.v.).

385 **Internal migration and the changing dowry in modern Greece.**
Peter S. Allen. In: *Greece: past and present.* Edited by John T. A. Koumoulides. Muncie, Indiana: Ball State University, 1979, p. 142-56.
The institution of the *proika*, or dowry, has long been a distinctive and important feature of rural Greek society. Traditionally, a son has not been free to marry unless and until he has seen his sisters married off with an appropriate dowry. The massive inflow of internal migrants from the villages to the cities in post-war Greece has inevitably affected traditional attitudes to the dowry. The author believes that under the impact of urbanization the dowry is declining in importance, yet it can still be an onerous obligation. 'In the majority of cases today the

Society. Anthropology

dowry no longer involves the devolution of land or other bases of livelihood; more typically, the dowry is made up of cash and domestic real estate; further, it has become inflated to the point that it sometimes comprises the near totality of a family's wealth instead of an equivalent portion as in the past'.

386 **'Honor' crimes in contemporary Greece.**
Constantina Safilios-Rothschild. *British Journal of Sociology*, vol. 20, no. 2 (June 1969), p. 205-18.

An analysis of the way in which social changes in Greece in recent years have led to some revision 'in the definition of what constitutes a dishonouring event as well as in what is an appropriate action in case of dishonour'. Nonetheless the persistence 'of the ideal of honour makes possible its use as a cover for criminal behaviour not necessarily resulting from strict moral standards or feelings of shame'.

387 **Attitudes of Greek spouses towards marital infidelity.**
Constantina Safilios-Rothschild. In: *Extramarital relations*. Edited by Gerhard Neubeck. Englewood Cliffs, New Jersey: Prentice-Hall, 1969. p. 77-93.

Based on research on a random sample of 250 Athenian families, the author advances the following hypotheses: '1. The better the husband-wife relationship, the less tolerated is marital infidelity, especially a wife's infidelity. The limiting factor is the presence of young children. 2. The greater the utilitarian dependence of one spouse upon the other, the greater the tendency of the dependent spouse to tolerate his (her) partner's infidelity. 3. The higher the spouse's educational achievement, the greater their deviation from traditionally prescribed behaviour in case of infidelity on the part of the marital partner. The direction of this deviation is toward greater tolerance on the part of well-educated husbands and towards less tolerance on the part of well-educated wives'.

388 **Lies, mockery and family integrity.**
Juliet Du Boulay. In: *Mediterranean family structures*. Edited by J. G. Peristiany. Cambridge, England: Cambridge University Press, 1976, p. 389-406.

'Deceit, therefore, and the avoidance of public mockery, appear as phenomena intimately connected with the structure of the value system and as part of the legitimate means by which the honour of a family is preserved and the prosperity of the house maintained.'.

389 **The implicative meaning of the Greek concept of philotimo.**
Vasso G. Vassiliou, George Vassiliou. *Journal of Cross-Cultural Psychology*, vol. 4, no. 3 (Sept. 1973), p. 326-41.

The authors conclude that when 'the individual moves from a less to a more highly complex milieu within Greece, his social conduct ceases to be regulated in ingroup norms, and role perceptions become more important. Consequently *philotimo* (or love of honour) is expressed in terms allowing for more individualized interpretation depending on the social context'. In short, 'the concept is gradually abstracted to where it is mainly associated with honesty'.

Society. Anthropology

390 **Honour and the devil.**
J. K. Campbell. In: *Honour and shame: the values of Mediterranean society*. Edited by J. G. Peristiany. London: Weidenfeld & Nicolson, 1965, p. 141-70.

A study of the conflict between 'the self-regarding values of honour' and 'the prescriptions of Christian charity and fellowship' among the 4,000 strong community of transhumant shepherds in northern Greece known as the Sarakatsanoi.

391 **The kindred in a Greek mountain community.**
J. K. Campbell. In: *Mediterranean countrymen: essays in the social anthropology of the Mediterranean*. Edited by Julian Pitt-Rivers. Paris: Mouton, 1963, p. 73-96.

A study of the 'cognatic kinship system' of the Sarakatsanoi transhumant shepherds which illuminates the 'moral values and political relations' of all rural Greeks.

392 **Folk model vs. actual practice: the distribution of spiritual kin in a Greek village.**
Stanley Aschenbrenner. *Anthropological Quarterly*, vol. 48, no. 2 (1975), p. 65-86.

A study of the role of the koumbaros (godparent or best man, although the obligations of the koumbaros are considerably greater than these terms might imply) in a Peloponnesian village.

393 **The idiom of family.**
Margaret E. Kenna. In: *Mediterranean family structures*. Edited by J. G. Peristiany. Cambridge, England: Cambridge University Press, 1976, p. 347-62.

A study, based on research on an Aegean island, which seeks to show how 'the idiom of family, used in relationships of wedding sponsorship and godparenthood (koumbaria), reconciles the ideal of family independence and self-sufficiency with the need for co-operative ties outside the family'.

394 **The role of kinship in the transmission of national culture to rural villages in mainland Greece.**
Ernestine Friedl. *American Anthropologist*, vol. 61, no. 1 (Feb. 1959), p. 30-38.

The author found that the dissemination of a national culture and its institutions in Greece was assisted by close contact between the rural and urban population and by 'upwardly mobile kin'.

Society. Anthropology

395 **Two case studies of marketing and patronage in Greece.**
J. K. Campbell. In: *Contributions to Mediterranean sociology. Mediterranean rural communities and social change.* Edited by J. G. Peristiany. Paris: Mouton, 1968, p. 143-54.

'Just as the peasant faces the administrator on unequal terms and attempts to protect his interest by developing patronage relationships with those who can introduce a measure of moral consideration into the administrator's handling of his affairs, so the same man as a small producer is generally in a weak bargaining position when he confronts the merchants who may purchase his produce. Again, he hopes to offset the consequences of his weak position by attempting to draw the merchant into a particular relationship implying some moral commitment which will modify the simple equation of power. Unhappily, as we shall see, the merchant does not often need, nor is it in his interest, to extend to a commercial client general protection of the kind sometimes enjoyed by political clients.'.

396 **Houses, fields and graves: property and ritual obligation on a Greek island.**
Margaret E. Kenna. *Ethnology*, vol. 15, no. 1 (Jan. 1976), p. 21-34.

A study, based on fieldwork in one of the islands of the Cyclades, of the way in which 'the pattern of naming, the system of inheritance, and beliefs about the fate of the soul relate to the value placed on the independence and self-sufficiency of the family and on the moral obligations of parents, children and koumbari (ritual kinsmen linked through weddings and baptisms). These principles and values are used to interpret, justify, and evaluate behaviour in different ways at various points in the domestic cycle'.

397 **The position of the coffee house in the social structure of the Greek village.**
John D. Photiadis. *Sociologia Ruralis*, vol. 5 (1965), p. 45-56.

The kapheneion, or coffee house, has traditionally been the focus of the (male) social life of the Greek village, with attendance at different coffee houses sometimes reflecting different political allegiances. This study of the village of Stavropolis found that the frequency with which male villagers attended the coffee house, combined with the village's physical isolation, resulted in the kapheneion constituting 'a cohesive social system which exerts strong control over its members'.

398 **The evil eye and bewitchment in a peasant village.**
Regina Dionisopoulos-Mass. In: *The evil eye.* Edited by Clarence Maloney. New York: Columbia University Press, 1976, p. 42-62.

Belief in the evil eye, namely that harm can be occasioned by looking at a person's property or person, is widespread in many parts of the world. This study focusses on contemporary evil eye beliefs in an island village. Attention is also given to the various protective devices that are worn to ward off the effects of the evil eye.

Society. Anthropology

399 **Tensions leading to conflict and the resolution and avoidance of conflict in a Greek farming community.**
Perry A. Bialor. In: *Contributions to Mediterranean sociology: Mediterranean rural communities and social change.* Edited by J. G. Peristiany. Paris: Mouton, 1968, p. 107-26.
A study of the factors leading to tensions in a rural Greek community and of the means by which these tensions are resolved.

400 **Name days and feasting: social and ecological implications of visiting patterns in a Greek village of the Argolid.**
Nicolas Gavrielides. *Anthropological Quarterly*, vol. 47, no. 1 (Jan. 1974), p. 48-70.
A study of 'the social and demographic dynamics' of the name day, the saint's day after which Greeks are, or, in the eyes of the Orthodox Church, should be, named. Particularly in rural areas a person's name day is the occasion for an elaborate ritual of visiting and hospitality, as are the various religious holidays of the church.

401 **Paratsoukli: institutionalized nicknaming in rural Greece.**
H. Russell Bernard. *Ethnologia Europaea. Revue internationale d'ethnologie européenne. A world review of European ethnology*, vol. 2-3 (1968-69), p. 65-74.
The practice of nicknaming is very common in Greece, particularly in rural areas. This is a study of the social function of nicknaming in the Dodecanesian island of Kalymnos. The author concludes that there is an inverse relationship between the size and discreteness of Greek communities and the strength and custom of nicknaming. He sees nicknames as a 'social integration factor' and as 'a powerful mode of social control'. 'They verify and constantly remind their bearers of their own socially unacceptable characteristics. By making such things as stinginess, rumor mongering, the persistent use of vulgar language and other anti-social characteristics the butt of constant joking, society continuously reminds itself of what it considers good and bad behavioral traits'.

402 **On aspects of child rearing in Greece.**
George Vassiliou, Vasso G. Vassiliou. In: *The child and his family.* Edited by E. James Anthony, Cyrille Koupernik. New York: Wiley-Interscience, 1970. vol. 1, p. 429-44.
An analysis of the ways in which traditional patterns of child rearing in Greece, formed in a pre-industrial environment, have failed to keep up with the rapid pace of socio-economic and technological development in the country, thereby generating 'conflicts that strain human relations and overtax the personality's synthetic capacities'.

Society. Anthropology

403 The options of Greek men and women.
Constantina Safilios-Rothschild. *Sociological Focus*, vol. 5, no. 2 (Feb. 1972), p. 71-83.

The author finds that, as in most developing and developed countries, women's liberation 'is an upper-middle and middle class phenomenon that for different reasons in each country does not easily permeate the other classes'.

404 The Cretans: a geographical analysis of some aspects of their physical anthropology.
D. F. Roberts. *Journal of the Royal Anthropological Institute of Great Britain and Ireland*, vol. 84, pts. 1-2 (Jan.-Dec. 1954), p. 145-57.

An anthropometric study based on data collected at the beginning of the present century and which proved 'of little assistance in specifying the original sources of the inhabitants of Crete'.

405 Values that inhibit modernization: the case of Greece.
Scott G. McNall. *Studies in Comparative International Development*, vol. 9, no. 3 (Fall 1974), p. 46-63.

The author argues that 'value systems that evolved during the period of subjugation to Turkish rule are maladaptive for responding to modernization'.

406 Ethnographic food habits research in Greece.
Margaret L. Arnott. *Ethnologia Europaea*, vol. 5 (1971), p. 204-10.

An account of the basic diet of the Greeks, which the author holds to be not much different from that of the ancient Greeks.

407 Field work in a Greek village.
Ernestine Friedl. In: *Women in the field: anthropological experiences*. Edited by Peggy Golde. Chicago: Aldine, 1970. p. 195-217.

A revealing insight into the experiences of an anthropologist and her classicist husband while undertaking during the mid-1950s the fieldwork in a Boeotian village that resulted in the pioneering study *Vasilika: a village in modern Greece* (q.v.).

Health and Welfare

408 **An analysis of the health and welfare services in Greece.**
Anne Wood-Ritsatakis. Athens: Center of Planning and Economic Research, 1970. 227p. bibliog. (Special Studies Series B no. 1).
Paints a somewhat gloomy view of the provision of health and welfare services in Greece, particularly in the rural areas.

409 **Social planning and policy alternatives in Greece. Income support and aid to families with dependent children (A.F.D.C.).**
Demetrius S. Iatridis. Athens: National Centre of Social Research, 1980. 320p. bibliog.
Indispensable for the study of social deprivation and social welfare in Greece.

410 **Health and healing in rural Greece: a study of three communities.**
Richard H. Blum, Eva M. Blum, assisted by Anna Amera, Sophie Kallifatidou. Stanford, California: Stanford University Press, 1965. 269p. bibliog.
Aims to provide the reader 'with an understanding of the health beliefs and practices of peasants and shepherds in rural Greece'. In seeking to explain the cultural factors affecting Greek attitudes to sickness and medicine, the book affords a fascinating insight into folk remedies and folk superstitions, e.g. the need to avoid 'the "heavy" shadow of the fig tree'.

411 **High life expectancy on the island of Paros, Greece.**
Jeff Beaubier. New York: Philosophical Library, 1976. 144p. bibliog.
An attempt, using both anthropological and medical techniques, to account for the absence of 'high mortality for the majority and extremely high longevity for a

substantial minority' among the inhabitants of the Aegean island of Paros. Among the reasons Beaubier advances for Paros' good 'health profile' are good nutrition, lack of high cholestorol levels, low smoking, high exercise and absence of excess weight problems. 'They approach life with verve and pride in self. The people are gregarious and have strong marriages. As a community they take part in religious and social activities. They are sensitive to changes in their bodily states and they practice health activities'.

412 A comparative study of the mortality of the population of Greece.

Vasilios G. Valaoras. *Human Biology*, vol. 8, no. 4 (Dec. 1936), p. 553-64.

A pioneering study of mortality statistics in Greece. The 1928 census revealed a distribution of the population 'distorted as to age and sex, there being an unusual excess of children and of females'. The author believed this was in part due to the upheavals consequent on the Balkan wars; the catastrophic Greek intervention in Asia Minor (1919-22) and the resulting exchange of populations.

413 Psychiatry in contemporary Greece.

Peter Hartocollis. *American Journal of Psychiatry*, vol. 123, no. 4 (Oct. 1966), p. 457-62.

A survey of the state of psychiatry in Greece in the mid-1960s. The author notes that 'possession by a demon is still a common belief concerning patients with hysterical crises or unpredictable temperament' among the population at large. He concludes that 'even though the professional attitude is enlightened and a conscientious effort is being made to change them from custodial into treatment centres, state hospitals throughout the country remain overpopulated and understaffed, enjoying little support from either the state or the public'.

414 Drinking practices and controls in rural Greece.

Richard H. Blum, Eva M. Blum. *British Journal of Addiction*, vol. 60, no. 1 (Aug. 1964), p. 93-108.

An interesting study of drinking practices in Greece. The authors conclude that, for the most part, the rural Greek is 'as temperate as Achilles of yore'.

Politics

General

415 **Politics in modern Greece.**
Keith R. Legg. Stanford, California: Stanford University Press, 1969. 367p. bibliog.
One of the few full-length academic studies of the Greek political system. Includes chapters on interest groups, political parties, politics at the parliamentary and extraparliamentary levels, occupational backgrounds and local connections of politicians and the composition of the political elite, whose resilience is such a pronounced feature of Greek politics. Places heavy stress, as do most observers be they political scientists, sociologists or anthropologists, on the importance of patron-client relationships. He concludes that so far 'the Greek system has not solved the basic questions of legitimacy, in that its people have never developed a loyalty to any office or institution for its own sake'. It is too early to say whether his gloomy prediction of 'unstable equilibrium', 'general malaise' with 'occasional chaotic outbursts' will prove correct. Significant changes have taken place in the political system since 1974, but the underlying patterns that have long characterized Greek politics still persist.

416 **The web of modern Greek politics.**
Jane P. C. Carey, Andrew G. Carey. New York, London: Columbia University Press, 1968. 240p. map. bibliog.
Somewhat superficial but useful as a preliminary introduction to the complexities of the Greek political system.

417 **Les forces politiques en Grèce.** (Political forces in Greece.)
Jean Meynaud, with the assistance of P. Merlopoulos, G. Notaras. Paris: Études de Science Politique, 1965. 530p.
One of the few serious monographs on post-war Greek politics, this book provides a detailed study of the Greek political system in the post-war period up until the election of George Papandreou's Centre Union government in February 1964. Contains very useful tables of electoral statistics.

Politics. The military

418 **The Greek political system: its strengths and weaknesses during a century of free political life.**
Thomas P. Trombetas. *Epitheorisis Koinonikon Erevnon. The Greek Review of Social Research*, no. 26-27 Jan.-Sept. 1976), p. 147-56.
An analysis of the politics of the first century of independent Greece.

419 **Grèce.**
Dimitri Kitsikis. In: *International guide to electoral statistics: Guide international des statistiques électorales. Vol. 1. National elections in Western Europe.* Edited by Stein Rokkan, Jean Meyriat. The Hague, Paris: Mouton, 1969, p. 163-82.
Greece was the first European country to introduce universal adult male suffrage, as early as 1844, although women did not acquire the right to vote in national elections until 1956. Dimitri Kitsikis provides a useful guide to electoral statistics in Greece, with summary tables of election results since 1926. In the post-war years the voting system, and in particular 'reinforced' proportional representation, has been used by the right to disadvantage its opponents, often with extraordinary results.

420 **Greek political reaction to American and Nato influences.**
Theodore A. Couloumbis. New Haven, Connecticut; London: Yale University Press, 1966. 250p.
A thorough analysis of the attitude of the political parties on NATO membership between 1952, when Greece became a member of the alliance, and the great political crisis of July 1965 which resulted in the downfall of George Papandreou's Centre Union government. The book has gained a new relevance with Greece's withdrawal from the military wing of NATO in the aftermath of the Turkish invasion of Cyprus in July 1974, again making Greek membership of the alliance a sensitive political issue.

421 **Post World War II Greece: a political review.**
Theodore A. Couloumbis. *East European Quarterly*, vol. 7, no. 3 (Fall 1973), p. 285-310.
A useful survey of Greece since the end of the Second World War.

The military

422 **The military in Greek politics: the 1909 coup d'état.**
S. Victor Papacosma. Kent, Ohio: Kent State University Press, 1977. 254p. bibliog.
Military intervention in the political process has been a recurrent feature of the Greek political system in the 20th century. This book provides a careful analysis

Politics. The military

of the coup of Goudi of 1909. This led to the emergence on the Greek political scene of the great statesman Eleftherios Venizelos and set the pattern for subsequent military intrusions into politics.

423 Some observations on the Greek military in the inter-war period, 1918-1935.
Thanos Veremis. *Armed Forces and Society*, vol. 4, no. 3 (May 1978), p. 527-41.

A useful article on the role of the military in inter-war Greece, a time when the political influence of the officer corps was at its height.

424 Allied politics and military interventions: the political role of the Greek military.
Nikolaos A. Stavrou. Athens: Papazisis, 1977. 196p.

The Greek military has a long and sorry record of direct intervention in the political process. This is a well-informed study of the political role of the military during the post-war period, concentrating more on the antecedents to the Colonels' coup of April 1967 than on the seven-year dictatorship itself, the longest period of outright military rule in the history of post-independence Greece. Stavrou finds, *inter alia*, that 'the Greek military is the most advanced of the political/social institutions and yet it is shown to have been conspiracy-prone, uni-ideological in attitudes, and uncritically committed to its allies'. He sees the civilian political leadership as 'a major contributor to the deviations in the role of the Greek military and the perpetuation of a climate of illegality in the armed forces', and he argues that 'if such a pattern of civilian-military relations persists, the probability of future adventures cannot be excluded'.

425 The role of the military in Greek politics.
George A. Kourvetaris. *International Review of History and Political Science*, vol. 8, no. 3 (Aug. 1971), p. 91-114.

Considering its relevance to Greek political life, political scientists and sociologists have only recently begun to investigate seriously the political role of the Greek military. This article raises some of the issues but much basic research still needs to be done.

426 The military and society in Greece.
James Brown. *European Journal of Sociology*, vol. 15, no. 2 (1974), p. 245-61.

'As long as the Greek military profession maintains a narrow social base of recruitment, it will possess a relatively uniform social and political outlook, which background conditions and fashions conservative political perspectives and sets limits on the links with other elite groups. As a result, these gaps in values, and the basic distrust that has long existed between these two elements of Greek society, heightened the suspicions of the coup leaders regarding the political chaos of 1965 to 1967. This, in turn, may well have precipitated the April 21st coup d'état.'.

Politics. The military

427 Professional self-images and political perspectives in the Greek military.
George Andrew Kourvetaris. *American Sociological Review*, vol. 36, no. 6 (Dec. 1971), p. 1043-57.

A study of the attitudes of the Greek military during the Colonels' regime. The author concludes that 'the shift from heroic to managerial styles of military leadership noted in the United States and other Western industrialized countries has not been paralleled in Greece. Rather, the modal self-image of the Greek officer is a synthesis of a primitive and indigenous heroic value system with a managerial ethic derived from the contemporary Western model'.

428 The Greek army officer corps: its professionalism and political interventionism.
George A. Kourvetaris. In: *On military intervention*. Edited by Morris Janowitz, Jacques van Doorn. Rotterdam: Rotterdam University Press, 1971, p. 154–201. (Contributions to Military Sociology 2. Studies presented at Varna International Sociological Conference 1970).

Based in part on interviews with middle and high ranking officers during the Colonels' dictatorship. Kourvetaris' interlocutors gave as their principal reasons for intervention the internal communist threat, the incompetence of the politicians and 'the moral decay and extreme forms of social inequality of the society at large'.

429 Greek service academies: patterns of recruitment and organizational change.
George A. Kourvetaris. In: *The military and the problem of legitimacy*. Edited by Gwyn Harries-Jenkins, Jacques van Doorn. Beverly Hills, California; London: Sage Publications, 1976, p. 113-39. (Sage Studies in International Sociology, no. 2).

The author concludes that 'historically and empirically the patterns of recruitment in the service academies did not evolve from the aristocratic model of Western European armies, but rather they closely paralleled those in the emerging nations and the armies of the 1950s. Because of this it can tentatively be suggested that the propensity of military intervention in Greek politics both in diachronic and synchronic terms might also parallel the frequency of military intervention in politics of the emerging nations'.

Politics. Communism

Communism

430 Revolution and defeat: the story of the Greek communist party.
D. George Kousoulas. London: Oxford University Press, 1965. 306p. bibliog.

A history of the Greek Communist Party (K.K.E.) from its foundation in 1918 to the aftermath of its failed bid for power in the Civil War of 1946-49. Banned in 1947, the K.K.E. split in 1968 into two wings, known as the Party of the Exterior (K.K.E.ex.), which is oriented towards Moscow, and the Party of the Interior (K.K.E.es.), whose policies are broadly Eurocommunist. The communists were legalized in 1974 and since then the Party of the Interior has attracted considerably fewer votes (three per cent) than the orthodox K.K.E. (nine per cent).

431 The dynamics of communism in eastern Europe.
R. V. Burks. Princeton, New Jersey: Princeton University Press, 1961. 244p.

Contains a considerable amount of information on communism in Greece and Macedonia.

432 Statistical profile of the Greek communist.
R. V. Burks. *Journal of Modern History*, vol. 27, no. 2 (June 1955), p. 153-58.

The author based his statistical profile on a questionnaire filled in by 586 'so-called repentant prisoners', out of some 10,000 communists held in Greek jails in the early 1950s following the defeat of the Democratic Army in 1949. Although the author is well aware of inevitable doubts as to the representative nature of the sample, the article throws interesting light on the socio-economic background of supporters of the left in Greece during the 1940s.

433 Greece: communism in a non-western setting.
Dimitri Kitsikis. In: *Communism and political systems in western Europe.* Edited by David E. Albright. Boulder, Colorado: Westview Press, 1979. p. 211-42.

An up-to-date study of communism and its political significance in present day Greece.

434 Yearbook on international communist affairs 1969-
Edited by Richard F. Staar. Stanford, California: Hoover Institution Press, 1970-. annual.

Contains annual surveys of developments within the Greek Communist Party (K.K.E.).

435 **The Greek Communist Party.**
Ilias Yannakakis. *New Left Review*, no. 54 (March-April 1969), p. 46-54.
An account, first published in Czechoslovakia in the summer of 1968, of the origins of the split that occurred in the Greek Communist Party (K.K.E.) in February 1968. The two wings that emerged were the Communist Party of the Exterior (K.K.E.ex.), which broadly adheres to the dictates of Moscow, and the Communist Party of the Interior (K.K.E.es.) which follows a Eurocommunist line.

436 **Greek communists and the Karamanlis government.**
Dimitri Kitsikis. *Problems of Communism*, vol. 26, no. 1 (Jan.-Feb. 1977), p. 42-56.
One of Constantine Karamanlis' first acts on his precipitate return to Greece in the summer of 1974 was to legalize the Greek Communist Party(ies) (K.K.E.), which had been banned since 1947. This move upset right wing Greeks and it represented a significant policy shift for Karamanlis. Whereas in the 1950s and 1960s he had sought to isolate and contain the far left, he now sought to integrate it into the political system. Kitsikis' article examines Karamanlis' policy towards the K.K.E. in historical perspective.

Politics since the 1950s

437 **Socioeconomic change and cabinet composition in Greece: 1946-1974.**
K. Koutsoukis. *Epitheorist Koinonikon Erevnon. The Greek Review of Social Research*, no. 32 (Jan.-April 1978), p. 74-79.
A statistical study of the composition of post-war Greek cabinets which illustrates 'some of the salient conflicts still ongoing in Greek society - urban versus rural cleavage, modernity versus tradition, and practical expertise versus generalists'.

438 **Consensus and cleavage: party alignment in Greece, 1945-1965.**
Thomas P. Trombetas. *Parliamentary Affairs*, vol. 17, no. 2 (Summer 1966), p. 295-311.
A study of Greek politics during the post-war period up until the great constitutional crisis of July 1965 which resulted in the downfall of George Papandreou's Centre Union government and paved the way for the Colonels' seizure of power in April 1967.

Politics. Politics since the 1950s

439 Political communication in Greece, 1965-1967: the last two years of a parliamentary democracy.
Demetrios G. Carmocolias. Athens: National Centre of Social Research, 1974. 167p. bibliog.

The author concludes that the mass media, and in particular the press, long famed for its rumbustious nature, contributed to political instability during the critical two years before the Colonels' take-over in April 1967 'by failing to provide sufficiently objective political information'.

440 Political change in a clientelistic polity: the failure of democracy in Greece.
Keith R. Legg. *Journal of Political and Military Sociology*, vol. 1, no. 2 (Fall 1973), p. 231-46.

The author argues that attempts to modernize George Papandreou's Centre Union party provoked the constitutional crisis of July 1965. 'However, a modernized Centre Union party, one that could seriously attempt the modernization of Greek society, was sufficiently threatening to provoke military intervention in 1967.'.

441 Political climate and political methods in contemporary Greece.
C. L. Doumas. *Southern Quarterly*, vol. 5, no. 2 (Jan. 1967), p. 151-68.

An analysis of the 'political culture' of Greece in the post-war period.

442 A tentative analysis of the power élite of Greece.
Christos L. Doumas. *Southern Quarterly*, vol. 4, no. 4 (July 1966), p. 374-408.

The purpose of this article is to offer 'a brief analysis of Greece's constitution and power structure' in the crucial mid-1960s.

443 Political implications of the modern Greek concept of self.
Adamantia Pollis. *British Journal of Sociology*, vol. 16, no. 1 (March 1965), p. 29-47.

The author argues that 'the Greek social order is predicated on a Hobbesian view of the nature of man' and that the Greek concept of self, and in particular the notion of *philotimo* (literally 'love of honour'), does not augur well for the future of democratic institutions in Greece.

444 The impact of traditional patterns on Greek politics.
Adamantia Pollis. *Epitheorisi Koinonikon Erevnon. The Greek Review of Social Research*, no. 29 (Jan.-April 1977), p. 1-14.

'An analysis of the Greek elites - the armed forces, the church hierarchy, the financial and economic oligarchy and the political elite - the interrelationship among them and the mechanisms employed for perpetuating their rule is essential for an understanding of the deterrents to change in Greece and hence the dynamics of Greek politics.'.

Politics. Politics since the 1950s

445 **Greece under military rule.**
Edited by Richard Clogg, George N. Yannopoulos. London: Secker & Warburg; New York: Basic Books, 1972. 272p. bibliog.

An analysis by various writers of the deleterious effects of the first five years of the Colonels' regime on almost every aspect of Greek life. Contains an extensive bibliography.

446 **Inside the Colonels' Greece.**
Athenian, *pseud. for* Rodos Roufos, translated from the French by Richard Clogg. London: Chatto & Windus; New York: W. W. Norton, 1972. 215p.

A well-informed and highly intelligent analysis of the Colonels' regime.

447 **Eyewitness in Greece: the colonels come to power.**
John A. Katris. St. Louis, Missouri: New Critics Press, 1971. 317p.

A racy, journalistic account of the background to the Colonels' coup of 21 April 1967.

448 **The death of a democracy: Greece and the American conscience.**
Stephen Rousseas, with the collaboration of Herman Starobin, Gertrud Lenzer. New York: Grove Press, 1968. 241p.

An account of the background to the Colonels' coup of 21 April 1967, particularly critical of the role of the U.S.A. in Greece.

449 **The origins of the Greek military coup, April 1967.**
D. George Kousoulas. *Orbis*, vol. 13, no. 1 (Spring 1969), p. 332-58.

An analysis of the background to the Colonels' takeover in 1967 whose unjustifiably gloomy conclusion is that 'the military coup was rendered inevitable by the breakdown of the democratic process'.

450 **Greek political perspectives.**
Marcus Wheeler. *Government and Opposition*, vol. 3, no. 3 (Summer 1968), p. 339-51.

A lucid attempt to set the Colonels' coup into 'the general perspective of recent Greek politics'.

Politics. Politics since the 1950s

451 **Crisis, revolution and military rule in Greece: a tentative analysis.**
Christos L. Doumas. *Southern Quarterly*, vol. 6, no. 3 (April 1968), p. 255-88.
An analysis of the early stages of the Colonels' regime, which argued that the West had 'little to gain from opposing the new regime', for this might impel it from the NATO alliance towards neutralism.

452 **Six years later: the Greek 'military' government revisited.**
Christos L. Doumas. *Southern Quarterly*, vol. 12, no. 1 (Oct. 1973), p. 51-79.
A sympathetic appraisal of the Greek Colonels' regime. The author believes that the Colonels, far from being inept 'politically or in organizational talent', were on the contrary 'well trained, educated, disciplined, and astute men who correctly assessed the prevalent political situation of the time'. The shambles which they made of Greece would scarcely seem to bear out such a judgement.

453 **Coups and countercoups in Greece, 1967-1973 (with postscript).**
Stephen G. Xydis. *Political Science Quarterly*, vol. 84, no. 3 (Fall 1974), p. 507-38.
A useful overview of the history of Greece under military rule.

454 **Aujourd'hui la Grèce.** (Greece today.)
Edited by Jean-Paul Sartre. *Les Temps Modernes*, no. 276 (no. 2), (1969), 363p.
The entire issue is devoted to the Colonels' Greece. The first part contains left-wing analyses of Greece's political, economic and social history, the monarchy, the constitution of 1968, the Colonels' educational policies, etc. The second part documents the repressive methods employed by the Colonels against their political opponents. The third part consists of translations of politically oriented poetry and prose by Greek authors. An impressive insight into the nature of the Colonels' regime two years after its establishment.

455 **Council of Europe. European Commission of Human Rights. The Greek Case. (Application no. 3321/67- Denmark v. Greece. Application no. 3322/67- Norway v. Greece. Application no. 3323/67- Sweden v. Greece. Application no. 3344/67- Netherlands v. Greece.) Report of the Commission.**
Strasbourg, France: Council of Europe, 1969. 2 vols. (4 pts.).
This is an unusual and perhaps unique document in international law, which throws a great deal of light on the Colonels' dictatorship. Following the coup of 21 April 1967, the governments of Denmark, Norway, Sweden and the Netherlands laid a complaint before the European Commission of Human Rights of the Council of Europe, of which Greece was also a member, alleging that the Greek regime was engaged in the torture of political prisoners and had suspended various articles of the constitution without sufficient justification. Following hearings

Politics. Politics since the 1950s

in Strasbourg and Greece, the Commission produced a report which found that torture in Greece was an administrative practice and there had been no state of emergency in April 1967 such as would have entitled the Greek regime, within the statutes of the Council of Europe, to suspend various articles of the constitution. In the face of almost certain expulsion by the Committee of Ministers of the Council of Europe, Greece withdrew in December 1969. The Commission's carefully documented report contains the evidence before it and the various legal arguments advanced on behalf of and against the Greek government. Seldom can a judicial body of this kind have been required to determine the facts of a particular political situation. The report was a powerful blow against the Colonels' regime and contributed substantially to its isolation within the international community. It fully justified the complaints of the Danish, Norwegian, Swedish and Netherlands governments, which took the lead in seeking to put pressure on the Colonels' regime, in sharp contrast to the inertia of the larger member countries of the Council of Europe.

456 **The Greek case before the European Human Rights Commission.**
James Becket. *Human Rights. Journal of the Section of the Individual Rights and Responsibilities, American Bar Association*, vol. 1, no. 1 (Aug. 1970), p. 91-117.
A useful commentary on the Greek case before the Human Rights Commission of the Council of Europe (see item above).

457 **Greece and the Council of Europe. the international legal protection of human rights by the political process.**
Howard D. Coleman. *Israeli Yearbook of Human Rights* (1972), p. 121-41.
A study by an international lawyer of the case mounted against Greece in the Council of Europe. He concludes that although the Council of Europe 'has rightfully stood as a model for other institutions in the sphere of protection of human rights', nonetheless the Council 'by acting before the process under the [European] Convention [on Human Rights] had been completed, substantially and needlessly interfered with the first steps for the collective enforcement of human rights in Greece'.

458 **Barbarism in Greece: a young American lawyer's inquiry into the use of torture in contemporary Greece, with case histories and documents.**
James Becket. New York: Walker & Co., 1970. 147p.
A revealing account of the repellent means used by the Colonels to keep themselves in power, written by a lawyer whose investigations on behalf of Amnesty International did much to focus international opprobrium on the regime.

459 **Torture in Greece: the first torturers' trial 1975.**
London: Amnesty International Publications, 1977. 98p.
The Greeks hold the rare distinction of not only having replaced a brutal, inefficient and unpopular dictatorship with a genuine plural democracy, but also of having sentenced the principal protagonists of the dictatorship, and the torturers on whom they relied, to long terms of imprisonment. Amnesty International has performed a signal service in publishing this account of the trial in August and

Politics. Politics since the 1950s

September 1975 of thirty-two members of the military police (E.S.A.) accused of torturing political prisoners. Based on verbatim newspaper accounts of the trial, the book paints a horrifying picture of the military regime's treatment of its opponents. Not the least of its merits is that it enables the Greekless reader to gain some insight into the crudely and narrowly nationalistic mentality of the torturers.

460 **Democracy at gunpoint: the Greek front.**
Andreas Papandreou. London: André Deutsch, 1971. 388p.

An insider's view of the background to the Colonels' coup of 21 April 1967 by the then *enfant terrible* of the Centre Union Party, headed by his father George Papandreou. Andreas Papandreou has since emerged as the leader of the radical, Marxist/populist Panhellenic Socialist Movement (P.A.S.O.K.), the largest opposition party and a very significant force in Greek politics. The author throws a lurid light on the alleged intrigues of the U.S. embassy in Greece. Affords a useful insight into the extraordinary complexity of Greek politics and the extent to which Greeks believe that their political system is manipulated by forces outside the country.

461 **Nightmare in Athens.**
Margaret Papandreou. Englewood Cliffs, New Jersey: Prentice Hall, 1970. 390p.

A revealing personal account of the background to and early months of the Colonels' regime by the American wife of a prominent Greek politician. Strongly critical of the American role in Greece.

462 **Journals of resistance.**
Mikis Theodorakis, translated from the French by Graham Webb. London: Hart-Davis MacGibbon, 1973. 334p.

An unhappy blend of autobiography, political polemic, contemporary history and musico-literary musings by Greece's best known living composer. Arrested by the Colonels, Theodorakis was allowed to leave Greece in 1970 thanks to the intervention of the French radical politician Jean-Jacques Servan-Schreiber. Perhaps the most valuable passages highlight the chronic factionalism of the Greek left. In the detention camp at Oropos he found no less than three communist factions which were scarcely on speaking terms with each other.

463 **I was born Greek.**
Melina Mercouri. London: Hodder & Stoughton, 1971. 224p.

Highly personal and more than a little corny autobiography of the actress and politician Melina Mercouri, who was stripped of her Greek citizenship for her opposition to the Greek Colonels. General Metaxas, the pre-war dictator, is described as a 'mean bastard', while the politician Constantine Karamanlis is 'a splendid hunk of a man'. She also records a somewhat improbable encounter with 'a Spetsai fisherman lightly perched on a plodding donkey reading Proust'.

464 **A piece of truth.**
Amalia Fleming. London: Jonathan Cape, 1972. 257p.

A spirited account of the Colonels' Greece by one of its most doughty and courageous opponents, Amalia Fleming, the Greek widow of Sir Alexander Flem-

Politics. Politics since the 1950s

ing. The book's great value lies in her deeply felt and moving account of her experiences at the hands of her interrogators in the military police following her attempt to engineer the escape of Alexandros Panagoulis, the would-be assassin of the dictator Col. Papadopoulos. Although she was not tortured herself she portrays with chilling accuracy the experiences of those who fell foul of the Colonels. Following world-wide protests she was deported from Greece and, in exile, waged an unceasing struggle against Greece's military dictators.

465 **Events, Greece 1967-1974.**
Compiled and edited by Michael Harlow. Athens: Anglo-Hellenic Publishing, 1975. 88p.

An anthology of prose and verse whose purpose is 'to present something of what it was like to live and write under the pall of the years 1967-1974', the years of the Colonels' dictatorship.

466 **The Greece of Karamanlis.**
Maurice Genevoix, with an introduction by Constantine Tsatsos. London: Doric Publications, 1973. 206p.

Despite its hagiographic tone, Genevoix's book has some value for an understanding of Constantine Karamanlis, one of Greece's outstanding 20th century politicians.

467 **On the Greek elections.**
Nicos P. Mouzelis. *New Left Review*, no. 107 (March-April 1978), p. 59-74.

An analysis of the significance of the elections of November 1977, which saw a dramatic increase in the vote for Andreas Papandreou's radical populist Panhellenic Socialist Movement (P.A.S.O.K.). With twenty-five per cent of the vote it almost doubled its share in the November 1974 election.

Constitution and Legal System

468 Constitution of the republic of Greece.
London: Press and Information Office, 1975.
An English translation of the constitution of July 1975, now in force in Greece.

469 Reflections on the Greek constitution.
Basil S. Markesinis. *Parliamentary Affairs*, vol. 27, no. 1 (Winter 1973-74), p. 8-27.
An analysis of the constitution of the 'presidential parliamentary republic' established by Col. Papadopoulos in the summer of 1973, in the aftermath of a naval mutiny and the abolition of the monarchy. Endorsed in an undemocratic referendum, this constitution was rendered still-born by Brig. Ioannidis' counter-coup of November 1973.

470 Recent political and constitutional developments in Greece.
Basil S. Markesinis. *Parliamentary Affairs*, vol. 28, no. 3 (Summer 1975), p. 261-77.
The reflections of a constitutional lawyer on the downfall of the Colonels' regime and the elections of November 1974, the first to be held for ten years.

471 The theory and practice of dissolution of parliament: a comparative study with special reference to the United Kingdom and Greek experience.
Basil S. Markesinis. Cambridge, England: Cambridge University Press, 1972. 283p. bibliog. (Cambridge Studies in International Law, no. 14).
Contains a considerable amount of useful material on Greek constitutional history.

Constitution and Legal System

472 The Greek crown and its ministers.
Basil S. Markesinis. *Parliamentary Affairs*, vol. 26, no. 1 (Winter 1972-73), p. 56-68.
A study of the often controversial role of the Greek monarchy in the constitutional life of the country. The author concludes that 'Greek kings adopted a personal interpretation of the Constitution and of their rights and duties under it'.

473 Greek law: three lectures delivered at Cambridge and Oxford in 1946.
Panagiotis J. Zepos. Athens, 1949. 119p.
A brief outline 'of the historical background of Modern Greek law and Modern Greek legal science' by a distinguished professor of law.

474 Twenty years of the Greek civil code: achievements and objectives.
Panagiotis J. Zepos. *Balkan Studies*, vol. 8, no. 2 (1967), p. 395-406.
An analysis of the working of the first twenty years of the Greek civil code of 1946.

475 The Greek penal code.
Translated by Nicholas B. Lolis, with an introduction by Giorgios Mangakis. South Hackensack, New Jersey: Fred B. Rothman; London: Sweet & Maxwell, 1973. 205p. (The American Series of Foreign Penal Codes, no. 18).
A translation of the Greek penal code, prefaced with a summary of its distinctive features.

476 Reform of family law in Greece.
Alkis Argyriadis. In: *The reform of family law in Europe (The equality of the spouses-divorce-illegitimate children).* Edited by A. G. Chloros. Deventer, Netherlands: Kluwer, 1978, p. 139-49.

477 The legal system and economic development of Greece.
A. A. Pepelasis. *Journal of Economic History*, vol. 19, no. 2 (June 1959), p. 173-98.
An interesting analysis of 'a neglected cause of economic backwardness' in modern Greece, namely her legal system.

Administration

478 **Reorganisation of public administration in Greece.**
Georges Langrod. Paris: Organisation for Economic
Co-operation and Development, 1965. 112p. (Problems of
Development).
The gloomy prognosis of this report is that 'at a moment when Greece is going
into the European Economic Community and will, consequently, have to enter
into competition with its member countries, it must be provided without delay
with an adequate administrative machine, and, in order to achieve this, give first
priority to its reform. It is, literally, the eleventh hour for understanding the
situation and going ahead with concrete and bold reforms without exaggerating or
indulging in "perfectionism" - but energetically and with continuity of ideas, to
avoid subjecting the country to a state of under-development'. Fifteen years later
the situation is not greatly improved and Greece's creaking bureaucratic structure
is still badly in need of radical reform.

479 **The ecology of Greek administration: some factors affecting
the development of the Greek civil service.**
Demetrios Argyriades. In: *Contributions to mediterranean
sociology. Mediterranean rural communities and social
change.* Edited by J. G. Peristiany. Paris: Mouton, 1968, p.
339-49.
A study of the composition of the notoriously cumbersome Greek bureaucracy.

Foreign Relations

480 **Foreign interference in Greek politics: an historical perspective.**
Theodore A. Couloumbis, John A. Petropoulos, Harry J. Psomiades. New York: Pella Publishing Co., 1976. 171p.

For a good part of its independent history Greek sovereignty has been more notional than real. This useful study focusses on the 'role of foreign powers in the formation and conduct of Greek foreign and fiscal policy, in the operation of the Greek political process, and in the development of Greek political institutions'.

481 **Balkan federation: a history of the movement toward Balkan unity in modern times.**
L. S. Stavrianos. Northampton, Massachusetts: Smith College, 1941-42. 338p. bibliog. (Smith College Studies in History, vol. 27, nos. 1-4).

A study of the various, for the most part still-born, movements to promote the unity of the Balkan peoples from the time of Catherine the Great onwards.

482 **The Greek foreign debt and the Great Powers 1821-1898.**
John A. Levandis. New York: Columbia University Press, 1944. 137p. bibliog.

In the 19th century the Greek state was crippled by a heavy burden of external debt, a burden which commenced during the War of Independence with the negotiation in the City of London of the Greek Loans of 1824 and 1825. In many respects during the 19th century Greece's independence was more notional than real and nowhere was her dependent relationship with regard to foreign powers more starkly revealed than in the problem of her foreign debts. As the author puts it in this admirable study: 'practically all Greek loans, in spite of the many safeguards offered, were floated at thirty per cent and often at forty per cent discount; their yields ranged from five to eight per cent, and interest and sinking fund charges were payable in gold. The acceptance by the borrowers of such onerous terms was due to urgent need. As a result the foreign debt was hastily and disadvantageously contracted. Most of the loan proceeds were appropriated to non income-creating purposes and particularly to expanding debt charges which

Foreign Relations

could not be met by an enfeebled Greek treasury. This eventually led to debt defaults. On such occasions the aggrieved creditors appealed to their respective governments, and demanded restitution through interference in the financial affairs of the borrowers'. After the bankruptcy of the Greek state in 1893 and its humiliating defeat in the Greco-Turkish war of 1897 the financial affairs of Greece were subject to the surveillance of an International Financial Commission of Control.

483 The Corfu incident of 1923: Mussolini and the League of Nations.
James Barros. Princeton, New Jersey: Princeton University Press, 1965. 339p. bibliog.

Following the murder in 1923 of the Italian members of the Greek-Albanian frontier commission, Mussolini, newly established in power in Italy, exploited Greece's weak international position by bombarding and occupying the island of Corfu. The intervention of the League of Nations brought about an Italian withdrawal, although Greece was obliged to pay a substantial indemnity to Italy. This was one of the League's few unequivocal successes in the inter-war period. Professor Barros' book is a thorough study of the subject.

484 The League of Nations and the Great Powers: the Greek-Bulgarian incident, 1925.
James Barros. Oxford, England: Clarendon Press, 1970. 143p.

Meticulous study, based on wide archival research, of the Greek-Bulgarian frontier incident of 1925, which precipitated a major crisis between the two countries. This was resolved following League of Nations mediation, with Greece being obliged to indemnify Bulgaria. The successful resolution of the crisis was one of the few unqualified successes of the League.

485 American foreign policy in Greece 1944-1949: economic, military and institutional aspects.
Michael Mark Amen. Frankfurt am Main, G.F.R.: Peter Lang, 1978. 310p. bibliog. (European University Papers, Series 31. Political Sciences vol. 13).

An analysis of American policy in Greece during the immediate post-war period. This the author sees as being essentially 'neo-imperialistic'.

486 Greece and the Great Powers 1944-1947: prelude to the 'Truman Doctrine'.
Stephen G. Xydis. Thessaloniki, Greece: Institute of Balkan Studies, 1963. 758p. bibliog.

During the critical three years covered by this massively documented book the role of Greece's chief external patron passed from Great Britain to the United States. The author analyses the way in which the U.S. administration moved from marked reluctance to become involved in the internal affairs of Greece to the interventionist policy enunciated in the 'Truman Doctrine' of March 1947. Fear of a communist take-over was, of course, the precipitant of this dramatic switch in policy, although through the famous 'percentages agreement' of May-October

1944 Stalin had agreed to a 'hands-off' policy in Greece in return for a free hand in Romania and Bulgaria.

487 The Truman Doctrine in perspective.
Stephen G. Xydis. *Balkan Studies*, vol. 8, no. 2 (1967), p. 239-62.

On 12 March 1947, President Truman, in requesting $400 million of emergency aid from the U.S. Congress for Greece and Turkey, enunciated what came to be known as the Truman Doctrine, by which the United States undertook to underwrite the efforts of 'free peoples' struggling to resist subversion by armed minorities. This marked the beginning of an eventually decisive U.S. involvement in the Greek Civil War on the side of the national government. This article examines the circumstances which gave rise to the Truman Doctrine.

488 From liberation to civil war: the U.S. and Greece, 1944-46.
John O. Iatrides. *Southeastern Europe*, vol. 3, pt. 1 (1976), p. 32-43.

A study of the transformation of the policy of the U.S. administration towards Greece from one of 'undiscriminating indifference', to one of 'holy wrath equally undiscriminating'. Greece, as a consequence, became a key battle ground in the Cold War.

489 Balkan triangle: birth and decline of an alliance across ideological boundaries.
John O. Iatrides. The Hague, Paris: Mouton, 1968. 211p. map. (Studies in European History, no. 12).

Given that Yugoslavia was the principal source of logistic support for the communist Democratic Army in the 1946-49 Civil War, it was somewhat surprising that, a few years later, Greece, Yugoslavia and Turkey should sign a treaty of friendship and cooperation (1953); followed by a formal military alliance (1954). Predictably, perhaps, this somewhat unnatural combination was short-lived. It soon broke up owing to growing tension between Greece and Turkey over Cyprus and as a result of the 1955 rapprochement between Moscow and Belgrade.

490 Greece and the United Nations.
Van Coufoudakis. *Epitheorisis Koinonikon Erevnon. The Greek Review of Social Research*, no. 24 (May-Aug. 1975), p. 292-301.

A study of Greece's relations with the United Nations, which have tended in the post-war years to revolve around the Cyprus problem.

491 Swan song of an eagle: America in Greece.
George Anastaplo. *Southwest Review*, vol. 50, no. 2 (Spring 1970), p. 105-25.

A prescient article warning of the danger to the long-term interests of the U.S.A. in Greece arising out of an over-identification with the Colonels' regime. With the return of democracy, the U.S.A. has, predictably and inevitably, incurred great odium for its willingness to give aid and comfort to a hated regime.

Foreign Relations

492 The wrong horse: the politics of intervention and the failure of American diplomacy.
Laurence Stern. New York: Times Books, 1977. 170p.

A journalistic, readable and very well-informed account of American policy towards Greece and Cyprus during the post-war period, with particular emphasis on the Colonels' dictatorship and the Cyprus crisis of 1974. The author is strongly critical of U.S. Secretary of State Henry Kissinger's role in the Cyprus crisis, but not, surprisingly, of that of James Callaghan, the British Foreign Secretary. Britain having in effect created the Cyprus problem reneged on her responsibilities to the people of Cyprus in refusing to intervene, as she was fully entitled to, in 1974 when the Turkish government sought joint action. Instead she allowed the Turks to take action alone, with disastrous consequences. Stern has clearly had access to information at the highest levels, although for obvious reasons, few of his strictures can be documented. The general picture he paints of ignorance and prejudice in the higher reaches of the State Department and C.I.A. is an alarming one.

493 Greek-American relations: a critical review.
Edited by Theodore A. Couloumbis, John O. Iatrides. New York: Pella, 1980. 263p. bibliog.

A comprehensive study of Greek-American relations, which have been thrown into sharp focus following the Turkish invasion of Cyprus and the concurrent collapse of the Colonels' dictatorship in 1974. The book's value is enhanced by a very comprehensive bibliography.

494 U.S. foreign policy toward Greece and Cyprus: the clash of principle and pragmatism.
Edited by Theodore A. Couloumbis, Sallie M. Hicks. Washington, D.C.: The Center for Mediterranean Studies and the American Hellenic Institute, 1975. 161p.

Contains a number of perceptive analyses of U.S. policy towards Greece and Cyprus in the post-war period, together with a transcript of the discussions to which they gave rise. Helps to explain the bitterness felt by many Greeks and Cypriots, a bitterness occasioned by U.S. support for the Colonels' junta and U.S. failure to head off the Turkish invasion of Cyprus in 1974.

495 The Aegean dispute.
Andrew Wilson. London: International Institute for Strategic Studies, 1979. 41p. (Adelphi Papers, no. 155).

A thorough analysis of the Aegean dispute that has bedevilled Greek-Turkish relations since 1973. The basic issue revolves around the delimitations of the two countries' respective continental shelves, but questions of flight control, territorial waters and the interpretation of treaties are also involved. The dispute, which involves complex questions of international law, brought Greece and Turkey, despite their common membership of the NATO alliance, to the brink of war in the summer of 1976.

496 Greek security considerations: a historical perspective.
Thanos Veremis. Athens: Papazisis, 1980. 128p.

The author presents 'a comprehensive picture of Greek security considerations and the effect of domestic factors in articulating them'. Particularly valuable is his

Foreign Relations

effort to place Greece's current security concerns within the historical context, without which they cannot properly be understood. Contains a useful appendix analysing the current state of the Greek armed forces.

497 The dispute between Greece and Turkey concerning the continental shelf in the Aegean.
Leo Gross. *American Journal of International Law*, vol. 71, no. 1 (Jan. 1977), p. 31-59.
A detailed study, from the perspective of international law, of the dispute between Greece and Turkey over the delineation of their respective continental shelves in the Aegean. The topic is also discussed in its wider political context by Andrew Wilson in *The Aegean dispute* (q.v.).

498 Macedonia: its place in Balkan power politics.
Elisabeth Barker. London, New York: Royal Institute of International Affairs, 1950. 129p. maps.
Although by now inevitably somewhat dated, this study constitutes an admirably balanced and lucid account of the Macedonian problem, that perennial 'Apple of Discord' between Greece, Yugoslavia and Bulgaria. The bitter polemics that frequently break out between Belgrade and Sofia demonstrate that the Macedonian question remains a potential destablizing force in the Balkans.

499 Nationalism and communism in Macedonia.
Evangelos Kofos. Thessaloniki, Greece: Institute for Balkan Studies, 1964. 251p. bibliog. maps.
Macedonia has long been the source of discord between Greece, Yugoslavia and Bulgaria. The Second World War added a further dimension of complexity to the problem with the establishment of communist regimes in Yugoslavia and Bulgaria and the defeat of a communist bid for power in Greece. The author provides a level-headed analysis of the Macedonian problem in the context of Balkan communism.

500 The progress of Greek nationalism in Cyprus, 1878-1970.
Peter Loizos. In: *Choice and change: essays in honour of Lucy Mair*. Edited by J. Davis. London: Athlone Press; New York: Humanities Press, 1974, p. 114-33.
The author argues that 'Greek nationalism in Cyprus, as symbolized by the enosis [union] platform has meant very different things, at different times, to different categories of people, and there is simply no intellectual short-cut to explaining this'.

501 The Cyprus revolt: an account of the struggle for union with Greece.
Nancy Crawshaw. London: George Allen & Unwin, 1978. 447p. bibliog. maps.
An exhaustive study of the enosis campaign for union with Greece in the 1950s. The author documents every twist and turn in the protracted process whereby an independent Cyprus, under tripartite British, Greek and Turkish guarantee, came

Foreign Relations

into existence in 1960. Inevitably the struggle for enosis had profound repercussions for Greek domestic politics in the 1950s.

502 **Cyprus: nationalism and international politics.**
Michael A. Attalides. Edinburgh: Q Press, 1979. 226p.

Cyprus constitutes the only substantial area of Greek settlement that is not incorporated within the bounds of the Greek state and the Cyprus question has inevitably loomed large in the external relations of Greece since the Second World War. The reasons for the failure of the campaign for enosis, or union with Greece, in the 1950s are carefully analysed, as are the unhappy history of the independent republic created in 1960 and the breakdown in relations between the majority Greek and minority Turkish population. The author, himself a Greek Cypriot, is remarkably objective in trying 'to grapple with the problem of how people living in a country with a potential of satisfying all their real human needs came to behave in most self-destructive ways, caught up in world power games which they only now begin to understand'.

Economy

General

503 Greece.
Adamantios A. Pepelasis. In: *Economic development: analysis and case studies.* Edited by Adamantios Pepelasis, Leon Mears, Irma Adelman. New York: Harper & Brothers, 1961, p. 500-22.
A useful concise history of the economic development of Greece.

504 The economy of Greece, 1944-66: efforts for stability and development.
Wray O. Candilis. New York, London: Praeger, 1968. 239p. bibliog. (Praeger Special Studies in International Economics and Development).
A comprehensive study of the Greek economy since the Second World War. Despite distortions in the pattern of development, the Greek economy has witnessed a remarkable rate of growth in the thirty years since the end of the Civil War.

505 OECD economic surveys: Greece.
Paris: Organisation for Economic Co-operation and Development, 1978. 72p.
Taken with the O.E.C.D. economic surveys on Greece for 1977 and 1976, this study provides a comprehensive analysis of the present state of the Greek economy. Despite an impressive, if uneven, record of economic growth during the post-war period, Greece has recently encountered serious economic difficulties engendered principally by the oil crisis, whose effects have been particularly felt in a country with few indigenous sources of energy. Overall, however, Greece's economic prospects look reasonably satisfactory. As the authors of this report conclude: 'in contrast to many other member countries [of the O.E.C.D.], Greece has pursued fairly expansionary demand management in recent years aimed at

Economy. General

achieving high levels of activity and employment. Policies in this regard have been broadly successful'.

506 **Economy of Greece 1976-78.**
Athens: Ch. Chronopoulos, G. Vassiliades and Co., with the cooperation of Hellenews, 1979. 456p.

A detailed compendium of information on the Greek economy during the three-year period 1976-78, with some comparative material from earlier years.

507 **Economic surveys: Greece.**
Paris: Organisation for Economic Co-operation and Development, 1962-. annual.

508 **Quarterly economic review: Greece.**
London: Economist Intelligence Unit, 1952-. quarterly.

The quarterly reviews, together with the annual supplement, form a useful, if expensive, guide to current trends in the Greek economy.

509 **Core-periphery problems in the Greek case.**
Mary Evangelinides. In: *Underdeveloped Europe: studies in core-periphery relations.* Edited by Dudley Seers, Bernard Schaffer, Marja-Lüsa Kiljunen. Hassocks, England: Harvester Press, in association with the Institute of Development Studies, 1979, p. 177-95.

The author considers the 'national socio-economic structure' of Greece to be characterized 'by a combination of underdevelopment phenomena typical of most formations of peripheral capitalism together with particular and exceptional manifestations of parasitic comprador activities'.

510 **Urbanization and development: the case of Greece.**
Evangelos C. Vlachos. *Rocky Mountain Social Science Journal*, vol. 6 (1969), p. 127-40.

A useful study of urbanization in Greece and its implications for development.

511 **Economic development issues: Greece, Israel, Taiwan and Thailand.**
Committee for Economic Development, with a foreword by Roy Blough. New York, London: Praeger, 1968. 216p. (Praeger Special Studies in International Economics and Development: Committee for Economic Development. Supplementary Paper no. 25).

The section on Greece, written by Diomedes D. Psilos, provides a clear and concise overview of the post-war development of the economy.

Economy. Regional

512 **Griechische Entwicklungsprobleme: Studien an einem kontinentaleuropäischen Entwicklungsland.** (Problems of Greek development: studies on a developing European country.)
Edited by Hans Jürgen Seraphim. Köln-Braunsfeld, G.F.R.: Institut für Siedlungs-und Wohnungswesen der Westfälischen Wilhelms-Universität, Münster, 1962. 82p. (Beiträge und Untersuchungen, vol. 56).
Contains essays on the social structure, economy and building industry.

513 **The image of the past and economic backwardness.**
Adamantios A. Pepelasis. *Human Organization*, vol. 17, no. 4 (Winter 1958-59), p. 19-27.
The author argues that the 'vivid sense of historical continuity' of the modern Greek, 'with its consequent emphasis on esoteric values and conditions irrelevant to modern reality, together with political instability and a perennial administrative disorganization -has been an important deterrent to the development of the country'.

Regional

514 **Le développement de la Grèce du nord depuis 1912.** (The development of northern Greece since 1912.)
Maria Negreponti-Delivanis. Thessaloniki, Greece: Institute of Balkan Studies, 1962. 189p. bibliog. (Society of Macedonian Studies. Institute of Balkan Studies, no. 61).
A study of the economy of northern Greece since the region was incorporated into the Greek state in 1912, at the time of the Balkan wars. Overall, the author takes an optimistic view of the region's economic progress.

515 **The changing economy of northern Greece since World War II.**
Paul P. Vouras. Thessaloniki, Greece: Institute of Balkan Studies, 1962. 227p. bibliog.
Another study of the economic development of northern Greece, this one limited to the period since the Second World War. Chapters deal with agriculture, livestock, fishing, forestry, mining, industry and handicrafts, electricity, transportation, ports and trade, and tourism.

Economy. Foreign aid

516 **Regional development strategy in southeast Europe: a comparative analysis of Albania, Bulgaria, Greece, Romania and Yugoslavia.**
George W. Hoffman. New York; Washington, D.C.; London: Praeger, 1972. 322p. bibliog. (Praeger Special Studies in International Economics and Development).
All five countries experienced long periods under Ottoman rule and this shared heritage has contributed to the varying degree of economic backwardness all have manifested until recent times. Since the Second World War, however, Greece, with its essentially laissez-faire economic system, has been the odd man out, although the economic policies of the four countries that experienced communist take-overs have not been monolithic. The author compares strategies for regional economic development in the countries of the Balkans and concludes that 'most of the countries of Southeast Europe lack comprehensive regional planning policies and some scholars question whether they have any regional policies at all'. In an epilogue the author considers various schemes for increased inter-Balkan economic cooperation: in the case of Greece, these have increased significantly since this book was written.

Foreign aid

517 **Greece: American aid in action, 1947-1956.**
W. H. McNeill. New York: Twentieth Century Fund, 1957. 240p. maps.
A clear and incisive account of the impact of the massive inflow of U.S. aid into Greece in the late 1940s and 1950s. At the same time it gives a remarkably full account of Greek life at a point when the country was just beginning its rapid, if uneven, economic advance of the last twenty years.

518 **American aid to Greece: a report on the first ten years.**
C. A. Munkman. London: Methuen; New York: Praeger, 1958. 306p.
A general, non-technical account to inform the 'ordinary taxpayer' of the results of the massive influx of U.S. aid into Greece during 1946-56.

519 **Analysis and assessment of the economic effects of the U.S. PL 480 program in Greece.**
G. Coutsoumaris, R. M. Westebbe, with D. D. Psilos, A. Michalakis, N. Xanthakis. Athens: Center of Planning and Economic Research, 1965. 293p. bibliog. (Special Studies Series, no. 1).
Some ten per cent, or almost 200 million dollars, of total U.S. aid to Greece between 1946 and 1963 was supplied under the Public Law 480 programme, which included the provision of dollars for local currency, emergency food aid, and the general provision of foodstuffs. The authors conclude that the P.L. 480 programmes made 'an important contribution to Greece's development effort'.

520 **Litton's 'noble experiment'.**
William W. McGrew. *Columbia Journal of World Business*, vol. 7, no. 1 (Jan.-Feb. 1972), p. 65-75.

An informative case-study of one of the several ill-fated attempts by the Colonels' regime to attract foreign investment in Greece. Signed amid much publicity in May 1967, the Litton Industries contract was cancelled in October 1969, after only a small amount of foreign capital had been attracted to Greece. Both the Colonels and Litton Industries had good reason to minimize the failure of this grandiose scheme to harness multi-national enterprise to economic development.

521 **Foreign skills and technical assistance in Greek development.**
Angus Maddison, Alexander Stavrianopoulos, Benjamin Higgins. Paris: Development Centre of the Organisation for Economic Co-operation and Development, 1966. 169p.

Greece has traditionally been an exporter of skills, many of her most talented and energetic citizens finding an outlet for their talents abroad. This study considers the potential of imported skills and technical assistance in the process of Greek development. The authors consider that in terms of the interaction of technical and capital assistance Greece has 'proved an almost classic example of a success story'.

522 **Manpower policy and problems in Greece.**
Paris: Organization for Economic Co-operation and Development, 1965. 51p. (Reviews of Manpower and Social Policies, no. 3).

This report calls, *inter alia*, for 'positive measures to promote the return and reintegration in the Greek economy of workers having acquired new skills and experiences abroad'.

European Economic Community

523 **Greece and the European Community.**
Edited by Loukas Tsoukalis. Farnborough, England: Saxon House, 1979. 172p.

A collection of essays on the implications for Greece of full membership of the European Economic Community. Particularly valuable for its analysis of the effects of entry on the industrial and agricultural sectors.

Economy. European Economic Community

524 **Common market and economic development: the E.E.C. and Greece.**
S. G. Triantis. Athens: Center of Planning and Economic Research, 1965. 232p. (Research Monograph Series, vol. 14).

Paints a gloomy picture of the economic effects of Greece's 1962 Treaty of Association with the E.E.C. and calls for its abrogation.

525 **Trade effects of economic association with the Common Market: the case of Greece.**
T. Hitiris. New York, London: Praeger, 1972. 172p. bibliog.

A technical study of the impact of the 1962 Treaty of Association with the E.E.C. on Greek trade.

526 **Greece and the European Economic Communities: the first decade of a troubled association.**
George N. Yannopoulos. Beverly Hills, California; London: Sage Publications, 1975. 35p. (Sage Research Papers in Social Sciences: Contemporary European Studies Series no. 90-019).

An examination of Greece's 1962 Treaty of Association with the E.E.C. and its economic impact on Greece. Particularly valuable in its analysis of the E.E.C. reaction to the Colonels' dictatorship and in demonstrating that the Common Market did not take such a tough line towards the junta as it claimed at the time and also subsequently.

527 **Greece's association with the European community: an evaluation of the first ten years.**
G. J. Kalamotousakis. In: *The EEC and the Mediterranean countries.* Edited by Avi Shlaim, G. N. Yannopoulos. Cambridge, England: Cambridge University Press, 1976, p. 141-60.

An optimistic view of the economic benefits of Greece's 1962 Treaty of Association with the E.E.C. The author goes so far as to refer to the 'economic miracle' which associate membership in the E.E.C. has brought.

528 **Griechenland und die Europäische Gemeinschaft. Erwartungen und Probleme des Beitritts.** (Greece and the European Community: expectations and problems of entry.)
Karl H. Buck. Bonn, G.F.R.: Europa Union Verlag, 1978. 235p. (Europäische Schriften des Instituts für Europäische Politik, vol. 50).

An analysis of the likely effects of Greek entry into the E.E.C.

Finance and Banking

529 **Industrial capital in Greek development.**
Howard S. Ellis, in collaboration with Diomedes D. Psilos, Richard M. Westebbe, Calliope Nicolaou. Athens: Center of Economic Research, 1964. 335p. (Research Monograph Series, vol. 8).

Greeks have traditionally preferred to invest their savings in real estate rather than in industry. This study explores the reasons for the low rate of capital investment in Greece and suggests some appropriate remedies. Among these the authors argue for a major shift in the educational system towards technical, business and economic education. Some not very convincing moves in this direction have recently been made. A significant fact to emerge from this study is the family nature of many corporate concerns in Greece. Of 1,400 corporations, a third had less than five shareholders, another third between five and nine, 213 between ten and twenty-five. Only 156 had more than twenty-five shareholders.

530 **Savings and investment in Greece.**
R. M. Westebbe. Athens: Centre of Economic Research, 1964. 48p.

The author concludes that 'despite the success in attaining and preserving internal monetary stability, the financial mechanism is not yet adequate to channel an increasing flow of private savings into productive uses'. Fifteen years later the situation has not much changed, with real estate rather than industrial investment benefiting from the relatively high rate of personal saving.

531 **Capital market in Greece.**
Diomedes D. Psilos. Athens: Centre of Economic Research, 1964. 254p. (Research Monograph Series, vol. 9).

An analysis of the problems involved in developing a capital market in Greece. The author takes a more sanguine view of the potential attractiveness of equities to savers than does George Maniatis (see following item).

Finance and Banking

532 Reliability of the equities market to finance industrial development in Greece.
George C. Maniatis. *Economic Development and Cultural Change*, vol. 19, no. 4 (July 1971), p. 598-619.

The author is sceptical about the ability of the limited equities market in Greece to absorb the very high rate of personal savings that has developed in recent years. 'Rigidities of an organic, institutional, technological and structural nature, as well as expediency, related to the demand for and the supply of equities, constitute serious barriers to the rapid development of the capital market'.

533 Emigration and capital formation: the case of Greece.
E. N. Botsas. *Balkan Studies*, vol. 10, no. 1 (1969), p. 127-34.

Emigrant remittances have long been an important constituent of the Greek balance of payments, but this study argues that capital formation would be accelerated if Greeks stayed at home rather than emigrated.

534 Greek monetary developments 1939-1948: a case study of the consequences of World War II for the monetary system of a small nation.
Dimitrios Delivanis, William C. Cleveland. Bloomington, Indiana: Indiana University, 1950. 196p. (Indiana University Publications. Social Science Series, no. 6).

A careful analysis of Greece's monetary experience from September 1939 to April 1948, a period during which she experienced rates of inflation of unimaginable proportions.

535 Monetary equilibrium and economic development, with special reference to the experience of Greece, 1950-1963.
Xenophon Zolotas. Princeton, New Jersey: Princeton University Press, 1965. 223p.

For the first twenty years after the end of the Civil War Greece enjoyed a remarkable degree of price stability before being engulfed, like the rest of the world, by the inflationary tides of the 1970s. The author, for many years governor of the Bank of Greece with overall responsibility for the country's fiscal policies, concludes that 'the maintenance of relative price stability and equilibrium in the balance of payments is not only compatible with a rapid and sustained development process but is, in fact, an indispensable prerequisite of it'.

536 Money and credit in a developing economy: the Greek case.
D. J. Halikias. New York: New York University Press, 1978. 307p.

An analysis of the effectiveness of the efforts of successive post-war Greek governments to promote economic development through the control of credit. The author concludes 'that the purpose and scope of the qualitative credit controls in Greece has been much wider than in most other countries'.

Finance and Banking

537 **Studies in Greek taxation.**
George F. Break, Ralph Turvey. Athens: Center of Planning and Economic Research, 1964. 250p. bibliog. (Research Monograph Series, vol. 11).

An analysis of the complex and inefficient system of taxation employed in Greece. Measures in recent years to make the system less inequitable and to clamp down on widespread evasion have met with mixed results.

538 **The distribution of tax burden by income groups in Greece.**
D. Karageorgas. *Economic Journal*, vol. 83, no. 330 (June 1973), p. 436-48.

This important article, written while the author was in prison for his opposition to the Colonels' dictatorship, demonstrates that 'the degree of inequality of income distribution in Greece remains very high in comparison to that of other countries'.

539 **Economic effects of value-added-tax substitution: Greece.**
Theodore A. Georgakopoulos. Athens: Center of Planning and Economic Research, 1976. 312p. bibliog. (Research Monograph Series, 21).

Historically a very large proportion of tax revenues in Greece has been raised through indirect rather than direct taxation. This has had obvious implications for the distribution of income. Greece's entry into the E.E.C. will entail a substantial restructuring of the Greek taxation system and the introduction of value added tax. The author considers the implications of such a change.

540 **The gold sovereign market in Greece - an unusual speculative market.**
N. A. Niarchos, C. W. J. Granger. *Journal of Finance*, vol. 27 (1972), p. 1127-35.

Up until 1965 there was a flourishing free market in gold sovereigns in Greece, and property transactions were frequently conducted in sovereigns. The authors of this article suggest that the sovereign was a favoured asset, even if it gave small or even negative returns over long periods, 'because its clientele was very risk-adverse because of lack of confidence in the currency following earlier politically and economically troubled periods'.

541 **Le développement industriel de la Grèce.** (The industrial development of Greece.)
Eleftherios A. Kartakis. Lausanne, Switzerland: Centre de Recherches Européennes, 1970. 207p. bibliog.

A useful survey of Greece's industrial development.

Finance and Banking

542 **Industrialisation, employment and income distribution in Greece: a case study.**
Dimitrios A. Germidis, Maria Negreponti-Delivanis. Paris: Organization for Economic Co-operation and Development, 1975. 204p. (Development Centre Studies, Employment Series no. 12). bibliog.

The authors conclude that 'structural changes, especially in industry, have not kept pace with Greece's economic growth. This finding is confirmed even more conclusively when the trend of the Greek economy is compared with that of the other developing economies of Southern Europe'. Although aggregate investment in Greek industry between 1950 and 1970 was considerable, there was an overwhelming preponderance of small production units.

Industry

543 The morphology of Greek industry: a study in industrial development.
George Coutsoumaris. Athens: Center of Economic Research, 1965. 430p. statistical tables.

'An empirical analysis and appraisal of the general structure and economic performance of Greek manufacturing industry'. Given the rapid pace of economic development in Greece over the past two decades this anatomy of Greek industry during the early 1960s is inevitably somewhat dated. However, many of the author's findings, e.g. the small size of many industrial units and the concentration of industrial development in the Athens and Thessaloniki regions, continue to be valid.

544 Fixed capital stock and future investment requirements in Greek manufacturing.
Rolf Krengel, Dieter Martens. Athens: Center of Planning and Economic Research, 1966. 138p. (Research Monograph Series, vol. 16).

The most significant fact to emerge from this study is the small scale of Greek industry. In 1958, for instance, only 5.31 per cent of manufacturing establishments employed more than ten people.

545 Greek industry in perspective.
Athens: Hellenic Industrial Development Bank, 1967. 187p.

A useful and clearly tabulated account of Greek industrial development since the First World War.

Industry

546 **Managerial attitudes of Greeks: the roles of culture and industrialization.**
L. L. Cummings, Stuart M. Schmidt. *Administrative Science Quarterly*, vol. 17, no. 2 (June 1972), p. 265-72.

The Greek managers who were the subject of this study displayed 'little belief in an individual's capacity for leadership and initiative, while advocating the practice of participative management'.

547 **Greek industrialists: an economic and social analysis.**
Alec P. Alexander. Athens: Center of Planning and Economic Research, 1964. 182p. (Research Monograph Series, vol. 12).

A study of the role of the entrepreneur in a society whose structure and values 'have generally been favourable to the development of entrepreneurial activity'. Accompanied by numerous tables of socio-economic data on Greek industrialists.

Agriculture

548 **The agricultural policy of Greece.**
Paris: Organisation for Economic Co-operation and
Development, 1979. 91p. (O.E.C.D. Agricultural Policy
Reports).
The agricultural sector of the Greek economy, although declining in importance, still contributed in 1977 a 17.2 per cent share of the gross domestic product. The important implications for the agricultural sector of Greek entry into the European Economic Community, and the structural changes these will necessitate, are fully analysed. As in other sectors of the Greek economy, state intervention in agricultural policy is considerable.

549 **Agriculture in a restrictive environment: the case of Greece.**
Adamantios A. Pepelasis, Kenneth Thompson. *Economic Geography*, vol. 36, no. 2 (April 1960), p. 145-57.
The authors conclude their study of the agricultural sector in Greece by urging that 'developmental policy should be directed primarily toward agriculture and those industries that provide agriculture with its inputs (e.g. fertilizers) or that process agricultural output'.

550 **Problems of the Greek rural economy.**
A. N. Damaskenides. *Balkan Studies*, vol. 6, no. 1 (1965), p. 21-34.
An analysis of the structure of the rural economy of Greece in the mid-1960s.

Agriculture

551 **Postwar growth in Greek agricultural production: a study in sectoral output change.**
Lawrence H. Shaw. Athens: Center of Planning and Economic Research, 1969. 392p. (Special Studies Series, no. 2).

The author finds that agricultural output has increased since the Second World War at an annual rate of five per cent and that the pattern of change in agricultural output during this period has shown considerable diversity.

552 **Problems of development: problems of agricultural co-operation: case study in Greece.**
J. Chombart de Lauwe, J. Poitevin. Paris: Organisation for Economic Co-operation and Development, 1965. 136p.

A study of the agricultural cooperative movement in Greece, with recommendations for its improvement.

553 **Farm fragmentation in Greece: the problem and its setting, with eleven village case studies.**
Kenneth Thompson. Athens: Center of Economic Research, 1963. 263p. bibliog. (Research Monograph Series no. 5).

Small and dispersed land holdings are common in Greece and inhibit the development of an efficient agriculture. This study analyses the implications of farm fragmentation for the agricultural sector of the economy.

554 **Labour shortages in Greek agriculture, 1963-1973.**
Adamantios A. Pepelasis. Athens: Center of Economic Research, 1963. 71p.

Demonstrates, *inter alia*, that, contrary to the generally held view of Greece as a country with a considerable degree of underemployment in the agricultural sector, Greece is suffering from a shortage of agricultural labour due to emigration, both external and internal, and a low birthrate.

555 **Labor shortages in Greek agriculture: a further look, 1963-1967.**
Adamantios A. Pepelasis. *The Journal of Developing Areas*, vol. 5, no. 1 (Oct. 1970), p. 17-26.

This study argues that Greek agriculture is prone to labour shortages rather than labour surpluses, the reverse of the generally accepted view. An indication of this trend is the fact that the daily wage of an agricultural labourer in cotton rose from fifty drachmas in 1962 to 150 in 1967, a rate of increase well in excess of price inflation.

Agriculture

556 Rural reconstruction in Greece: differential social prerequisites and achievements during the development process.
D. Weintraub, M. Shapira. Beverly Hills, California; London: Sage Publications, 1975. 80p. bibliog. (Sage Studies in Comparative Modernization, no. 3).

The authors note that despite the many obstacles to change and development that exist in Greece, nonetheless their data indicates massive achievements in agricultural growth. 'This was made possible first and foremost by the flexibility of the rural society in terms of its freehold system and open stratification, and in terms of individual accessibility to change'.

557 Rural development in Greece.
Abraham Rozenman, G. N. Sykianakis. In: *Rural development in a changing world*. Edited by Raanan Weitz, Yahuda H. Landau. Cambridge, Massachusetts: M.I.T. Press, 1971, p. 501-14.

Largely devoted to an examination of the comprehensive ten year development plan for the island of Crete, prepared by Israeli and Greek planners on behalf of the Organisation for Economic Co-operation and Development during the early 1960s.

558 Greek agricultural cooperatives within the framework of the Greek social fabric.
John E. Tsouderos. Chicago: Fund for International Cooperative Development, 1961. 123p.

An informative study of the cooperative movement in Greece, although now necessarily somewhat out of date. Includes a brief history of the cooperative movement in Greece. The first modern cooperative was founded at Almyros in Thessaly in 1900.

559 'The thrice-ploughed field': cultivation techniques in ancient and modern Greece.
Hamish A. Forbes. *Expedition*, vol. 19, no. 1 (Fall 1976), p. 5-11.

A study demonstrating that for all the dramatic changes that have taken place in recent years in Greek agriculture, in the Argolid at least, 'the technology and techniques of cultivation remain largely unchanged'.

560 The thousand year road.
Harold Koster. *Expedition*, vol. 19, no. 1 (Fall 1976), p. 19-28.

An account of shepherding practice in the Argolid, which has remained fundamentally unchanged over the centuries.

Agriculture

561 **The pursuit of wild edibles, past and present.**
Mary Clark Forbes. *Expedition*, vol. 19, no. 1 (Fall 1976), p. 12-18.

An interesting account of the part played by wild edibles, particularly wild greens or horta, in the Greek diet, with some consideration of the evidence that they figured in the diet of the ancient Greeks.

562 **Stewards of the land: the American farm school and modern Greece.**
Brenda L. Marder. New York: Columbia University Press, 1979. 234p.

A history of the American Farm School in Thessaloniki. Founded in 1904, the School has played an important role in the dissemination of new agricultural techniques.

563 **Greece: a guide to official statistics of agriculture, population, and food supply.**
Compiled by Annie M. Hannay. Washington, D.C.: Department of Agriculture. Bureau of Agricultural Economics, 1932. 142p.

564 **Development of the highland economy and the timber industry in Greece.**
W. Ryser, J. Vodoz. Paris: Organization for Economic Co-operation and Development, 1960. 83p. (Problems of Development).

The first section by W. Ryser considers the economic development of the mountain regions of Greece; the second, by J. Vodoz, considers the development of the timber industry in Epirus.

Transport

565 **The Greek merchant marine (1453-1850).**
Edited by Stelios A. Papadopoulos. Athens: National Bank of Greece, 1972. 504p.
This superbly produced and illustrated book is indispensable for the study of the early history of the Greek merchant marine, now such a formidable force in world shipping. Especially valuable is George Leon's introductory chapter.

566 **The economics of tramp shipping.**
B N. Metaxas. London: Athlone Press, 1971. 268p. bibliog. appendices.
Although this is an academic study of the economics of tramp shipping in general, the fact that Greece has one of the largest merchant fleets in the world and that the author is Greek means that there is much of interest to the reader interested specifically in the Greek merchant marine. This is an important factor in the Greek economy but not as significant as it should be, for much Greek-owned shipping sails under flags of convenience. In 1949, for instance, total tonnage of Greek owned ships flying the Greek flag was 1,301,512, that of Greek owned ships flying the Panamanian flag a mere 50,016: by 1967 the respective figures were 7,665,297 and 12,382,836.

567 **Panama and Greek ships: for shipowners, shipbrokers and everybody in shipping.**
Gunnar M. Grønvald. Oslo: The author, 1956. 3rd ed.
A detailed list of the various Greek owned shipping companies registered in Panama in the mid-1950s. Now out of date, but significant as an indicator of the vast number of Greek ships flying under the Panamanian (and other) flags of convenience.

Transport

568 **La marine marchande des Grecs en 1967.** (The Greek merchant marine in 1967.)
Pierre-Yves Péchoux. *Information Géographique*, no. 3 (1968), p. 121-32.
A useful study of the Greek merchant marine as it stood in 1967, including ships under Greek ownership sailing under flags of convenience.

569 **Greece.**
Supplement to: *Lloyd's List*, (14 June 1977).
Contains much information on the Greek merchant marine.

570 **Aristotle Onassis.**
Nicholas Fraser, Philip Jacobson, Mark Ottoway, Lewis Chester. London: Weidenfeld & Nicolson, 1977. 372p.
The life and loves of a modern Maecenas. Entertaining and informative analysis, gossipy in the 'Insight' mould of journalism, of the chequered rise of Aristotle Socrates Onassis from a modestly affluent background in Smyrna to vast riches. Describes Onassis' sometimes dubious business dealings in the course of which he built up an enormous tanker fleet, together with his controversial relations with the Greek Colonels towards the end of his life. Much spicy detail about Onassis' exotic private life, his love for Maria Callas, his marriage to Jackie Kennedy and about his long-standing feud with his equally wealthy erstwhile brother-in-law, Stavros Niarchos. Complements rather than supersedes, Willi Frischauer, *Onassis* (London: Bodley Head, 1968).

571 **National transportation study: domestic transport flows.**
Basil P. Coukis. Athens: Center of Planning and Economic Research, 1969. unpaginated.
A detailed analysis, profusely illustrated with maps and charts, of the internal transport network in Greece. Her internal communications, by land and sea, have always been unusually problematic.

Labour Movement and Trade Unions

572 **Trade unionism in Greece: a study in political paternalism.**
Christos Jecchinis. Chicago: Roosevelt University, Labor Education Division, 1967. 205p.

The trade union scene in Greece is one of exceptional complexity. Jecchinis' book, although by now somewhat out of date, is the only book in English dealing with the topic.

573 **Une organisation socialiste ottomane: la fédération ouvrière de Salonique (1908-1912).** (An Ottoman socialist organization: the workers' federation of Thessaloniki.)
Paul Dumont. *Études Balkaniques*, vol. 11, no. 1 (1975), p. 76-88.

Socialism barely took root in the economically underdeveloped Ottoman Empire before its demise. This study focusses on the largely Jewish-dominated Federation of Thessaloniki, which was one of the earliest and best organized, if relatively insignificant socialist groups in the Greek lands.

574 **The Greek labor movement and the bourgeois state, 1910-1920.**
George B. Leon. *Journal of the Hellenic Diaspora*, vol. 4, no. 4 (Winter 1978), p. 5-28.

A study of the nascent Greek labour movement at a crucial phase of its development.

Labour Movement and Trade Unions

575 **The Greek socialist movement and the First World War: the road to unity.**
George B. Leon. Boulder, Colorado: East European Quarterly; New York: Columbia University Pres, 1976. 204p. (East European Monographs, no. 18).

Detailed account, based on wide range of sources, of the fragmented Greek left during the First World War. '...the very crisis which shattered the unity of the major European socialist parties and of the International served as a catalyst for the strengthening, radicalization, and ultimate unification of the Greek socialist movement'.

Statistics

576 **Statistiki epiteris tis Ellados.** (Statistical yearbook of Greece.)
Athens: National Statistical Service, 1930-. annual.

An annual compendium of statistics which may be supplemented by reference to the Monthly Statistical Bulletin of the National Statistical Service and the Monthly Statistical Bulletin of the Bank of Greece.

577 **Statistikai meletai 1821-1971. I statistiki kata ta 150 eti apo tis palingenesias tis Ellados.** (Statistical studies. Statistics during the 150 years since the rebirth of Greece.)
M. Khouliarakis, E. Makris, E. Gritsopoulos, M. Gevetsi, A. Agiopetritis. Athens: Ethnikon Kentron Koinonikon Erevnon, 1972. 351p. bibliog.

A most useful historical overview of the various statistical surveys that have been undertaken in Greece since independence.

Environment

578 **Vasileion tis Ellados. Ypourgeion syntonismou. Rhythmistiki meleti anaptyxeos poleos kai periokhis Kalamatas.** (Kingdom of Greece. Ministry of Coordination. Master plan of the town and region of Kalamata.)
Athens: National Technical University of Athens, Town Planning Centre, 1971. 194p.

A detailed development plan for Kalamata, the principal town in the southern Peloponnese, and its hinterland.

579 **Mykonos and Patmos.**
Paul J. Mitarachi, Robert Ernest. *Perspecta: The Yale Architectural Journal*, vol. 6 (1960), p. 78-87.

'While the cityscape of Mykonos is purely popular in origin and remains humble in its scale and anonymous in its expression, Patmos shows itself to be the result of a cultural continuity.'.

580 **Hydra: a Greek island town: its growth and form.**
Constantine E. Michaelides. Chicago, London: University of Chicago Press, 1967. 93p. bibliog.

This 'visual presentation of the morphological growth of a town' is one of the few studies in English of the development of a particular community in Greece from a town planning and architectural perspective. Contains many maps, plans and illustrations.

Education

581 A sketch of the history of education in Greece.
J. Gennadius. Edinburgh: World Federation of Education, 1925. 47p.
A useful brief survey of the history of education in Greece.

582 Greek education: reorganization of the administrative structure.
Kalliniki Dendrinou Antonakaki. New York: Teachers' College, Columbia University, 1955. 274p. bibliog.
Now inevitably somewhat out of date; but still useful for the study of Greek educational history.

583 Greece.
In: *Tradition and change in education: a comparative study.* Edited by Andreas M. Kazamias, Byron G. Massialas. Englewood Cliffs, New Jersey: Prentice-Hall, 1965. (Foundations of Education Series), p. 107-15.
A useful brief survey of the educational system of Greece on the eve of George Papandreou's effort to introduce basic reforms during his short-lived government of 1964-65. The authors stress its highly centralized nature.

584 Classification of educational systems in OECD member countries: Canada, Greece, Yugoslavia.
Paris: Organisation for Economic Co-operation and Development, 1973. 80p.
Contains a useful classification (as of 1971) of the structure of the Greek educational system.

Education

585 **OECD: education and development, country reports: the Mediterranean regional project: Greece.**
Paris: Organisation for Economic Co-operation and Development, 1965. 195p.
Provides a comprehensive view of the Greek educational system of the mid-1960s, with proposals for future policy.

586 **The 'renaissance' of Greek secondary education.**
Andreas M. Kazamias. *Comparative Education Review*, vol. 3, no. 3 (Feb. 1960), p. 22-27.
An analysis of the report of a 1959 government committee set up by Constantine Karamanlis to inquire into the state of secondary education. The author's cautious use of inverted commas proved justified. The very limited nature of the 1959 reform proposals are in marked contrast to the reforms of 1975-77, which, for all their limitations, indicate how far the educational views of the Greek right have changed in the last twenty years.

587 **Plans and policies for educational reform in Greece.**
Andreas M. Kazamias. *Comparative Education Review*, vol. 11, no. 3 (Oct. 1967), p. 331-47.
A useful analysis of the various reform proposals advanced in post-war Greece, culminating with Papandreou's 1964 reforms which were systematically dismantled under the Colonels' dictatorship. Despite this setback the author is justified in concluding that the 1964 reforms may well have constituted 'the beginning of a silent social and pedagogical revolution in Greek modernization'.

588 **Attitudes, sociometric status and ability in Greek schools.**
Calliope Moustaka. Paris: Mouton, 1967. 151p.
A study in the 'micro-sociology' of a Greek school.

589 **The movement for reform: a historical perspective.**
Alexis Dimaras. *Comparative Education Review*, vol. 22, no. 1 (Feb. 1978), p. 11-20.
A useful overview of the historical basis of the movement for educational reform in Greece by a leading authority on the subject.

590 **Current education reforms: an overview.**
F. K. Voros. *Comparative Education Review*, vol. 22, no. 1 (Feb. 1978), p. 7-10.
A useful tabulation of the principal reform measures of the 1975-77 period. These include the seemingly definitive establishment of the dimotiki, or spoken language, as the language of instruction throughout all levels of the education system; the de-emphasis of the teaching of classical Greek literature in the original; the increase in compulsory schooling from six to nine years; the reorganization of teacher training; the reorganization and expansion of technical and vocational education; the introduction of new and more up-to-date textbooks.

Education

591 Values underlying the 1976-1977 educational reform in Greece.
P. K. Persianis. *Comparative Education Review*, vol. 22, no. 1 (Feb. 1978), p. 51-59.
The author argues that two fundamental values underlay the educational reform measures of 1976-77, these being democratization and modernization: the first was inspired by the need to prevent a relapse into dictatorship, the second by the need to overhaul the country's social, economic and political institutions.

592 Educational demoticism.
E. P. Papanoutsos. *Comparative Education Review*, vol. 22, no. 1 (Feb. 1978), p. 46-50.
The author, who was very closely involved in George Papandreou's attempted educational reforms of 1964, considers the language question which constitutes' the major issue around which the educational policy of the nation revolves and which is so baffling to outsiders. The issue between the artificial pseudo-classical katharevousa and the living dimotiki, or popular language, has apparently been resolved by the government's decision in 1976 to make the dimotiki the official language not only of education but of the state. But it will be many decades before the disastrous effects of the language question are finally erased.

593 The politics of educational reform in Greece: law 309/1976.
Andreas M. Kazamias. *Comparative Education Review*, vol. 22, no. 1 (Feb. 1978), p. 21-45.
A fascinating account of the attitudes adopted by the various political parties and interest groups to the Karamanlis government's efforts to reform the educational system. Predictably, perhaps, the further to the left the political party, the stronger the criticism. The author concludes his analysis with a telling quotation by Mr. Karamanlis' minister of education, George Rallis: 'the bill is not at all above party politics. The law plan bears the seal of the New Democracy'. But what is perhaps most remarkable about the reform measures in the context of post-war Greek politics is that measures of this kind should have been introduced by a right-wing government at all.

594 Economic implications of raising the school leaving age.
George Psacharopoulos. *Comparative Education Review*, vol. 22, no. 1 (Feb. 1978), p. 71-79.
The education act of 1976 provided for the raising of the period of compulsory schooling from six to nine years, with full effect from the school year 1980-81. The author analyses the economic implications of this measure and concludes that the overall economic impact is likely to prove beneficial, but that problems will be caused by inadequate funding and resistance on the part of some parents to the sending of their children to school for three years after the age of twelve.

595 Those whom reform forgot.
Maria Eliou. *Comparative Education Review*, vol. 22, no. 1 (Feb. 1978), p. 60-70.
The author points to the various groups whose interests are largely neglected in the educational reform measures of 1976-77: those living in isolated rural areas; ethnic and linguistic minorities (with the exception of the Turks of Western

Education

Thrace); and, the largest category, women. Two out of every three failing to complete elementary school are girls. A striking fact to emerge from her study is the very high rate (for a European country) of illiteracy. According to the 1971 census some 14.2 per cent of the population, mostly women, were illiterate. Despite her strictures against the 1976 reforms, the author does concede, however, that with their enactment Greece 'ceased to turn its back stubbornly on the process of change'.

596 **Democratization of education in contemporary Greece: selected aspects.**
Jane Lambiri-Dimaki. *Epitheorisi Koinonikon Erevnon. The Greek Review of Social Research*, no. 29 (Jan.-April 1977), p. 55-64.
A consideration of the extent to which Greek education can be considered to be 'democratic' and 'open'.

597 **The situation of the universities in Greece.**
George V. Haniotis. *Minerva*, vol. 16, no. 2 (Winter 1968), p. 163-84.
A study of Greek higher education as it stood when the Colonels came to power. Many of the problems diagnosed by the author have yet to be resolved.

598 **Equality of opportunity in the Greek higher education system: the impact of reform policies.**
Georgia K. Polydorides. *Comparative Education Review*, vol. 22, no. 1 (Feb. 1978), p. 80-93.
The author concludes that there was a measure of progress towards greater equality of access to higher education in the aftermath of the 1964 reforms, but that this progress was not generally sustained, and that in fact the trend toward greater equality of opportunity has in some cases been reversed in recent years.

599 **A quantitative analysis of the demand for higher education.**
George Psacharopoulos, Costas Soumelis. *Higher Education*, vol. 8 (1979), p. 159-77.
A study based on a sample of 7,425 secondary school children in Greece, which finds, *inter alia*, that scholastic achievement is closely related to the level of parents' education.

600 **Problems of development: adult education techniques in developing countries: a Greek case study.**
Pierre Fourré, in collaboration with Constantine Theodossopoulos. Paris: Organisation for Economic Co-operation and Development, 1959. 137p.
A handbook for those engaged in the education of adults in Greece.

Education

601 Student activism in Greece: a historical and empirical analysis.
George Psacharopoulos, Andreas M. Kazamias. *Higher Education*, vol. 9 (1980), p. 127-38.

Most observers agree that it was the students' occupation of the Athens Polytechnic in November 1973, and its brutal suppression by the military dictatorship, that precipitated the downfall of the Colonels' regime in the summer of 1974. The authors offer an 'historical background of student politics in Greece and present the results of a quantitative model attempting to explain present student activism'. They also speculate on the 'future direction of student activism given the extension of educational opportunities to rural students'.

602 Estimating shadow rates of return to investment in education.
George Psacharopoulos. *Journal of Human Resources*, vol. 5, no. 2 (Winter 1970), p. 34-50.

An article, based on Greek data, whose purpose is 'to suggest the use of the social marginal product of labor on the benefits side for the estimation of the rate of return on investment in education, instead of the observed market earnings'.

603 Greece.
Constantine Soumelis. In: *Individual demand for education. Demande individuelle d'éducation.* Paris: Organization for Economic Co-operation and Development, 1979. p. 249-334.

The author finds, *inter alia*, that 'although demand for education in general, and more particularly for post-secondary education, is strongly manifested not only in the number of candidates but also in their persistence in attempting to enter a post-secondary institution and in their taking refuge abroad to study, the supply of places, which has always been controlled by the State, was constantly kept at a relatively low level'.

Science

604 **The search for a national scientific policy in Greece.**
George V. Haniotis. *Minerva*, vol. 3, no. 3 (Spring 1965), p. 312-20.
A survey of government efforts to develop a coherent science policy for Greece.

605 **Science and development: national reports of the pilot teams, Greece.**
Paris: Organisation for Economic Co-operation and Development, 1968, 208p.
A study which clearly demonstrates 'that the 20th century scientific revolution has not entered Greek life in anything like the people's and the economy's capacity and desire to absorb it. For the first time in modern Greece, however, the need, the will and the means to utilise the results of scientific research and technological development in order to achieve a higher level of social and economic welfare are simultaneously being realised...'.

The Arts

Visual arts

606 **Art of the Byzantine era.**
David Talbot Rice. London: Thames & Hudson, 1963. 286p. bibliog.
A well-written and well-illustrated account of the art and architecture of the Byzantine Empire by a leading authority. Particularly useful for the extraordinary renaissance in fresco and mosaic decoration which flowered during the declining centuries of the empire.

607 **Folk art in Greek Macedonia.**
Alke Kyriakidou-Nestoros. *Balkan Studies*, vol. 4, no. 1 (1963), p. 15-36.
A concise, illustrated survey of the folk art of Greek Macedonia, with particular reference to the collections of the Folklore Museum of Northern Greece and the Folklore Museum of the University of Thessaloniki.

608 **Exhibition of Greek folk art catalogue.**
Popi Zora. Athens: Ministry of Culture and Sciences. 48p. bibliog.
The handsomely illustrated and informative catalogue of an itinerant exhibition of folk art from the collections of the Museum of Greek Folk Art in Athens.

609 **Works of art in Greece, the Greek islands and the Dodecanese: losses and survivals in the war.**
Compiled by the Monuments, Fine Arts and Archives Sub-Commission of the Central Mediterranean Force. London: H.M. Stationery Office, 1946. 64p.
An invaluable but little-known guide to the effect of the occupation and the fighting that followed liberation on Greece's artistic heritage. The buildings of the

The Arts. Visual arts

Acropolis in Athens, for instance, suffered some minor damage during the fighting in Athens in December 1944 between British troops and E.L.A.S. guerillas.

610 **Histoire picturale de la guerre de l'indépendance hellénique par le Général Makriyannis.** (Pictorial history of the Greek War of Independence by General Makriyannis.)
Notice historique de S.E.M. Johannes Gennadius, préface de Fred Boissonas. Geneva: Editions d'Art Boissonas; Paris: Jean Budry, 1926. unpaginated.

Magnificent reproductions of the paintings of the Greek War of Independence commissioned by General Ioannis Makriyannis (see following item).

611 **The War of Independence in pictures: copies by Demetrios Zographos from originals by his father Panayiotis Zographos commissioned by General Makriyannis and presented to Her Majesty Queen Victoria through her minister at Athens Sir Edmund Lyons 1839.**
Edited by H. A. Lidderdale. Birmingham, England: University of Birmingham Centre for Byzantine Studies, 1976. 33p. bibliog.

The twenty-four pictures included in the exhibition constitute one of the four sets of paintings commissioned by General Makriyannis, a hero of the War of Independence, for presentation to King Otto and to the ministers of the three protecting powers, Great Britain, France and Russia. They depict a number of the major battles of the War of Independence and are masterpieces of primitive painting. They are accompanied by copious notes in which Makriyannis recounts details of the various hostilities. H. A. Lidderdale has provided useful explanatory notes to the pictures which form part of the royal collection in Windsor Castle.

612 **Ellines zographoi tou 19ou aiona.** (Greek painters of the 19th century.)
E. K. Phrantziskakis. Athens: Commercial Bank of Greece, 1957. 157p.

An illustrated guide to the generally rather uninspired Greek painters of the 19th century.

613 **Geschichte der griechischen Malerei des 19ten Jahrhunderts.** (A history of Greek painting in the 19th century.)
Stelios Lydakis. Munich, G.F.R.: Prestel Verlag, 1972. 379p. bibliog. (Materialen zur Kunst des neuzehnten Jahrhunderts, vol. 7).

A copiously illustrated and annotated study of the rather undistinguished group of Greek painters who studied and painted in Munich in the 19th century.

The Arts. Individual artists

614 **Greek art and architecture 1945-1967: a brief survey.**
Dimitris A. Fatouros. *Balkan Studies*, vol. 8, no. 2 (1967), p. 421-35.
A concise, illustrated survey of the principal trends in Greek art and architecture in the first two decades after the Second World War.

615 **Introduction à la peinture néo-héllenique.** (An introduction to modern Greek painting.)
Tony Spiteris. Athens, 1962. 85p. bibliog.
A guide to modern Greek painting.

616 **Arte dopo il 1945: Grecia.** (Art since 1945: Greece.)
Tony Spiteris, translated by Francesco Golisano. Milan, Italy: Cappelli, 1971. 123p.
A useful illustrated (black-and-white only) survey of post-war Greek art, with potted biographies of leading artists.

617 **Greece: an approach to contemporary art.**
Dimitris A. Fatouros. In: *Art of our time. Painting and sculpture throughout the world.* Edited by Will Grohmann. London: Thames & Hudson; New York: Abrams, 1966, p. 250-57.
A brief overview of contemporary art in Greece.

618 **Modern art in Greece and some contemporary Greek painters.**
Marinos Kalligas. *The Connoisseur*, (May 1962), p. 39-43.
A brief survey of the state of contemporary Greek art.

Individual artists

619 **Theophilos.**
Edited by Yannis Tsarouchis. Athens: Commercial Bank of Greece, 1966. 305 plates.
A superbly illustrated study of Theophilos (Khatzimikhail), (1868-1934), perhaps the best known of Greek primitive painters. His pictures admirably capture the atmosphere of provincial Greece in the late 19th and early 20th centuries.

The Arts. Architecture

620 **Theophilos, Kontoglou, Ghika and Tsarouchis: four painters of 20th century Greece.**
Introduction by Nicos Hadjinicolaou. London: Wildenstein, 1975. 46p. 33 plates.

The catalogue of an exhibition of four of the most significant painters of modern Greece, organized in connection with the Greek Month held in London in November 1975. Contains an informative introduction setting the four painters within the overall context of modern Greek painting.

621 **Eight artists: eight attitudes: eight Greeks. Stephen Antonakos, Vlassis Caniaris, Chryssa, Jannis Kounellis, Pavlos, Lucas Samaras, Takis, Costas Tsoclis.**
Introduction by Christos M. Joachimides. London: Institute of Contemporary Arts, 1975. 90p. plates.

The lavishly illustrated catalogue of an exhibition of the work of eight avant-garde Greek artists held in London in November 1975 in connection with the Greek Month.

622 **Ghika: paintings, drawing, sculpture.**
Stephen Spender, Patrick Leigh Fermor, with an introduction by Christian Zervos. London: Lund Humphries, 1964. 69p. plates. biographical notes. bibliog.

A magnificent compendium of the paintings of one of Greece's foremost painters, some of whose best pictures are inspired by his native island of Hydra.

Architecture

623 **Early Christian and Byzantine architecture.**
Richard Krautheimer. Harmondsworth, England: Penguin Books, 1965. 390p. glossary.

A comprehensive, scholarly and well-illustrated account of the development of early Christian architecture in the eastern Mediterranean region.

624 **Shelter in Greece-Oikismoi stin Ellada.**
Edited by O. B. Doumanis, Paul Oliver. Athens: Architecture in Greece Press, 1979. 2nd ed. 173p.

A study of the Greek dwelling.

The Arts. Handicraft and design

625 **Neoklassiki arkhitektoniki stin Ellada.** (Neoclassical architecture in Greece.)
Introduction by J. Travlos. Athens: Commercial Bank of Greece, 1967. 282p.

A splendidly illustrated account of neoclassical architecture, for a century or more the 'official' architectural style of the new state. Alas, growing prosperity, rapid urbanization and escalating property values have resulted in the destruction of many fine examples of this style.

626 **Greece.**
Orestes Doumanis. *World Architecture*, vol. 1 (1964), p. 117-23.

A brief introduction to post-war developments in Greek architecture.

627 **Traditional houses in modern Greece.**
J. M. Wagstaff. *Geography*, vol. 50, pt. 1 (Jan. 1965), p. 58-64.

A study of traditional houses, many of which have disappeared during the course of the present century as a result of war, occupation, civil war, exchange of populations, improved communications (which have made standardized building materials more readily available), and rapid modernization.

628 **The architecture of Chios: subsidiary buildings, implements and crafts.**
A. C. Smith, edited by Philip P. Argenti. London: Alec Tiranti, 1962. 171p. map.

A detailed study of the remarkably rich post-classical architecture of the island of Chios about which, thanks to the work of Philip Argenti, vastly more literature is available in English than on any other Greek island. Essential for the study of Greek domestic architecture.

Handicraft and design

629 **Greek handicraft.**
Edited by S. A. Papadopoulos. Athens: National Bank of Greece, 1969. 332p. bibliog.

A handsomely produced and illustrated introduction to Greek handicrafts, covering areas such as stone sculpture, woodcarving, pottery, weaving, embroidery, metalwork, silverwork and carpetmaking. Includes a particularly valuable list of museums where examples of the richness and variety of Greek popular art may be viewed.

The Arts. Handicraft and design

630 **The Byzantine tradition in church embroidery.**
Pauline Johnstone. London: Alec Tiranti, 1967. 144p. plates.

Very few of the rich embroideries of the Byzantine era have found their way into western museums. Pauline Johnstone's well-illustrated study throws important light on this aspect of the Byzantine decorative arts.

631 **Catalogue of a collection of old embroideries of the Greek islands and Turkey.**
A. J. B. Wace. London: Burlington Fine Arts Club, 1914. 61p.

A useful guide to the extraordinarily fine embroideries of the Greek islands.

632 **Greek island embroidery.**
Pauline Johnstone. London: Alec Tiranti, 1961. 58p.

A well-illustrated and clearly written guide to an aspect of Greek folk art which has only recently begun to be properly appreciated.

633 **Victoria and Albert Museum: a guide to Greek island embroidery.**
Pauline Johnstone. London: H.M. Stationery Office, 1972. 111p. bibliog. map.

A well-illustrated (though unfortunately not in colour) guide to the popular embroidery of the Greek islands, based on the embroideries in the Victoria and Albert Museum, London. Most of these came from the collection formed by the distinguished neo-Hellenist, R. M. Dawkins.

634 **Greek contemporary handweaving.**
M. Matthews. *Ciba Review*, no. 2 (1969), p. 2-32.

A comprehensive account of all aspects of contemporary handweaving in Greece. 'If students want to learn techniques which are commonplace today but may be forgotten in twenty years time, if they want to save for posterity and industry aesthetic values which have taken centuries to evolve, they must make the effort to visit and learn from the masters still alive and working today'.

635 **From spindle to loom: weaving in the southern Argolid.**
Joan Bouza Koster. *Expedition*, vol. 19, no. 1 (Fall 1976), p. 29-39.

An account of traditional weaving techniques still practised in Greece. The author is pessimistic about the future of this skilled craft.

636 **Modern Greek coins, 1828-1968.**
Jean-Paul Divo. Zurich: Bank Leu; Amsterdam: Jacques Schulman, 1969. 100p. bibliog.

'A detailed description of every known Greek and Cretan coin from the time of Capodistrias until the present time (with valuations).'.

The Arts. Music and dance

637 **A collection of the modern coins of Greece: coins of Crete; coins of the Ionian Islands; historical medals.**
London: Spink, 1979. 48p.
Well-illustrated catalogue of an auction sale by Spink & Son held on 17 May 1979. Indispensable for the study of modern Greek coinage.

Music and dance

638 **A history of Byzantine music and hymnography.**
Egon Wellesz. Oxford, England: Clarendon Press, 1961. 2nd ed. 461p. bibliog.
A scholarly history of Byzantine music, a tradition which is still very much alive in the music of the Orthodox Church.

639 **Ellinika laika mousika organa.** (Greek popular musical instruments.)
Phoivos Anogeianakis. Athens: National Bank of Greece, 1976. 400p. bibliog.
A superbly illustrated account of the development of popular musical instruments, of which the *bouzouki* is the most familiar outside Greece.

640 **Griechenland: Volksmusik und neuere Musik.** (Greece: folk and modern music.)
Minos E. Dounias. In: *Musik in Geschichte und Gegenwart: allgemeine Enzyklopädie der Musik.* Kassel, G.F.R.: Bärenreiter-Verlag, 1956. cols. 882-905. bibliog.
A useful brief survey of folk music and modern music in Greece.

641 **Greek folk music: a selective and annotated discography.**
Lucy Durán. *Mandatophoros*, no. 6 (May 1975), p. 9-23.
A most useful guide which aims to give 'an accurate picture of Greek folk-music as it is performed today by both professional and non-professional musicians'.

642 **Road to rebetika: music from a Greek sub-culture: songs of love, sorrow and hashish.**
Gail Holst. Athens: Anglo-Hellenic Publishing, 1977. 2nd ed. 175p. bibliog. discography.
The 'rebetika' songs of the Greek underworld have now become something of a cult. This book provides a fascinating insight into an Oriental aspect of Greek popular culture which is fast disappearing. The second edition helpfully contains the Greek texts (with translations) of many rebetika songs and a most useful discography.

The Arts. Music and dance

643 **Rebetika: songs from the old Greek underworld.**
Edited by Katherine Butterworth, Sara Schneider. Athens: Komboloi, 1975. 168p.
A collection of essays exploring the music, dances and lyrics of the 'rebetika', the songs of the *mangas* or *rebetis*, the hard man of the urban underworld.

644 **New music in Greece.**
Nicolas Slonimsky. *Musical Quarterly*, vol. 51, no. 1 (Jan. 1965), p. 225-35.
A survey of the contemporary music scene in Greece. Composers such as Yannis Xenakis and Nikos Mamangakis have acquired a very considerable international reputation.

645 **Nikos Skalkottas.**
John G. Papaioannou. In: *European music in the twentieth century*. Edited by Howard Hartog. Harmondsworth, England: Penguin Books, 1961, p. 336-44.
A useful short account of the works of Nikos Skalkottas, perhaps the best known Greek composer of modern music in the 20th century.

646 **Mikis Theodorakis: music and social change.**
George Giannaris. London: Allen & Unwin, 1973. 322p. bibliog. discography.
A musico-political biography of the man generally acknowledged to be Greece's greatest living musician, who with his fellow musician Manos Hadzidakis, has stimulated a revival of interest in Greece's traditional popular music. Left-wing politics have always loomed large in Theodorakis' life and his political activities, including his persecution during the Colonels' dictatorship, are fully described.

647 **Folk dances of the Greeks: origins and instructions.**
Theodore Petrides, Elfleida Petrides. Folkestone, England: Bailey Bros. & Swinfen, 1974. 79p.
An illustrated practical guide to Greek folk dancing.

648 **Greek dances.**
Ted Petrides. Athens: Lycabettus Press, 1975. 104p.
An account of Greek folk dances by one of the country's leading experts.

649 **Dances of Greece.**
Domini Crosfield. London: Max Parrish, 1948. 40p.
A guide, with music and a description of the steps, to Greek folk dances.

Theatre and film

650 **Le théâtre grec moderne de 1453 à 1900.** (Modern Greek theatre from 1453 to 1900.)
M. Valsa. Berlin: Akademie Verlag, 1960. 384p. (Berliner Byzantinische Arbeiten, vol. 18).
A scholarly history of the Greek theatre up to the beginning of the present century.

651 **The contemporary Greek cinema.**
Mel Schuster. Metuchen, New Jersey; London: Scarecrow Press, 1979. 360p. bibliog. selected filmography.
Greece is scarcely a country noted for the excellence of its films. But in recent years a handful of Greek directors have begun to win international recognition in addition to Michael (*Zorba the Greek*) Cacoyannis, who is a Cypriot, and Costa (Z) Gavras, who for many years has lived outside Greece. Theodore Angelopoulos, for instance, has won considerable acclaim for his four hour marathon *O Thiasos* ('The travelling players') (1975) set in the Greece of the occupation and Civil War, as has Pandelis Voulgaris' for his *Happy day* (1976). Actresses such as Irene Pappas and Melina Mercouri have also made their mark outside Greece. This entertaining book tells you all you need to know, and probably more, about the Greek cinema.

652 **Humour and status reversal in Greek shadow theatre.**
Loring M. Danforth. *Byzantine and Modern Greek Studies*, vol. 2 (1976), p. 99-111.
An analysis of the inner meaning of the Greek shadow puppet theatre, which revolves around the adventures of Karaghiozis, the personification of *poniria*, or cunning, who is forever outwitting the Turk. Although, with rapid modernization, the once-popular Greek shadow theatre is very much on the decline, there has in recent years been something of a revival of interest on the part of the urban intelligentsia in this pristine manifestation of folk culture.

653 **Modern Greek humor: a collection of jokes and ribald tales.**
Ethelyn G. Orso. Bloomington, Indiana: Indiana University Press, 1979. 262p. bibliog.
A thorough study of modern Greek humour by an anthropologist. Includes chapters on political jokes, anti-clerical jokes, ethnic slur jokes and *sókin* (dirty) jokes, replete with four-letter words. Contains an appendix of insulting gestures.

654 **O kosmos tou Karaghiozis: figoures.** (The world of Karaghiozis: figures.)
Ap. Giagannos, Ar. Giagannos, I. Diglis. Athens: Ermis, 1976. 2 vols.
A superbly illustrated guide to the various stock characters of the much-loved but now nearly defunct shadow theatre, based on the adventures of Karaghiozis.

The Arts. Folklore

Folklore

655 **État actuel des études folkloriques èn Grece.** (The present state of folklore studies in Greece.)
Demetrios Loukatos. In: *Actes du IIe Congrès International des Études du Sud-Est Européen.* Athens: Greek Committee of AIESEE, 1972. Vol. 1, p. 551-82.

A useful overview of the development and present state of folklore studies in Greece during the present century, with details of periodicals and institutions concerned with the study of folklore.

656 **Modern Greek folktales.**
Translated from the Greek by R. M. Dawkins. Oxford, England: Clarendon Press, 1953. 487p.

A collection of eighty-four folktales, admirably translated, from various parts of the Greek world. In an interesting introduction Dawkins attempts a basic classification of the different story types.

657 **More Greek folktales.**
Translated from the Greek by R. M. Dawkins. Oxford, England: Clarendon Press, 1955. 178p.

A further selection of folktales, admirably chosen and selected by one of Britain's foremost authorities on the modern Greek language, drawn from various parts of the Greek world including Thrace, Pontos and Asia Minor.

658 **Folktales of Greece.**
Edited by Georgios A. Megas, translated from the Greek by Helen Colaclides, foreword by Richard M. Dorson. Chicago, London: University of Chicago Press, 1970. 287p. bibliog.

A collection of Greek folktales grouped under the following headings: animal tales; wonder tales; tales of kindness rewarded and evil punished; tales of fate; jokes, anecdotes, and religious tales; legends.

659 **Forty-five stories from the Dodekanese.**
Edited and translated from the manuscripts of Jacob Zarraftis by R. M. Dawkins. Cambridge, England: Cambridge University Press, 1950. 560p. glossary.

Forty-five folk tales from the Dodecanese islands, prefaced by three introductory chapters on the art of story-telling in the Dodecanese, on the general context of the stories and on their value.

The Arts. Folklore

660 Two studies on modern Greek folklore.
Stilpon P. Kyriakides, translated from the German and Greek by Robert A. Georges, Aristotle A. Katranides. Thessaloniki, Greece: Institute for Balkan Studies, 1968. 132p.

Two short studies by one of the pioneers of academic folklore studies in Greece.

661 Macedonian folklore.
G. F. Abbott. Cambridge, England: Cambridge University Press, 1903. Reprinted, Chicago: Argonaut Publishers, 1969. 372p. appendices.

A detailed account of the folklore of Macedonia at the beginning of the 20th century, with chapters on the folklore associated with the seasons, birth, marriage, death, on spirits and spells, legends concerning Alexander the Great and Philip of Macedonia, etc.

662 The folk lore of Chios.
Philip P. Argenti, H. J. Rose. Cambridge, England: Cambridge University Press, 1949. 2 vols.

A truly thorough account of almost all aspects of daily life on the island of Chios. Folklore is here interpreted very broadly.

663 Modern Greek folklore and ancient Greek religion: a study in survivals.
John Cuthbert Lawson. Cambridge, England: Cambridge University Press, 1910. Reprinted, New York: University Books, 1964. 620p.

Through a study of the folklore of the modern Greeks the author sought survivals of the religious beliefs and practices of the ancient Greeks. For example, he links the Centaurs of the Ancient World with the *kallikantzaroi*, the demons who are today held to haunt the twelve days of Christmas. Although some of his claims are undoubtedly exaggerated, this is an interesting and worthwhile pioneering study.

664 Morality, courtship, and love in Greek folklore.
Constantina Safilios-Rothschild. *Southern Folklore Quarterly*, vol. 29, no. 4 (Dec. 1965), p. 297-308.

'Morality and love in the traditional Greek culture can be understood only when examined in the context of "honor". Behavior is guided by the consideration of potential consequences for one's honor; anything that may lead to dishonor is painstakingly avoided. Being honored or dishonored very often proves to be a matter of life and death. This extreme concern and literally "love of honor", expressed in *philotimo*, constitutes a central characteristic of the Greek national character.'.

Folk customs, costumes, cookery

665 Greek calendar customs.
G. A. Megas. Athens: Press and Information Department, Prime Minister's Office, 1958. 159p.

A useful study of the various traditional customs associated with the Orthodox religious cycle.

666 The customs and lore of modern Greece.
Rennell Rodd. London: David Stott, 1892. 2nd ed. 305p.

An interesting early account of the customs, beliefs and popular culture of the Greek peasantry. The author believed that there was 'probably no country in Europe where such a wealth of lore and fancy still governs the daily life of the people, where superstition is so historic and so interesting as it is here'.

667 The Anastenaria: Thracian firewalking festival.
Anne Gault Antoniades. Athens: Society of Thracian Studies, 1954. 22p. (Thracian Archives, no. 36).

A study of the firewalkers of the Thracian village of Langada who annually, on the feast of Saints Constantine and Helen, walk on hot coals. Some have seen in this custom a link with the ancient cult of Dionysos.

668 Ellinikes phoresies - Greek costumes - Costumes grecs.
Ioanna Papantoniou. Nafplion, Greece: The Peloponnesian Folklore Foundation, 1976. unpaginated.

An illustrated guide to women's regional dress in the Greek lands. Gives a good impression of the richness of traditional costume.

669 Ellinikes phoresies. (Greek costumes.)
Ioanna Papantoniou. Nafplion, Greece: The Peloponnesian Folklore Foundation, 1974. unpaginated.

A companion volume to the above item, illustrating the richly embroidered men's traditional dress.

670 Greek regional costumes.
A. Hadjimihali. *Ciba Review*, no. 2 (1969), p. 35-44.

A brief survey of regional costume in Greece.

671 The costumes of Chios: their development from the XVth to the XXth century.
Philip P. Argenti. London: Batsford, 1953. 338p.

An exceptionally well-illustrated and exhaustive guide to the traditional costumes of Chios by one of the island's most devoted native sons. Chios has always been a prosperous island, and this prosperity is reflected in the richness of its costumes.

The Arts. Folk customs, costumes, cookery

672 **Greek cooking.**
Robin Howe. London: André Deutsch, 1960. 282p.
No one would claim that Greek cuisine is one of the great cuisines of the world, yet good meals can be had in Greece. This clearly written cookery book is a useful guide to the preparation of the most common Greek dishes.

673 **The home book of Greek cookery: a selection of traditional Greek recipes.**
Joyce M. Stubbs. London: Faber & Faber, 1963. 159p.
A comprehensive and clear introduction to Greek cooking.

Sport

674 The first modern Olympics.
Richard D. Mandell. Berkeley, Los Angeles: University of California Press, 1976. 194p.

An entertaining account of the revival of the Olympic idea in modern times. The first modern Olympic games were held in Athens in 1896 thanks to the initiative of the French Baron Pierre de Coubertin and to the generosity of a wealthy Greek, George Averoff, who paid for the restoration of the Panathenian stadium. This handsome reconstruction is one of the more attractive features of the modern city of Athens.

Literature

General literary history and criticism

675 **A history of modern Greek literature.**
Linos Politis. Oxford, England: Clarendon Press, 1973. 338p. bibliog.

A useful, if somewhat woodenly written, history of the literature of a country whose literary output has always seemed disproportionate to its size. Politis' text is comprehensive in scope, beginning with the rise of literature in demotic Greek in the 11th century, although his coverage of post-Second World War literary developments is somewhat perfunctory. His treatment of the language question which has so bedevilled Greek cultural life is clear and concise. As he points out, Greek *diglossia*, the co-existence of the demotic with the purified *katharevousa*, is 'not easily comprehensible to a foreigner (or to any reasonable man)'. The book contains useful chronological tables.

676 **A history of modern Greek literature.**
C. Th. Dimaras, translated from the Greek by Mary P. Gianos. London: University of London Press, 1974; Albany: State University of New York Press, 1972. 539p. bibliog.

Constantine Dimaras' history enjoys something of the status of a classic in Greece. The English version is marred by an unsatisfactory translation, but still provides a useful overview of the remarkably rich literature of modern Greece.

Literature. General literary history and criticism

677 **Fair Greece! Sad relic! Literary philhellenism from Shakespeare to Byron.**
Terence Spencer. London: Weidenfeld & Nicolson, 1954. Reprinted 1971. 312p. bibliog.

A scholarly and brilliantly written account of the literary contacts between England and Greece in the 300 or so years before the outbreak of the Greek War of Independence in 1821.

678 **Disaster and fiction: modern Greek fiction and the Asia Minor disaster of 1922.**
Thomas Doulis. Berkeley, California; London: University of California Press, 1977. 313p. bibliog.

An analysis of the impact of the disastrous defeat of the Greek armies in Asia Minor in 1922 on the Greek novel. A classic example of the genre is George Theotokas' *Argo*.

679 **The ritual lament in Greek tradition.**
Margaret Alexiou. Cambridge, England: Cambridge University Press, 1974. 274p. bibliog.

A fascinating study of the ritual lament as it has evolved from ancient times to the present day.

680 **The marble threshing floor: studies in modern Greek poetry.**
Philip Sherrard. London: Vallentine, Mitchell, 1956. 258p.

A study of the poetry of Dionysios Solomos, Kostis Palamas, Constantine Cavafy, Anghelos Sikelianos and George Seferis.

681 **Folk poetry of modern Greece.**
Roderick Beaton. Cambridge, England: Cambridge University Press, 1980. 229p. bibliog.

A scholarly study of the rich corpus of modern Greek folk poetry.

682 **The songs of Greece.**
H. Pym. London: Sunday Times, 1968. 96p.

An illustrated collection of translations of Greek folk songs.

Anthologies

683 The Penguin book of Greek verse.
Introduced and edited by Constantine A.
Trypanis. Harmondsworth, England: Penguin Books, 1971.
630p. bibliog.

Examples of Greek poetry from Homer to Elytis, with the Greek originals accompanied by 'plain prose' translations.

684 Medieval and modern Greek poetry: an anthology.
C. A. Trypanis. Oxford, England: Clarendon Press, 1951.
285p. glossary.

A selection, in the original Greek, of poetry from the Byzantine, Ottoman and post-independence periods, accompanied by a substantial introduction.

685 Four Greek poets: C. P. Cavafy, George Seferis, Odysseus Elytis, Nikos Gatsos.
Translated and edited by Edmund Keeley, Philip
Sherrard. Harmondsworth, England: Penguin Books, 1966.
110p.

A selection in translation of the poetry of four of Greece's leading poets, with notes.

686 Six poets of modern Greece.
Selected and translated with introductions by Edmund
Keeley, Philip Sherrard. New York: Alfred A. Knopf,
1961. 185p. bibliog.

Translations of the poetry of Cavafy, Sikelianos, Seferis, Antoniou, Elytis and Gatsos.

687 Modern Greek poetry: translation, introduction, an essay on translation, and notes.
Kimon Friar. New York: Simon & Schuster, 1973. 780p.

Contains translations, prefaced by a lengthy introduction and extensive notes, of poetry by Cavafy, Kazantzakis, Varnalis, Sikelianos, Ouranis, Papatsonis, Kariotakis, Seferis, Themelis, Karelli, Embiricos, Panayotopoulos, Vafopoulos, Pappas, Boumi-Pappas, Antoniou, Baras, Sarandaris, Calas, Pendzikis, Prevelakis, Ritsos, Kavadhias, Karandonis, Melissanthi, Matsas, Engonopoulos, Elytis, Gatsos, Vrettakos.

688 Eighteen texts: writings by contemporary Greek authors.
Edited by Willis Barnstone. Cambridge, Massachusetts:
Harvard University Press, 1972. 187p.

When originally published in Greece in 1970 as *Dekaokhto Keimena* (Eighteen texts), this book created a sensation. For the first time during the Colonels' dictatorship a number of Greece's most respected literary figures, including Nobel

Literature. Major writers

prize winning poet, George Seferis, broke their self-imposed silence. The book rapidly went through several impressions. Of uneven literary quality, most of the contributions have an implicit or explicit political message. Outstanding is Kay Cicellis' *Brief dialogue*.

689 **Contemporary Greek literature.**
Descant, vol. 8, no. 2 (1977), 101p.
An issue of this Canadian literary journal devoted solely to modern Greek literature in translation. Contains extracts of the work of many contemporary writers.

Major writers

690 **Loukis Laras: reminiscences of a Chiote merchant during the War of Independence.**
D. Bikelas, translated from the Greek by J. Gennadius. London: Macmillan, 1881. 273p.
A fascinating historical novel set in the time of the Greek War of Independence.

691 **The poems of C. P. Cavafy.**
C. P. Cavafy, translated from the Greek by John Mavrogordato, with an introduction by Rex Warner. London: Hogarth Press, 1951; New York: Grove Press, 1952. 199p.
A translation of some of Cavafy's poems, in which the translator seeks to 'represent the rhymes and the rhyme patterns of the original'.

692 **The complete poems of Cavafy.**
C. P. Cavafy, translated from the Greek by Rae Dalven, with an introduction by W. H. Auden. London: Hogarth Press; New York: Harcourt, Brace & World, 1961. 234p. bibliog.
The second translation of the poetic works of Cavafy.

693 **Collected poems.**
C. P. Cavafy, edited by George Savidis, translated from the Greek by Edmund Keeley, Philip Sherrard. Princeton, New Jersey: Princeton University Press; London: Hogarth Press, 1975. 447p. bibliog.
A nearly complete edition of Cavafy's poetry, with facing Greek texts and excellent English translations.

Literature. Major writers

694 **Selected poems.**
C. P. Cavafy, translated from the Greek by Edmund Keeley, Philip Sherrard. Princeton, New Jersey: Princeton University Press, 1972. 98p. bibliog.
A selection of Cavafy's 'most significant and characteristic' poems.

695 **Passions and ancient days.**
C. P. Cavafy, translated from the Greek and introduced by Edmund Keeley, George Savidis. New York: Dial Press, 1971; London: Hogarth Press, 1975. 68p.
Late additions to the corpus of Cavafy's poetry, with the original Greek texts and English translations in parallel.

696 **Cavafy: a critical biography.**
Robert Liddell. London: Duckworth, 1974. 222p. bibliog.
A lively and well-written biography of perhaps the greatest Greek poet of modern times, C. P. Cavafy, whom E. M. Forster once graphically described as standing at a slight angle to the universe. The poet par excellence of the Greek diaspora, Cavafy spent part of his childhood in Liverpool and most of his adult life in Alexandria.

697 **Cavafy's Alexandria: study of a myth in progress.**
Edmund Keeley. London: Hogarth Press; Princeton, New Jersey: Princeton University Press, 1977. 196p. bibliog. map.
An exploration of the significance of the myth of Alexandria to the poetry of Cavafy, who lived in the city for most of his life. The appendices contain a useful chronology of the composition of Cavafy's poems.

698 **Constantine Cavafy.**
Peter A. Bien. New York, London: Columbia University Press, 1964. 48p. bibliog.
A useful brief introduction to the life and works of the greatest of the poets of modern Greece, a country which has produced more than its fair share. 'Unable to look upward to heaven for his answers, he looked backward into history and inward into his own psyche. What he found in both places was awful...cowardice, disillusion, sordidness, contradiction, paradox'.

699 **Analogies of light: the Greek poet Odysseus Elytis.**
Books Abroad. An International Literary Quarterly, vol. 49, no. 4 (Autumn 1975), p. 627-716.
Contains an anthology of the Nobel prize-winning Elytis' poetry, together with a number of critical essays, including a brief appreciation of his poetry by Lawrence Durrell.

Literature. Major writers

700 **The axion esti (It is meet): an International Poetry Forum selection.**
Odysseus Elytis, translated from the Greek and annotated by Edmund Keeley, George Savidis. Pittsburgh, Pennsylvania: University of Pittsburgh Press, 1974. 159p. bibliog.

A translation of what is perhaps Elytis' greatest poetic work to date, together with the original Greek text. This secular oratorio has been set to music by Mikis Theodorakis.

701 **The sovereign sun: selected poems.**
Odysseus Elytis, translated from the Greek with an introduction and notes by Kimon Friar. Philadelphia, Pennsylvania: Temple University Press, 1974. 200p. bibliog.

A collection of translations of some seventy of Elytis' best-known poems. In October 1979 Elytis was awarded the Nobel Prize for poetry which 'against the background of Greek tradition depicts with sensuous strength and intellectual clarity modern man's struggle for freedom and creativity'.

702 **Christ recrucified.**
Nikos Kazantzakis, translated from the Greek by Jonathan Griffin. New York: Simon & Schuster, 1953; Oxford, England: Cassirer, 1954. 470p.

A superb novel set in Asia Minor as the Greek presence became untenable with the clash of rival Greek and Turkish nationalism. Published in the U.S.A. as *The Greek passion*.

703 **The fratricides.**
Nikos Kazantzakis, translated from the Greek by Athena Gianakas Dallas. New York: Simon & Schuster, 1964; Oxford, England: Cassirer, 1967. 254p.

One of Kazantzakis' less familiar novels.

704 **Freedom and death.**
Nikos Kazantzakis. Oxford, England: Cassirer, 1956. 472p.

A novel set in 19th century Crete, when the islanders launched repeated struggles to overthrow Ottoman rule and achieve the dream of *enosis*, or union with the Greek kingdom.

705 **The last temptation.**
Nikos Kazantzakis, translated from the Greek with a note on the author and his language by P. A. Bien. Oxford, England: Cassirer; New York: Simon & Schuster, 1961. 519p.

A novel, based on the life of Christ, which, like many of his other works, upset the hierarchy of the Orthodox Church in Greece. In the words of his translator, Kazantzakis 'wished to make Jesus a figure for a new age, while still retaining

Literature. Major writers

everything in the Christ-legend which speaks to the conditions of all men of all ages'.

706 Zorba the Greek.
Nikos Kazantzakis, translated from the Greek by Carl Wildman. London: John Lehmann, 1952; New York: Simon & Schuster, 1953. 315p.

Made into a film, starring Anthony Quinn as Zorba, by Michael Cacoyannis in 1964, this novel more than any other has been responsible for the somewhat absurd concept of the 'Super Greek'.

707 Travels in Greece: journey to the Morea.
Nikos Kazantzakis, translated from the Greek by F. A. Reed. Oxford, England: Cassirer, 1966. 190p.

The novelist's impressions of the Peloponnese, based on five visits between 1915 and 1937. In the words of the translator: 'travel in the Peloponnesos reveals to him with frightening intensity the pitiful plight of his race. With the same eye that has feasted on the riches of the Orient and gazed at Russia's interminable snowy expanse, he now searches about him trying to discover Greece's true face, among the malaria-stricken peasants and the stagnant-souled householders of the provinces'.

708 Report to Greco.
Nikos Kazantzakis, translated from the Greek by P. A. Bien. New York: Simon & Schuster; Oxford, England: Cassirer, 1965. 512p.

Kazantzakis, in his own introduction, describes *Report to Greco* as not being 'an autobiography. My personal life has some value, extremely relative, for myself and no one else. The sole value I acknowledge in it was its effort to mount from one step to the next and reach the highest point to which its strength and doggedness could bring it: the summit I named the Cretan Glance. Therefore, reader, in these pages you will find the red track made by drops of my blood, the track which marks my journey among men, passions and ideas'.

709 Nikos Kazantzakis: a biography based on his letters.
Helen Kazantzakis, translated from the Greek by Amy Mims. New York: Simon & Schuster; Oxford, England: Cassirer, 1968. 589p.

A biography of one of Greece's best known writers of this century, based on his letters.

710 Kazantzakis: the politics of salvation.
James F. Lea, with a foreword by Helen Kazantzakis. University, Alabama: University of Alabama Press, 1979. 207p. bibliog.

An analysis of Kazantzakis' political and social philosophy. The author argues that Kazantzakis' politics 'represents an alternative to ideology and the basis for a politics of existential hope beyond absolutist claims, illusory secular faiths, and destructive nihilistic despair'.

Literature. Major writers

711 **Nikos Kazantzakis.**
Peter A. Bien. New York: Columbia University Press, 1972. 48p. (Columbia Essays on Modern Writers, no. 62).
A useful short survey of Kazantzakis' writings by a scholar who has translated a number of his novels.

712 **Kazantzakis and the linguistic revolution in Greek literature.**
Peter A. Bien. Princeton, New Jersey: Princeton University Press, 1972. 291p.
A scholarly study of the central role which demotic Greek (often in some rather odd forms) played in the artistic inspiration of the novelist Nikos Kazantzakis. Prefaced by a lengthy and clear analysis of the language question in Greece, the struggle between the demotic, or commonly spoken language, and the *katharevousa*. The latter was a 'purified' form of the language propounded by 19th century pedants as more befitting the descendants of the ancient Hellenes than the 'crude' demotic. Inevitably the language question has assumed political overtones in Greece and Bien's analysis is as good an introduction as any to this extraordinary politico-cultural phenomenon, virtually without parallel elsewhere in the world.

713 **The Cretan glance: the world and art of Nikos Kazantzakis.**
Morton P. Levitt. Columbus, Ohio: Ohio State University Press, 1980. 187p. bibliog.
A study of the writings of the Cretan Nikos Kazantzakis, perhaps the best-known of Greek novelists outside the country.

714 **Nikos Kazantzakis: a check list of primary and secondary works supplementing the Katsimbalis bibliography.**
Peter A. Bien. *Mandatophoros*, no. 5 (Nov. 1974), p. 7-53.
A massively detailed bibliography of Kazantzakis' writings, their numerous translations, and the huge secondary literature of criticism that they have generated. Bien is the translator of a number of Kazantzakis' major works.

715 **Life in the tomb.**
Stratis Myrivilis, translated from the Greek by Peter A. Bien. Hanover, New Hampshire: University Press of New England, 1977. 325p. maps.
Based on the fictionalized experiences of an army sergeant on the Macedonian front in 1917, the book is described by its translator as 'the single most successful and most widely read serious novel in Greece in the period since the Great War'. Its circulation was forbidden during the Metaxas dictatorship and subsequent Axis occupation of Greece.

716 **The mermaid madonna.**
Stratis Myrivilis, translated from the Greek by Abbott Rick. London: Hutchinson, 1959. 288p.
A novel of island life by one of Greece's leading novelists set in his native island of Mytilini.

Literature. Major writers

717 The schoolmistress with the golden eyes.
Stratis Myrivilis, translated from the Greek by Philip Sherrard. London: Hutchinson, 1964. 288p.

A modern rendering of the legend of Sappho by one of Greece's leading novelists.

718 The twelve words of the gypsy.
Kostis Palamas, translated with an introduction by Frederic Will. Lincoln, Nebraska: University of Nebraska Press, 1964. 205p.

This is a translation of the most famous poem of one of the leading poets of modern Greece. This translation had been much criticized on grounds of accuracy but, unusually in the case of modern Greek literature, the Greekless reader has a choice of three versions of Palamas' epic masterpiece. (See following two items).

719 The twelve lays of the gypsy.
Kostis Palamas, translated with an introduction by George Thomson. London: Lawrence & Wishart, 1969. 146p.

The translator quotes a telling observation of the poet George Seferis on Palamas' place in Greek literature: 'With Palamas Greek literature enters at last on its regular path. Of the two traditions which have maintained themselves continuously since the period of the first Koine [the language of the Gospels]; the one, illustrious but lifeless, the learned tradition, comes to an end, in the life of poetry, with Kavafis [Cavafy]; the other, despised but living, the popular tradition, after taking fire from Tartarus and light from Elysium, breaks into the upper world with Palamas. With him, for the first time after 2,000 years, the two lines converge and become one'.

720 The twelve words of the gypsy.
Kostis Palamas, translated from the Greek by Theodore Ph. Stephanides, George C. Katsimbalis. London: Translators, 1974. 194p.; Memphis, Tennessee: Memphis State University Press, 1975. 314p. glossary.

A lively and fluent translation. The American edition conveniently gives the original Greek text as well as the translation.

721 Kostis Palamas.
Thanasis Maskaleris. New York: Twayne Publishers, 1972. 156p. bibliog. (Twayne World Authors Series, no. 197).

A study of the man who 'contributed more than any other writer to the establishment of the vernacular idiom as the literary language of modern Greece'. He was, par excellence, the poet of the *Megali Idea* (Great Idea), the vision of once again reuniting all the Greek peoples within the bounds of a single polity. His best known poem *The twelve lays of the gipsy* has been translated into English (see preceding three entries).

Literature. Major writers

722 **The murderess.**
Alexandros Papadiamantis, translated from the Greek by George X. Xanthopoulides. London, Athens: Doric Publications, 1977. 167p.
A remarkable novel by one of Greece's most original literary talents.

723 **The sun of death.**
Pandelis Prevelakis, translated from the Greek by Philip Sherrard. London: John Murray, 1965. 206p.
A novel set in the author's native island of Crete during the First World War.

724 **The tale of a town.**
Pandelis Prevelakis, translated from the Greek by Kenneth Johnstone. London, Athens: Doric Publications, 1976. 119p.
A novel of small-town life on the island of Crete, at the time when the exchange of populations agreed between Greece and Turkey meant the departure of the Greek-speaking Muslims of Crete and their replacement by Greek refugees from Asia Minor.

725 **Selected poems.**
Yannis Ritsos, translated from the Greek by Nikos Stangos, with an introduction by Peter A. Bien. Harmondsworth, England: Penguin Books, 1974. 207p.
A selection of the prolific output of Yannis Ritsos, perhaps the leading poet of the Greek left. Bien's introduction is particularly helpful in setting Ritsos' poetic output in the context of his personal experiences.

726 **Ritsos in parentheses.**
Yannis Ritsos, translated and introduced by Edmund Keeley. Princeton, New Jersey: Princeton University Press, 1979. 175p.
A selection of the poetry of Yannis Ritsos, with facing Greek and English texts and biographical data on the poet.

727 **Eighteen short songs of the bitter motherland.**
Yannis Ritsos, translated from the Greek by Amy Mims, with illustrations by Yannis Ritsos, edited with an introduction by Theofanis G. Stavrou. St. Paul, Minnesota: North Central Publishing, 1974. 60p.
Sixteen of these songs were written in an island prison camp in September 1968, while Ritsos was imprisoned by the Colonels. Parallel Greek (handwritten) and English texts.

Literature. Major writers

728 **Scripture of the blind.**
Yannis Ritsos, translated from the Greek with an introduction by Kimon Friar, Kostas Myrsiades. Columbus, Ohio: Ohio State University Press, 1979. 251p.

The Greek texts, with an English translation, of a series of poems written during a two-month period of the Colonels' dictatorship between 28 September and 28 November 1972.

729 **Yannis Ritsos: bibliography.**
Ninetta Makrynikola. *Mandatophoros*, no. 12 (May 1978), p. 12-87.

Vast bibliography of the Lenin Prize winning poet Yannis Ritsos, including translations into foreign languages and secondary literature.

730 **Pope Joan.**
Emmanuel Royidis, translated from the Greek by Lawrence Durrell. London: André Deutsch, 1960. 163p.

A translation of Emmanuel Royidis' remarkable novel, *Papissa Ioanna*, first published in 1886. A satire based on the papacy of the allegedly female Pope John VIII, its publication scandalized the church authorities in Greece. Royidis was excommunicated and *Papissa Ioanna* was banned. It enjoyed a huge success, however, in France. A brilliantly written and amusing novel.

731 **The flaw.**
Antonis Samarakis, translated from the Greek by Peter Mansfield, Richard Burns. London: Hutchinson, 1966. 208p.

Although written in 1966, before the Colonels' coup, and set in an unspecified totalitarian state, Samarakis' novel graphically prefigures the police state atmosphere of the Colonels' Greece.

732 **Collected poems 1924-1955.**
George Seferis, translated from the Greek and edited and introduced by Edmund Keeley, Philip Sherrard. Princeton, New Jersey: Princeton University Press, 1967; London: Jonathan Cape, 1969. 490p. bibliog.

Contains the Greek texts together with translations of the poems of the Nobel Prize winning poet, George Seferis. In the words of the translators: 'one senses really the whole of the Greek past, as it is represented in poetry from the age of Homer down to the contemporary period in his poetic output'.

733 **A poet's journal: days of 1945-51.**
George Seferis, translated from the Greek by Athan Anagnostopoulos, introduction by Walter Kaiser. Cambridge, Massachusetts: Belknap, 1974. 206p.

The journal of one of the greatest Greek poets of the 20th century, George Seferis. Covering the years 1945-51, a period of considerable political turmoil,

Literature. Major writers

this diary is essential reading for an understanding of Seferis both as a man and as a poet.

734 **On the Greek style: selected essays in poetry and Hellenism.**
George Seferis, translated from the Greek by Rex Warner, Th. D. Frangopoulos, with an introduction by Rex Warner. London: Bodley Head; Boston: Atlantic-Little Brown, 1966. 196p.

A series of essays by George Seferis on various literary topics.

735 **Angelos Sikelianos.**
Translated and introduced by Edward Keeley, Philip Sherrard. London: George Allen & Unwin, 1980. 75p.

A selection of Sikelianos' poems, together with biographical data.

736 **Landscape of death. The selected poems of Takis Sinopoulos.**
Translated from the Greek with an introduction by Kimon Friar. Columbus, Ohio: Ohio State University Press, 1979. 288p.

A bilingual edition of the poems of one of Greece's leading contemporary poets.

737 **Dionysios Solomos.**
Romilly Jenkins. Cambridge, England: Cambridge University Press, 1940. 186p.

A well-written study of the life and poetry of Dionysios Solomos (1798-1857), a native of Zante in the Ionian Islands and best known as the author of Greece's national anthem, *The hymn to liberty*. Like another of Greece's greatest poets, Cavafy, Greek was not Solomos' first language. He was the scion of a noble Zantiot family and his first language was Italian. Such has been the remarkable growth of interest in the English-speaking world in modern Greek literature, that the author's gloomy claim that barely a dozen persons in England in his time knew the name of Solomos certainly no longer holds good.

738 **Dionysios Solomos.**
M. B. Raizis. New York: Twayne Publishers, 1972. 158p. (Twayne World Authors Series, no. 193).

A study of one of Greece's greatest poets, whose *Hymn to liberty* is the country's national anthem. It has been translated, among others, by Rudyard Kipling.

739 **The third wedding.**
Costas Taktsis, translated from the Greek by Leslie Finer. London: Alan Ross, 1967. 303p.

A fine novel which incidentally throws revealing light on contemporary Greek society.

Literature. Major writers

740 **Argo.**
George Theotokas, translated from the Greek by E. Margaret Brooke, Ares Tsatsopoulos. London: Methuen, 1951. 357p.

A novel set in Istanbul and Athens at the time of The Catastrophe, the disastrous defeat of the Greek armies in Asia Minor in 1922. Theotokas graphically captures the turbulent atmosphere of this troubled period of Greek history.

741 **George Theotokas.**
Thomas Doulis. Boston: Twayne Publishers, 1975. 185p. bibliog. (Twayne World Authors Series, no. 339).

A study of one of modern Greece's most distinguished writers of prose. Regrettably only one of his novels, *Argo* (see item above), has been translated into English.

742 **Drifting cities: a trilogy.**
Stratis Tsirkas, translated from the Greek by Kay Cicellis. New York: Alfred A. Knopf, 1974. 710p.

A powerful novel set against the political turmoil of the Greek community in Egypt during the Second World War.

743 **Aeolia.**
Ilias Venezis, translated from the Greek by E. D. Scott-Kilvert. London: William Campion, 1949; New York: Vanguard Press, 1957. 260p.

A novel full of nostalgia for the lost Eden of Anatolia before the expulsion of the Greeks in 1922. As Lawrence Durrell eloquently puts it in his preface: 'the golden ambience of Aeolia springs out of an imaginative reconstruction of a way of life which has vanished, the re-valuation of an inheritance which has been forfeited'.

744 **Elias Venezis.**
Alexander Karanikas, Helen Karanikas. New York: Twayne Publishers, 1969. 158p. bibliog. (Twayne World Authors Series, no. 74).

Venezis was born in Ayvalik in Asia Minor and memories of his childhood and the catastrophic defeat of the Greek armies in 1922 are a prominent theme of his novels. *Aioliki gi (Aeolian land)*, a nostalgic account of life in Asia Minor before the catastrophe put an abrupt end to a 2,000 year Greek presence in Anatolia, has been translated into English (see preceding item).

Printing and Publishing

745 **Buchproduktion und Buchdistribution in Griechenland: Probleme und Eigentümlichkeiten des griechischen Buch und Verlagswesen.** (Book production and distribution in Greece: problems and characteristics of the organization of publishing.)
E. Winters Ohle. Bochum, G.F.R.: University of Bochum, 1979. 263p. (Bochumer Studien zur neugriechischen und byzantinischen Philologie, vol. 2).
An account of the ill-organized but very lively book trade in Greece.

746 **The Greek book, 1476-1825.**
Francis R. Walton. Athens: Dixième Congrès International des Bibliophiles, 1977. 46p.
A useful brief overview of the history of Greek printing (much of it carried on outside the Greek lands) during the period of Turkish rule.

747 **Portrait of a bibliophile XII: Joannes Gennadius, 1844-1932.**
Francis R. Walton. *The Book Collector*, vol. 13, no. 3 (Autumn 1964), p. 305-26.
A fascinating account of Joannes Gennadius, for many years Greek minister in London and an assiduous bibliophile. His personal library forms the basis of the Gennadius Library of the American School of Classical Studies at Athens, one of the richest and most efficiently run libraries in Greece.

Printing and Publishing

748 **The Greek press at Constantinople in 1627 and its antecedents.**
R. J. Roberts. *The Library*, vol. 22, no. 1 (March 1967), p. 13-43.
A thorough account of the brief and troubled history of the first Greek printing press in Constantinople, set up by Nikodimos Metaxas in 1627.

749 **Nikodemos Metaxas, the first Greek printer in the eastern world.**
Evro Leyton. *Harvard Library Bulletin*, vol. 15, no. 2 (April 1967), p. 140-68. bibliog.
Another study of the short-lived Metaxas press in Constantinople. The author concludes that it was 'almost a miracle that, considering the turbulent political and religious climate in which he [Metaxas] found himself at the time of his stay in Constantinople, he managed to print anything at all'.

Mass Media

General

750 **The newspapers of Greece.**
Kenneth E. Olson. In: *The history makers. The press of Europe from its beginnings through 1965.* Baton Rouge, Louisiana: Louisiana State University Press, 1966, p. 253-69.
A summary of the history and present state, as of the mid-1960s, of the flourishing newspaper industry in Greece. Greeks appear to be among the most avid newspaper readers in the world.

751 **Istoria tou ellinikou typou.** (History of the Greek press.)
K. Mager. Athens: A. Dimopoulos, 1957-60. 3 vols.
A detailed history of the Greek press since 1870.

752 **The Greek press under the colonels.**
Robert McDonald. *Index on Censorship*, vol. 3, no. 4 (Winter 1974), p. 27-41.
A useful study of the impact of the Colonels' regime on the Greek press, elements of which in normal times enjoy a freedom bordering on licence.

753 **Summary of world broadcasts.**
Reading, England: B.B.C. Monitoring Service, 1948-. daily.
Provides a convenient means of keeping abreast of major policy statements and commentaries broadcast on the state radio, and also of commentaries on events of Greek concern broadcast by other radio stations.

Newspapers

754 Eleftheros Kosmos. (Free World.)
Athens.
A newspaper of the far right. Circulation approximately 10,000. Circulation figures are approximate for this and following newspapers cited, which relate to the Athens-Piraeus area only.

755 Estia. (Hearth.)
Athens.
An old-established newspaper of the far right. Circulation approximately 8,000.

756 Akropolis.
Athens.
Right-wing popular daily. Circulation approximately 32,000.

757 Apoyevmatini. (Afternoon.)
Athens.
The afternoon sister paper to *Akropolis*. Circulation approximately 96,000.

758 Kathimerini. (Daily.)
Athens.
An old-established conservative daily, owned by the redoubtable Helen Vlachos, who closed her newspapers down rather than submit to censorship during the Colonels' regime. With a circulation of approximately 17,000, *Kathimerini* is perhaps Greece's nearest equivalent to a newspaper of record.

759 Mesimvrini. (Midday.)
Athens.
The afternoon counterpart to *Kathimerini*, but of a more popular nature. Circulation approximately 38,000.

760 To Vima. (Tribune.)
Athens.
An old-established newspaper which has traditionally supported the Venizelist centre. Published by the Lambrakis group, it has a circulation of approximately 32,000.

761 Ta Nea. (The News.)
Athens.
Like *To Vima* a part of the Lambrakis group, *Ta Nea* is a mass circulation afternoon paper with a more sensationalist approach than its morning counterpart. Circulation approximately 165,000.

Mass Media. Weeklies and monthlies

762 **Proini.** (Morning.)
Athens.
A daily of the radical left, with a circulation of approximately 20,000.

763 **Eleftherotypia.** (Free Press.)
Athens.
An afternoon newspaper of the radical left, the sister paper of *Proini*. Broadly supports Andreas Papandreou's P.A.S.O.K. Circulation approximately 93,000.

764 **Avghi.** (Dawn.)
Athens.
The official daily of the Communist Party of the Interior (K.K.E.es.). Circulation approximately 5,000.

765 **Rizospastis.** (Radical.)
Athens.
The official daily of the Communist Party (K.K.E.). Circulation approximately 18,000.

766 **Ellinikos Vorras.** (Greek North.)
Thessaloniki.
One of the most important provincial newspapers. Right-wing in outlook.

767 **Makedonia.**
Thessaloniki.
The other main newspaper of Greece's second city, Thessaloniki.

Weeklies and monthlies

768 **Nea Poreia.** (New Course.)
Athens. weekly.
A weekly that reflects the views of the Nea Dimokratia (New Democracy) Party. Circulation approximately 40,000.

769 **Exormisi.** (Sortie.)
Athens. weekly.
The official party weekly of P.A.S.O.K. Circulation approximately 30,000.

Mass Media. Weeklies and monthlies

770 **Politika Themata.** (Political Themes.)
Athens, 1973/74-. weekly.
A moderately conservative weekly, which ran into trouble when it commenced publication in 1973 during the last months of the Colonels' regime. Circulation approximately 8,500.

771 **Epikentra.** (Focal Points.)
Athens, 1978-. bi-monthly.
A moderately conservative bi-monthly, reflecting the views of the more liberal wing of Mr. Karamanlis' Nea Dimokratia. Circulation approximately 10,000.

772 **Anti.**
Athens, 1972/74-. fortnightly.
A radical fortnightly that commenced publication under the Colonels, only to have its first issue confiscated. It recommenced publication in September 1974 and now has a circulation of approximately 15,000.

773 **O Politis.** (The Citizen.)
Athens, 1976-. monthly.
A well-produced political and cultural monthly, broadly reflecting the viewpoint of the Communist Party of the Interior (K.K.E.es.). Circulation approximately 4,300.

774 **Oikonomikos Tachydromos.** (Economic Courier.)
Athens, 1926-. weekly.
Greece's leading financial and economic weekly, published by the Lambrakis group, circulation approximately 12,000.

775 **Tachydromos.** (Courier.)
Athens, 1930-. weekly.
Established in 1930 and published by the Lambrakis group, this weekly general interest magazine has a weekly circulation of approximately 65,000.

776 **Epikaira.** (Current Events.)
Athens, 1969-. weekly.
A general interest weekly, with a circulation of approximately 45,000.

777 **Nea Estia.** (New Hearth.)
Athens, 1927-. fortnightly.
An old-established literary fortnightly, with a circulation of approximately 4,000.

778 **Zygos.** (Balance.)
Athens, 1973-. bi-monthly.
A bi-monthly art magazine, with a circulation of approximately 5,500.

Mass Media. Weeklies and monthlies

779 **Athenian.**
Athens.
An intelligent and well-produced English language monthly which provides a comprehensive guide to current attractions, restaurants, etc. in Athens, accompanied by articles on various aspects of Greek life. As useful for the tourist as for the permanent resident.

780 **Greece: Background-News-Information.**
London: Press and Information Office, Greek Embassy, 1974-. fortnightly.
Provides a useful current chronicle of events in Greece.

Professional Periodicals

781 The Annual Register of World Events.
London: Longman, 1758-. annual.
The *Annual Register*, which was first published in 1758 by Edmund Burke and has now reached vol. 220, offers a convenient brief summary of the previous year's events in Greece.

782 Modern Greek Society: a Social Science Newsletter.
Edited by Nikiforos P. Diamandouros, George Mavrogordatos. Providence, Rhode Island: P.O. Box 9411, Providence, Rhode Island 02940, U.S.A., 1973-. bi-annual.
An excellent publication which, with its social science bias, admirably complements *Mandatophoros* (see following item). Contains bibliographies, lists of theses completed or in progress, details of current research, information on research resources, lists of recent publications, reports and information about recent and impending conferences bearing on modern Greek studies (particularly in North America). Read in conjunction with *Mandatophoros*, it provides comprehensive coverage of the whole range of modern Greek studies in the western world.

783 Mandatophoros: Bulletin of Modern Greek Studies.
Amsterdam: Bizantijns-Nieuwgrieks Seminarium, University of Amsterdam, 1972-. bi-annual.
A most useful publication produced initially under the auspices of the School of Hellenic and Roman Studies of the University of Birmingham, England, and now of the Bizantijns-Nieuwgrieks Seminarium of the University of Amsterdam. Contains periodic bibliographies, summaries of theses and lists of recent publications in the fields of language, literature, history, geography, music etc., but generally eschews the social sciences, which are, however, well covered by *Modern Greek Society* (see preceding item). Provides a convenient means of keeping abreast of the surprisingly wide and growing range of modern Greek studies in Europe.

Professional Periodicals

784 Balkan Studies.
Thessaloniki, Greece: Institute of Balkan Studies, 1960-. bi-annual.

A scholarly journal devoted to all aspects of Balkan history and society, the bulk of whose articles are devoted to Greece and are written in English.

785 Epitheorisis Koinonikon Erevnon: the Greek Review of Social Research.
Athens: Social Science Centre, 1969-. tri-annual.

Contains many useful articles, frequently in English, on different aspects of Greek society.

786 Byzantine and Modern Greek Studies.
Oxford, England: 1975-. annual.

A scholarly journal published in cooperation with the Modern Greek Studies Association of the United States and Canada. Covers all aspects of Byzantine and modern Greek studies but does not include book reviews.

787 Journal of the Hellenic Diaspora.
New York, 1974-. quarterly.

A radical journal devoted to the study of Greek history and society.

788 Scandinavian Studies in Modern Greek.
Gothenburg, Sweden: University of Gothenburg, Department of Modern Greek, Södra Vägen 61, S-412 54 Gothenburg, Sweden; Copenhagen: University of Copenhagen, Department of Modern Greek, Njalsgade 94, 2300 Kobenhavn S, Denmark, 1977-. annual.

Contains articles, mainly in English, on various aspects of modern Greek language, literature and history.

Encyclopaedias

789 **Megali elliniki enkyklopaideia.** (Great Greek Encyclopaedia.)
Pavlos Drandrakis. Athens: O Phoinix, 1956-65. 2nd ed. 28 vols.

790 **Eleftheroudaki synchronos enkyklopaideia, meta plirous lexikou tis ellinikis glossis.** (Eleftheroudakis' contemporary encyclopaedia, with a complete dictionary of the Greek language.)
Athens: Nikas, 1965-67. 3rd ed. 12 vols.

791 **Thriskeftiki kai ithiki enkyklopaideia.** (Religious and moral encyclopaedia.)
Athens: Martinos, 1962-68. 12 vols.

Bibliographies

General

792 **Vivliographia ton ellinikon vivliographion 1791-1947.**
(Bibliography of Greek bibliographies 1791-1947.)
G. I. Phousouras. Athens: Vivliopoleion tis 'Estias' (Estia Bookshop), 1961. 284p.

A useful compilation which includes booksellers' catalogues, although, as the author points out, the bibliographer in Greece who aims at comprehensiveness faces many problems.

793 **Elliniki vivliographia 1972.** (Greek bibliography 1972.)
Athens: Vivliographiki Etaireia tis Ellados (Bibliographical Society of Greece), 1975. 686p.

Intended as the first volume of the national bibliography of Greece, the first such undertaking to enjoy official sponsorship. Compiled at the National Library of Greece, which is theoretically the repository of all printed material in Greece, although at present only some sixty per cent of the country's printed output is deposited. It is to be hoped that this most valuable undertaking will not meet with the delays that have befallen its pioneering and equally valuable predecessor, the *Bulletin analytique de bibliographie hellénique* (see following item). Volumes for 1973 and 1977 were published in 1976 and 1977 respectively.

794 **Bulletin analytique de bibliographie hellénique.** (Analytical bulletin of Greek bibliography.)
Athens: Institut Français d'Athènes, 1947-. irregular.

Extremely useful coverage of the whole range of publishing activity (including some 500 periodicals) in Greece. Its usefulness, however, is lessened by the substantial delays that attend its publication.

Bibliographies. General

795 Greece: a selected list of references.
Anne Duncan Brown, Helen Dudenbostel Jones. Washington, D.C.: Library of Congress. Division of Bibliography, 1943. 101p.

A checklist, now inevitably outdated, but still of considerable value, of books, pamphlets and periodical articles relating to Greece. Entries are listed under the following headings; bibliographies, general, geography and climate, description and travel, history, politics and government, economics, people, the First World War, the Second World War, Athens, Macedonia, and islands of Greece.

796 Valkaniki vivliographia. (Balkan bibliography.)
Edited by K. A. Dimadis. Thessaloniki, Greece: Institute of Balkan Studies, 1973-. occasional.

Contains material in all the Balkan languages, and English, on Greece.

797 Bibliographie d'Etudes Balkaniques. (Bibliography of Balkan Studies.)
Sofia, Bulgaria, 1968-. annual.

Covers all the Balkan countries and includes a section on Greece.

798 Modern Greek culture: a selected bibliography (in English, French, German, Italian).
Edited by C. Th. Dimaras, C. Koumarianou, L. Droulia. Athens: National Hellenic Committee of the International Association for South Eastern European Studies, 1974. 4th rev. ed. 119p.

A comprehensive listing of works on the geography, history, language and literature of Greece in the major Western languages.

799 Southeastern Europe: a guide to basic publications.
Edited by Paul L. Horecky. Chicago, London: Chicago University Press, 1969. 755p.

Includes an annotated listing of some 600 titles, in Greek and other languages, relating to Greece, covering topics such as reference aids and bibliographies; general and descriptive works; the land; the people; history; the state; diplomacy and foreign relations; the economy; society; intellectual and cultural life; religion; and education.

800 Diavazo. (I Read.)
Athens, 1976-. bi-monthly.

A useful way of keeping abreast of the remarkably lively, if somewhat haphazard publishing scene in Greece.

Historical writings and travels

801 Greek historical periodicals related to modern Greek history.
Katerina Gardikas. *Modern Greek Society*, vol. 5, no. 2 (May 1978), p. 22-29.

A useful checklist of the numerous periodicals published in Greece concerned with modern Greek history, both national and regional. Some, such as *Balkan Studies*, regularly contain articles in English.

802 Quinze ans de bibliographie historique en Grèce (1950-1964), avec une annexe pour 1965. (Fifteen years of historical writing in Greece 1950-1964, with a supplement for 1965.)
Athens: Centre de Recherche Néo-Hellénique de la Fondation Royale de la Recherche Scientifique, 1966. 293p.

A comprehensive listing of the output of Greek historians between 1950 and 1965.

803 Cinq ans de bibliographie historique en Grèce (1965-1969), avec un supplément pour les années 1950-1964. (Five years of historical bibliography in Greece, 1965-69: with a supplement for 1950-64.)
Athens: Comité National Hellénique de l'Association Internationale des Études du Sud-est Européen, 1970. 134p.

A useful guide to Greek historical writing during the 1960s.

804 Quatre ans de bibliographie historique en Grèce (1970-1973), avec un supplément pour les années 1965-1969. (Four years of historical writing in Greece 1970-1973, with a supplement for the years 1965-1969.)
Athens: Comité National Hellénique de l'Association Internationale d'Études du Sud-Est Européen, 1974. 151p.

A comprehensive listing of the output of Greek historians between 1965 and 1973, which complements the preceding item.

805 Literaturbericht über die Geschichte Neu-Griechenlands, 1453-1945. Veröffentlichungen 1945-1970. (A review of the literature on the history of modern Greece, 1453-1945, published between 1945 and 1970.)
Edgar Hösch. *Historische Zeitschrift*, Sonderheft 5 (1973), p. 421-535.

A comprehensive, annotated bibliography of post-war writings, principally in Greek, on modern Greek history.

Bibliographies. Historical writings and travels

806 **Voyages and travels in Greece, the Near East and adjacent regions made previous to the year 1801, being part of a larger catalogue of works on geography, cartography, voyages and travels, in the Gennadius Library in Athens.**
Shirley Howard Weber. Princeton, New Jersey: American School of Classical Studies, 1953. 208p. (Catalogues of the Gennadius Library, no. 2).

A listing of the very comprehensive collection of early travel accounts of Greece housed in the Gennadius Library of the American School of Classical Studies in Athens. Its usefulness is enhanced by a topographical index.

807 **Voyages and travels in the Near East made during the XIX century. Being a part of a larger catalogue of works on geography, cartography, voyages and travels, in the Gennadius Library in Athens.**
Shirley Howard Weber. Princeton, New Jersey: American School of Classical Studies at Athens, 1952. 252p. (Catalogues of the Gennadius Library, no. 1).

A catalogue of the very rich holdings of 19th century travel accounts of the Near East in the Gennadius Library. A particularly useful feature of the volume is the topographical index.

808 **Les voyageurs français en Grèce au XIXe siècle (1800-1900).** (French travellers in Greece in the 19th century 1800-1900.)
Eugène Lovinesco. Paris: Honoré Champion, 1909.

A study of 19th century French travellers in Greece.

809 **Le voyage de Grèce: bibliographie des voyageurs français en Grèce au XXe siècle, 1900-1968.** (Travel in Greece: a bibliography of French travellers in Greece in the 20th century.)
Maurice Lebel. Sherbrooke, Quebec: Éditions Paulines, 1969. 61p.

A comprehensive listing of 20th century travel accounts of Greece written in French, which complements Eugène Lovinesco's checklist for the 19th century (see item above).

Bibliographies. Library catalogues

Library catalogues

810 **Vivliothikes kai arkheia stin Ellada: symvoli sti meleti tis pnevmatikis istorias tou neou Ellinismou.** (Libraries and archives in Greece: a contribution to the study of the intellectual history of modern Hellenism.)
Spyros Kokkinis. Athens: Petros Tzounakos, 1970. 2nd ed. 332p. bibliog.
A detailed guide to the libraries and archives of Greece.

811 **East central and southeast Europe: a handbook of library and archival resources in North America.**
Edited by Paul L. Horecky, David H. Kraus. Santa Barbara, California; Oxford, England: Clio Press, 1976. 468p.
A guide to the holdings of university and other libraries in the United States in the field of east central and southeast European studies. Particularly impressive are the collections of the University of Cincinnatti (approximately 20,000 items) and of the Widener Library at Harvard University (approximately 30,000 items) (see items below).

812 **Catalog of the modern Greek collection at the University of Cincinnati.**
Boston, Massachusetts: G. K. Hall, 1978. 5 vols.
Contains some 70,000 entries from the catalogue of one of the most extensive collections on modern Greece in the United States. Supersedes *The modern Greek collection in the library of the University of Cincinnati: a catalogue.* Edited by Niove Kyparissiotis (Athens: Estia, 1960. 387p.).

813 **Catalog of the Gennadius Library, American School of Classical Studies, Athens.**
Boston: G. K. Hall, 1968. 7 vols.+supplement, 1973.
The catalogue of the superb library relating to modern Greece run by the American School of Classical Studies in Athens. Its original core was the personal library of Ioannes Gennadius, a great bibliophile who for many years was Greek minister in London.

814 **The modern Greek collection in the Harvard College library.**
Evro Leyton. *Harvard Library Bulletin*, vol. 19, no. 3 (July 1971), p. 221-43.
An account of the very extensive holdings on modern Greece in the Harvard Library.

Bibliographies. Specialized

815 **The Finlay papers: a catalogue.**
J. M. Hussey. London: British School of Archaeology at Athens with Thames & Hudson, 1973. 200p.

George Finlay first went to Greece in the 1820s and lived in Athens until his death in 1875. An acute if somewhat jaundiced observer of the politics of the emergent Greek state, Finlay left an archive which is an indispensable resource for the historian of 19th century Greece. It is now housed in the library of the British School at Athens.

Specialized

816 **Modern Greek society: continuity and change: an annotated classification of selected sources.**
Evangelos C. Vlachos. Fort Collins, Colorado: Colorado State University, 1969. 177p. (Department of Sociology and Anthropology Special Monography Series, no. 1).

An invaluable and comprehensive annotated listing of works bearing on the study of Greek society. The entries are organized within the following framework: the sociological perspective in the study of modern Greek society; the Greek people; form and extent of groupings in Greece; culture and personality; nature and characteristics of Greek institutions; social change and development; conformity, deviance and social disorganization.

817 **Modern Greek studies in the West: a critical bibliography of studies on modern Greek linguistics, philology and folklore, in languages other than Greek.**
Donald C. Swanson. New York: New York Public Library, 1960. 93p.

A comprehensive, thorough and most useful bibliography.

818 **Language and area studies: east central and southeastern Europe: a survey.**
Edited by Charles Jelavich. Chicago, London: University of Chicago Press, 1969. 483p. bibliog.

A guide to special training available in the United States in the languages and cultures of Eastern Europe, including Greece: recommendations are also made as to how this training might be improved.

819 **On Greece and Cyprus: theses index in Britain (1949-1974).**
Roussos Koundouros. London: Greek Press and Information Office, 1977. 23p.

A useful checklist of theses completed at British universities in the post-war period and relating to Greece and Cyprus.

181

Bibliographies. Specialized

820 **La Grèce moderne et sa littérature: orientation bibliographique en allemand, anglais, français, italien.**
(Modern Greece and her literature: a bibliographic guide in German, English, French and Italian.)
C. Th. Dimaras, C. Coumariano, L. Droulia. Athens, 1966. 81p.

A most useful bibliography extracted from the French translation of C. Th. Dimaras' classic *History of modern Greek literature.*

821 **Philhellénisme: ouvrages inspirés par la guerre de l'indépendence grecque 1821-1833.** (Philhellenism: works inspired by the Greek War of Independence 1821-1833.) Loukia Droulia. Athens: Centre de Recherches Néo-Helléniques de la Fondation Nationale de la Recherche Scientifique, 1974. 314p.

A listing of some 2,000 contemporary works in various languages inspired by the struggle for Greek independence during the 1820s. This vast outpouring is an accurate reflection of how much the cause of the embattled Greeks attracted the sympathy of liberal opinion in Europe.

822 **Bibliography of Chios: from classical times to 1936.**
Philip P. Argenti. Oxford, England: Clarendon Press, 1940. 836p.

A comprehensive listing of works on all aspects of the island of Chios, by a native son and one of its most assiduous historians. Includes sections on geography, topography, archaeology, political and social history.

823 **Bibliographical article: present day Greece.**
L. S. Stavrianos, E. P. Panagopoulos. *Journal of Modern History*, vol. 20, no. 2 (June 1948), p. 149-58.

A useful survey of writings, mainly in Greek, on Greece during the Second World War and the immediate post-war period.

824 **Greece under Axis occupation, 1941-44: a bibliographical survey.**
Hagen Fleischer. *Modern Greek Society*, vol. 5, no. 1 (1977), p. 4-47; vol. 6, no. 1 (1978), p. 13-40.

An exhaustive and usefully annotated bibliography of contemporary publications relating to the Axis occupation and subsequent studies of the wartime resistance in all relevant languages. An indispensable aid to the study of Greece during the Second World War, a period which left a deep impression on the subsequent political development of the country.

Bibliographies. Specialized

825 A bibliographic guide to materials on Greeks in the United States, 1890-1968.
Michael N. Cutsumbis. New York: Center for Migration Studies, 1970. 100p.

A useful listing of materials relating to the history of the Greek community in the United States, the largest and most prosperous of the communities of the Greek diaspora. Available from 209 Flagg Place, Staten Island, New York 10304.

826 An annotated bibliography on Greek migration.
Evangelos C. Vlachos. Athens: Social Sciences Centre, 1966. 126p. (Research Monographs on Migration, no. 1).

A useful annotated guide to the literature on Greek emigration, a topic of vital concern to a country that has traditionally seen a significant part of its productive population take the path of *xeniteia*, or migration to foreign parts. Until 1924 the United States was the favoured destination of Greek migrants. In the post-war period Greek permanent migration, as opposed to the migration of Greek *Gastarbeitern* to seek temporary employment in the industrialized countries of western Europe and particularly West Germany, has tended to be concentrated on Canada and Australia. Significant Greek communities are also to be found in South Africa, some of the countries of South America and New Zealand.

827 Bibliography of anthropological sources on modern Greece and Cyprus.
Peter S. Allen, Perry A. Bialor. *Modern Greek Society: a newsletter*, vol. 4, no. 1 (Dec. 1976), p. 6-60.

A comprehensive listing of the surprisingly large corpus of anthropological writings on modern Greece and Cyprus published in recent years.

828 Visual anthropology in Greece: an annotated filmography.
Peter S. Allen. *Modern Greek Society*, vol. 5, no. 2 (May 1978), p. 15-21.

A useful list, with details of how films may be rented or purchased, of the surprisingly large number of films of anthropological interest relating to Greece that have been made in recent years.

829 Symvoli gia mia diskographia tis neoellinikis poiisis kai pezographias. (A contribution to a discography of modern Greek poetry and prose.)
Christos Alexiou. *Mandatophoros*, no. 6 (May 1975), p. 31-36.

A useful listing of recordings of Greek poetry and prose, including recordings of such poets as Seferis, Varnalis, Ritsos and Elytis reading their own poetry. Part 2 of this discography (*Mandatophoros*, no. 9 (Nov. 1976), p. 35-46) includes settings of Greek poetry to music.

Bibliographies. Specialized

830 **Greek architecture and the decorative arts from the 15th to the 20th centuries: a select bibliography.**
Jennifer Scarce. *Mandatophoros*, no. 13 (June 1979), p. 48-60; no. 14 (Nov. 1979), p. 5-15.

Index

The index is a single alphabetical sequence of authors (personal and corporate), titles of publications and subjects. Index entries refer both to the main items and to other works mentioned in the notes to each item. Title entries are in italics. Numeration refers to the items as numbered.

A

Abbot, G. A. 266
Abbott, G. F. 661
Adamantios Korais: a study in Greek nationalism 137
Adams, Walter 243
Adelman, Irma 503
Administration, Public 4, 478–479
Administrative districts 40
Adult education
  techniques 600
Aegean: a sea guide to its coasts and islands 88
Aegean dispute 495
Aegean Greece 63
Aegean islands 6, 87
  20th century 63
  folklore 34
  guide books 86, 88–89
  life and customs 34, 36
  travellers' accounts 63
  Venetian rule, 15th century 130
Aegean memories 169
Aegean quest: a search for Venetian Greece 130
Aeolia 743
Aerial photographs
  archaeological sites 97

Affair of the heart 53
After the Odyssey: a study of Greek Australians 284
Agapitidis, S. 241
Agiopetritis, A. 577
Agricultural development 24, 364, 549
  20th century 551, 556–557
  cooperative movement 552, 558
  Crete 557
  E.E.C. membership implications 523, 548
  Macedonia 21
  mountain regions 564
  problems of farm fragmentation 553
  timber industry 564
Agricultural policy of Greece 548
Agriculture 40, 515
  20th century 554
  education 562
  history 559
  labour shortages 554
  Peloponnese 26
  policy 548–549
  statistics 563
  Thessaly 24

185

AHEPA - American Hellenic Educational Progressive Association 281
Alastos, D. 163
Albania
  Greek occupation, 1940-41 184
Albright, David E. 433
Alchoholism
  rural areas 414
Alexander, A. P. 547
Alexander the Great
  legends 661
Alexandria
  Greek community 292
  in C. P. Cavafy's poems 697
Alexiou, C. 319, 829
Alexiou, Margaret 132, 679
Allbaugh, L. G. 32
Allen, H. B. 21
Allen, P. S. 385, 827—828
Allied politics and military interventions: the political role of the Greek military 424
Allied secret service in Greece 168
Amen, M. M. 485
Amera, A. 376, 410
American aid to Greece: a report on the first ten years 518
American Farm School, Thessaloniki 562
American foreign policy in Greece 1944-1949: economic, military and institutional aspects 485
American School of Classical Studies, Gennadius Library 747
American travellers' accounts
  18th century 147
  19th century 147
Amnesty International
  Greek infringement of human rights, 1967 458—459
Amsterdam University, Bizantijns-Nieuwgrieks Seminarium 783
Anagnostopoulos, A. 733
Analysis and assessment of the economic effects of the U.S. PL 480 program in Greece 519
Analysis of the health and welfare services in Greece 408
Anastaplo, G. 491
Anastenaria 667
Anastenaria: Thracian firewalking festival 667

Anatomy of a church. Greek orthodoxy today 329
Anchored in God: an account of life, art, and thought on the Holy Mountain of Athos 350
Ancient Greece from the air 97
Ancient Greek literature 112
Ancient Greeks 107
Anderson, M. S. 105
Andreades, K. G. 246
Andrews, K. 12—13, 60
Anecdotes 658
Angelopoulos, Theodore 651
Angelos Sikelianos 735
Angus, S. 321
Animal husbandry 40
Animals
  folklore 658
Ankori, Z. 356
Annotated bibliography on Greek migration 826
Annual Register of World Events 781
Anogeianakis, P. 639
Anthony, E. James 402
Anthropology 98, 379, 381—382
  bibliographies 827
  Crete 404
  Cyprus 827
  films 828
Anton, J. P. 143
Antonakaki, K. D. 582
Antonakos, Stephen 621
Antoniades, A. G. 667
Antoniou 686—687
Apodimoi Ellines 257
Apple of discord: a survey of recent Greek politics in their international setting 182
Archaeological sites 40, 53, 72—76, 78
  aerial photographs 97
  Athens 77
  Bronze Age 96
  Crete 68
  Mycenaean 95
Archaic society 106—107
Archer, Margaret Scotford 360
Architecture 100, 624, 627
  19th century 625
  20th century 614, 626
  ancient 99
  bibliographies 830
  Byzantine 623
  Chios 628
  early Christian 623
  Mykonos 579

neoclassical 625
Patmos 579
Architecture of Chios: subsidiary buildings, implements and crafts 628
Archives
  directories 810
  Finlay papers 815
Archives depositories, American
  directories 811
Argenti, Eustratios 335
Argenti, P. P. 216, 245, 628, 662, 671, 822
Argo 678, 740, 741
Argyriades, D. 479
Argyriadis, A. 476
Aristotle Onassis 570
Armed forces 124, 359
  military attitudes in 20th century 424
  political attitudes in 20th century 422−423, 425−429, 444
  security 496
Arnott, M. L. 406
Aroumanians 249−250
Arpajolu, A. 320
Art
  19th century 612−613
  20th century 614−615, 617−618, 621
  ancient 100
  Byzantine 606, 630
  Christian 354
  folk 608
  folk, Macedonia 607
  post-war 616
Art, Classical 107, 109
  impact of World War II 609
Art, Decorative
  bibliographies 830
Art of the Byzantine era 606
Art periodicals
  circulation and policy 778
Arte dopo il 1945: Grecia 616
Artists
  20th century 616
Arvanito-Vlachs 249
Aschenbrenner, S. 392
Asia Minor
  Greek offensive, 1921 170
  population exchanges 174
Asia Minor disaster, 1922
  impact on the Greek novel 678

Asia Minor Greeks 175−176, 743−744
  20th century 58
  language 308
Assimilation of Greeks in the United States, with special reference to the Greek community of Anderson, Indiana 273
Astyphilia 227−232
Athenagoras I 264
Athenian 446
Athens 14
Athens 6, 12−14
  American School of Classical Studies 747
  archaeological sites 77
  bibliographies 795
  Gennadius Library 747
    catalogues 806−807, 813
  guide books 56, 77−78
  history 221
  industrial workers 365
  industry 543
  maps and atlases 77
  Museum of Greek Folk Art 608
  Social Science Centre 785
  urbanization 228−230
Athens alive, or the practical tourist's companion to the fall of man 13
Athens, Greater
  migrant population 234
  refugee population 234
Athens Polytechnic
  student occupation, 1973 601
Athos and its monasteries 347
Athos, the Holy Mountain 349
Athos, Mount 52, 346, 348−350, 352
  bibliographies 354
  history 347, 354
  population 353
  travellers' accounts 351
Athos: the mountain of silence 352
Attalides, M. A. 360, 502
Attica 6
Attitudes, sociometric status and ability in Greek schools 588
Auden, W. H. 692
Augustinos, G. 160
Australia
  bibliographies 826
  Greek community 283−286
  Greek immigrants 826

187

Auty, P. 190
Averoff, George 674
Axion esti: an International Poetry Forum selection 700

B

Baddeley, J. 288
Baelen, J. 218
Baggally, J. W. 136
Bakalopoulos, A. E. 217
Baker Street Irregular 196
Balance of payments 535
 importance of emigrants' remittances 533
Balkan exchange of minorities and its impact upon Greece 174
Balkan federation: a history of the movement toward Balkan unity in modern times 481
Balkan federation movements
 history 481
Balkan languages
 general use of Greek alphabet 309
Balkan triangle: birth and decline of an alliance across ideological boundaries 489
Balkan Wars, 1912-13 122
Balkans
 history 103−104
 politics 498
 regional economic cooperation 516
Balkans and Hellenism 17
Ballads, Klephtic 136
Bandits
 ballads 136
Bank of Greece
 Monthly Statistical Bulletin 576
Bankruptcy, State, 1893 482
Baras 687
Barbarism in Greece: a young American lawyer's inquiry into the use of torture in contemporary Greece, with case histories and documents 458
Barker, E. 189, 498
Barnstone, W. 688
Barros, J. 483−484
Basdekis, A. 344
Battle of Navarino 148
Baxevanis, J. J. 228, 232
Beaton, R. 681
Beaubier, J. 411

Becket, J. 456, 458
Behavioural patterns 401
Belgium
 short-term migrant workers from Greece 239
 short-term migrant workers returning to Greece 239
Beliefs and superstitions 376
Bent, J. T. 34
Bergwelt Griechenlands: ein Führer für Wanderer und Bergsteiger 92
Bernard, H. Russell 35−36, 270, 401
Bialor, P. A. 134, 399, 827
Bibliographic guide to materials on Greeks in the United States, 1890-1968 825
Bibliographical Society of Greece 793
Bibliographie d'Etudes Balkaniques 797
Bibliographies 783, 795−797, 799−800
 20th century 823
 anthropology 827
 architecture 830
 Athens 795
 bibliographies 792, 795, 799
 booksellers' catalogues 792
 Chios 822
 climate 795
 culture 798−799, 816, 820
 Cyprus 827
 decorative art 830
 diplomacy 799
 economics 795, 799
 education 799
 emigrants to Australia 826
 emigrants to Canada 826
 emigrants to Federal Republic of Germany 826
 emigrants to Latin America 826
 emigrants to South Africa 826
 emigrants to the U.S.A. 826
 emigrants to western Europe 826
 emigration 826
 folklore 817
 foreign relations 799
 French travellers' accounts 808−809
 geography 795, 798
 German occupation, 1941-44 824
 government 795
 Greek community in the U.S.A. 825
 Greek islands 795
 Greek language 798
 historical periodicals 801

history 795, 798−799, 802−804, 823
Italian loan words in modern
    Greek 302
linguistics 817
literature 798, 820−821
Macedonia 795
maps and atlases 43
modern history 805
Mount Athos 354
Nikos Kazantzakis 714
Ottoman rule 103
periodicals 794
Philhellenism 821
philology 817
politics 795
reference works 799
religion 799
rural settlement 20
social change 816
social science 782, 816
society 799, 816
state 799
topography 795, 799
travel 795
travellers' accounts 806−807
voyages 806−807
War of Independence, 1821-27 143, 821
World War I 795
World War II 795, 823−824
Yannis Ritsos 729
Bibliography, National 793−794
Bibliography of Chios: from classical times to 1936 822
Bickford-Smith, R. A. H. 159
Bien, C. 319
Bien, P. A. 319, 698, 705, 708, 711−712, 714−715, 725
Bikelas, D. 690
Bintliff, J. L. 18
Biography
    Greek Canadians 289
Birmingham University, School of Hellenic and Roman Studies 783
Birth rate 223, 225−226
Births 40
    folklore 661
Bizantijns-Nieuwgrieks Seminarium, University of Amsterdam 783
Blight of Asia 172
Blough, R. 511
Blue Guides: Crete 80
Blue Guides: Greece 72
Blum, E. M. 376, 410, 414

Blum, R. H. 376, 410, 414
Boardman, J. 111
Boeotia
    economic factors affecting population movements 230
    life and customs 383
    migration to the cities 230
Boissonas, F. 610
Bolitho, G. 151
Book trades 745
Books 800
    production 745
Booksellers' catalogues
    bibliographies 792
Botsas, E. N. 237, 533
Bottomley, G. 284
Boucas, Philip 154
Boumi-Pappas 687
Bouzouki 639
Bower, L. 151
Bowman, J. 81
Bowra, M. 110, 112
Bradford, E. 85
Brailsford, H. N. 215
'Brain drain'
    emigration 243−244
Break, G. F. 537
Brief dialogue 688
Brigandage 145
    19th century 155
Britain's Greek empire: reflections on the history of the Ionian Islands from the fall of Byzantium 154
British and American philhellenes 146
British Institute in Athens 56
British military mission to the Greek resistance 192−193
British policy in south-east Europe in the Second World War 189
British policy towards wartime resistance in Yugoslavia and Greece 190
British School at Athens 53−54, 68
British School of Archaeology at Athens, Library
    Finlay papers 815
Broadcasts
    daily summaries, 1948 to date 753
Bronze Age civilization 96
    Messenia 98
Brooke, E. M. 740
Brown, A. D. 795
Brown, J. 426
Browning, R. 297

189

Buchproduktion und Buchdistribution in Griechenland: probleme und Eigentümlichkeiten des griechischen Buch-und Verlagswesen 745
Buck, K. H. 528
Buckley, C. 186
Building industry 512
Bulgaria
 claims to Macedonia 213, 498−499
 strife over Macedonia 215
Bulgarian-Greek frontier incident, 1925 484
Bulletin analytique de bibliographie hellénique 793, 794
Bureaucracy 478−479
Burgel, G. 33, 365
Burks, R. V. 431−432
Burn, A. R. 75, 109
Burn, M. 75
Burnley, I. H. 287
Burns, R. 731
Bury, J. B. 108, 116
Business
 conditions 5
 political attitudes in 20th century 444
Butterworth, K. 643
Byford-Jones, W. 201
Byron, George Gordon, 6th baron 146
Byzantine civilization 117
 history 114−116
Byzantine culture
 research 786
Byzantine tradition 117
 architecture 623
 art 606
 embroidery 630
 hymns 638
 music 638
Byzantine tradition in church embroidery 630
Byzantium
 Turkish conquest, 1453 127
Byzantium and Byzantinism 117

C

Cabinet
 20th century 437
 history 437

Cacoyannis, Michael 651, 706
Cairo
 Greek community 292
Calas 687
Callaghan, James
 Cyprus crisis, 1974 492
Callas, Maria 570
Cambridge mediaeval history, vol. 4. The Byzantine Empire. Pt. 1: Byzantium and its neighbours. Pt. 2: Government, church and civilization 115
Campbell, J. K. 375, 390−391, 395
Campbell, John 1, 207
Camping
 guide books 91
Canada
 bibliographies 826
 Greek community 289−291
 Greek immigrants 826
Candilis, W. O. 504
Caniaris, Vlassis 621
Capital investment
 in industry 529−530, 544
 in real estate 529−530
Capital market
 development 531−532
 retarded by emigration 533
Capital market in Greece 531
Capitalism 359
Capo d'Istria, Giovanni Antonio 150
Capodistria: the founder of Greek independence 150
Cappadocia
 dialect 308
Carey, A. G. 416
Carey, J. P. C. 416
Carmocolias, D. G. 439
Carney, T. F. 219
Carpetmaking 629
Carter, F. W. 18
Case study in guerilla war 191
Castles 66
Castro, F. P. 253
Catalog of the Gennadius Library, American School of Classical Studies, Athens 813
Catalog of the modern Greek collection at the University of Cincinnati 812
Catalogue of a collection of old embroideries of the Greek islands and Turkey 631
Cavafy: a critical biography 696

Cavafy, Constantine P. 680, 685−687, 691−697, 719
Cavafy's Alexandria: study of a myth in progress 697
Cavarnos, C. 350
Censorship 772
  Colonels' regime, 1967-74 752, 758
Census, 1961 39−40
Census, 1963 41
Centralization 39
Centre Union party 438, 440, 460
Cervi, M. 184
Chaconas, S. G. 137
Chandler, G. 203
Changing economy of northern Greece since World War II 515
Chapters on mediaeval and renaissance visitors to Greek lands 45
Charles II, King of England 296
Chester, L. 570
Child rearing 402
Chios 690
  architecture 628
  bibliographies 822
  emigrants to Great Britain 296
  folklore 662
  German occupation, 1941-44 216
  Jewish community 245
  life and customs 662
  regional costumes 671
  Roman Catholic community 245
Christ recrucified 702
Christian art 354
Christie, A. 91
Chronologies 781
  modern literature 675
Chryssa 621
Church, Byzantine 114−116
Churchill, Sir Winston 186, 189
Cicellis, Kay 688, 742
Cincinnati University Library
  modern Greek collection 811−812
Cinema 651
Cinq ans de bibliographie historique en Grèce, avec un supplément pour les années 1950-1964 803
Cities 17
Cities of the world: Athens 12
City-state civilization 107, 110
Civil code, 1946
  history 474

Civil-military relations 161
Civil service 478−479
Civil War, 1946-49 181, 183, 188, 200
  background 202−203
  effects on population 60
  history 204
  impact on the Orthodox Church 338
  personal accounts 205
  United Nations policy 207
  U.S. involvement 487−488
Civilization
  influence overseas 111
Class structure 359
  history 360
Classical art
  impact of World War II 609
Classical landscape with figures 8
Classification of educational systems in OECD member countries: Canada, Greece, Yugoslavia 584
Cleveland, W. C. 534
Climate
  bibliographies 795
Climbing
  guide books 92
Clogg, R. 120, 138−139, 190, 445−446
Coffee houses
  London 296
  Stavropolis 397
Coins 100
  modern 636−637
Colaclides, H. 658
Coleman, H. D. 457
Colettis, O. M. 92
Collected poems 693
Collected poems 1924-1955 732
Collection of the modern coins of Greece: coins of Crete; coins of the Ionian Islands; historical medals 637
Colloquial Greek 326
Colonels' regime, 1967-74 121, 123, 426−428, 445−446, 448, 450−459
  and Litton Industries 520
  background 447, 449, 460−461
  downfall 470
  E.E.C. membership 526
  foreign investment 520
  impact on the press 752
  opponents 462−465, 538
  relations with Onassis 570
  setbacks in educational system 587
  U.S. support 491−494

191

Colossus of Maroussi 57
Come over into Macedonia: the story of a ten-year adventure in uplifting a war-torn people 21
Commerce 515
　management 546
Committee for Economic Development 511
Common market and economic development: the E.E.C. and Greece 524
Communications 3, 40, 70, 176, 515
　internal 571
Communism 431, 433−435, 462, 486
　Balkan movements 498−499
　Macedonia 431
　military opposition 428
　statistics 432
Communist movements
　20th century 181−182, 188, 191, 200, 203−205
　'second round', 1944-45 200−201
Communist Party, Greek - K.K.E. 188, 431, 433−436, 764−765, 773
　history 430
Companion guide to the Greek islands 85
Companion guide to southern Greece: Athens, the Peloponnese, Delphi 78
Complete poems of Cavafy 692
Condit, D. M. 191
La condition industrielle à Athènes Études sociogéographique 365
Condominas, Georges 382
Conflict, Social 399
Consciousness and history: nationalist critics of Greek society 1897-1914 160
Constantelos, D. J. 355
Constantine and Helen, Saints
　firewalking festival 667
Constantine Cavafy 698
Constantine, King of the Hellenes 167
Constantinople
　first Greek printing press 748−749
　Turkish conquest, 1453 127
Constitution of the republic of Greece 468
Constitutional history 471
Constitutions 4, 472
　1968 454
　1973 469

1975 344, 468
20th century 442
　impact on the Orthodox Church 344
Contemporary Greek cinema 651
Contemporary Greek literature 689
Continental shelf
　dispute with Turkey 495, 497
Contossopoulos, N. G. 304
Contributions to Mediterranean sociology: Mediterranean rural communities and social change 382
Cookery 672−673
Cooperatives, Agricultural 552, 558
Copenhagen University, Department of Modern Greek 788
Corcyra
　guide books 82−84
　incident, 1923 483
Corfu 84
Corfu (see also Ionian islands)
　guide books 82−84
　incident, 1923 483
　life and customs 62
Corfu incident of 1923: Mussolini and the League of Nations 483
Costumes of Chios: their development from the XVth to the XXth century 671
Costumes, Regional 670
　Chios 671
　men 669
　women 668
Coubertin, Pierre de, Baron 674
Coufoudakis, V. 490
Coukis, B. P. 40, 571
Couloumbis, T. A. 420−421, 480, 493−494
Coumariano, C. 820
Council of Europe 455−456
　defense of human rights 457
Council of Europe. European Commission of Human Rights. The Greek Case. Report of the Commission 455
Coups d'état 453
　army officers, 1967 426
　counter-coup, 1973 469
　Military League, 1909 422
Coutsoumaris, G. 243, 519, 543
Cowan, G. 115
Crafts 515

Crawley, C. W. 15, 141
Crawshaw, N. 501
Credit controls
  20th century 536
Cretan glance 708
Cretan glance: the world and art of Nikos Kazantzakis 713
Cretan runner: his story of the German occupation 195
Crete 6
  20th century 67, 69, 557
  agricultural development 557
  anthropology of the inhabitants 404
  archaeological sites 68
  culture 66
  enosis movement 122
  German invasion, 1941 187
  guide books 80−81
  history 66
  kidnapping of General Kreipe, 1944 194
  life and customs 69
  living conditions 32
  maps and atlases 80
  Mesara plain 33
  modern coins 636−637
  novels 704, 723−724
  Pobia 33
  travellers' accounts 67, 69
  World War II 186, 195
Crete: a case study of an underdeveloped area 32
Crighton, W. 310
Crime
  misuse of honour concept 386
Crosfield, D. 649
Cruickshank, C. 185
Cultivation techniques
  history 559
Culture 1, 3−4, 10, 13, 65, 177, 206, 381, 394
  19th century 133
  bibliographies 798−799, 816, 820
  Crete 66
  history 132
  history, 1453-1669 128
  influence overseas 111
Cummings, L. L. 546
Current events 779−780
Currie, J. 90
Customs
  Orthodox Church 665
  peasant 666

Customs and lore of modern Greece 666
Cutsumbis, M. N. 825
Cyclades 34
Cyclades or life among the insular Greeks 34
Cypriot Greek: its phonology and inflections 299
Cypriot Greek language
  phonology and inflections 299
Cyprus
  20th century 494, 501−502
  anthropology 379, 827
  bibliographies 827
  crisis, 1974 492
  enosis movement 500−502
  history 500−502
  impact of War of Independence 149
  impact on NATO membership 420
  relations with the U.S.A. 494
  sociology 379
  theses 819
  Turkish claims 489
  Turkish invasion 420
Cyprus and the war of Greek independence 1821-1829 149
Cyprus: nationalism and international politics 502
Cyprus revolt: an account of the struggle for union with Greece 501
Cyril V, Ecumenical Patriarch 336

D

Dakin, D. 122, 140, 146, 213
Dallas, A. G. 703
Dalven, R. 692
Damaskenides, A. N. 550
Dances, Folk 647−649
Dances, Modern 643
Dances of Greece 649
Danforth, L. M. 652
Dangerous hour: the lore of crisis and mystery in rural Greece 376
Darby, H. C. 15
Davenport, W. W. 14
Davies, Dorothy 6
Davis, J. 500

Dawkins, R. M. 308, 348, 633, 656—657, 659
de Jongh, B. 78
Death
  folklore 661
  statistics 40
Death of a democracy: Greece and the American conscience 448
Debts, Foreign
  history 482
Deceit
  connection with honour concept 388
Decentralization 19
Decorative art
  bibliographies 830
Defence 4
Dekaokhto Keimena 688
Delivanis, D. 534
Delphi 6
  guide books 78
Democracy at gunpoint: the Greek front 460
Demography (see Population)
Demotic Greek 319
Denham, H. M. 88—89
d'Espérey, Louis Franchet 165
Detention camps
  Oropos 462
Detroit's Greek community 267
Development of the highland economy and the timber industry in Greece 564
Le développement de la Grèce du nord depuis 1912 514
Le développement industriel de la Grèce 541
Diamandouros, N. P. 143, 782
Diaspora 9
Diavazo 800
Dicks, B. 3
Dictionaries 790
  modern demotic Greek 311
  modern Greek 310, 312—315
Diet 406
Diglis, I. 654
Dikhasmos, 1914-17 164, 168—169
Dilessi murders 155
Dimadis, K. A. 796
Dimaras, A. 589
Dimaras, C. Th. 676, 798, 820
Dimen, M. 379
Dimitras, E. 239
Dimographikai exelixeis en Elladi 1950-1980: demographic trends in Greece 1950-1980 223

Dionisopoulos-Mass, R. 398
Dionysios Solomos 737—738
Diplomacy
  bibliographies 799
Directories
  American archives depositories 811
  American libraries 811
  archives 810
  libraries 810
  museums 4, 629
Disaster and fiction: modern Greek fiction and the Asia Minor disaster of 1922 678
Discographies
  folk music 641
  George Seferis 829
  literature 829
  Odysseus Elytis 829
  poetry 829
  rebetika 642
  Varnalis 829
  Yannis Ritsos 829
Dishonour concept 386, 388
Districts, Administrative 40
Divided land: an Anglo-Greek tragedy 203
Diving techniques 35
Divo, Jean-Paul 636
Djaferis, S. 313
Dobratz, B. A. 372
Dodecanese: diversity and unity in island politics 37
Dodecanese islands 37
  folklore 659
  Italian occupation 15
  World War II 198
Dontas, D. N. 156
Doren, D. McN. 69
Dorson, R. M. 658
Doulis, T. 678, 741
Doumanis, O. B. 624, 626
Doumas, C. L. 441—442, 451—452
Dounias, M. E. 640
Dowling, T. E. 296
Dowry system 384—385
  Boeotia 383
  Vasilika 373
Drakatos, C. G. 226
Drama, Modern
  history 650
Drandrakis, P. 789
Drifting cities: a trilogy 742
Droulia, L. 798, 820—821
Du Boulay, J. 374, 388

Dumont, P. 252, 573
Durán, L. 641
Durrell, L. 62, 64, 75, 86, 699, 730, 743
Dynamics of communism in eastern Europe 431

E

E.A.M. -National Liberation Front 188, 201
Early Christian and Byzantine architecture 623
East central and southeast Europe: a handbook of library and archival resources in North America 811
Eastern Churches 331
Eastern Orthodox Church 214
Eastern question 1774-1923: a study in international relations 105
Eastern question, the last phase: a study in Greek-Turkish diplomacy 173
Economic development 19, 211, 235, 362−363, 382, 503, 522, 541
 20th century 180, 454, 504−508, 510−512, 514−515, 520−521, 535−536, 543
 agriculture 564
 Balkan cooperation 516
 credit controls 536
 E.E.C. membership implications 524, 526−528
 foreign investment 520
 foreign technical assistance 521
 industry 542
 legal drawbacks 477
Economic development issues: Greece, Israel, Taiwan and Thailand 511
Economic effects of value-added-tax substitution: Greece 539
Economic geography 15
Economic surveys: Greece 507
Economics
 bibliographies 795
Economics of tramp shipping 566
Economy 1−4, 361
 20th century 504−508
 bibliographies 799
 history 128, 503
 rural 550
 underdevelopment 509, 513
 World War II 199

Economy and finance of Greece under occupation 199
Economy and population movements in the Peloponnesos of Greece 232
Economy of Greece, 1944-66: efforts for stability and development 504
Economy of Greece 1976-78 506
Economy, Rural 556
Ecumenical Patriarchate
 17th century 334
 18th century 336
 19th century 337
 history 332−334, 336−337
Eddy, C. B. 175
Eden, Anthony, Earl of Avon 185
Edmonds, Mrs. 145
Education 3, 40, 176, 361, 454, 588
 20th century 583
 administration 582, 584−585
 adult 600
 agricultural 562
 bibliographies 799
 compulsory schooling 590, 594
 democratization 596
 history 581, 583, 589
 reform 582−583, 585, 587, 589−591, 593, 595−596
 social benefits 602
 system 244
 technical 590
 vocational 590
Education act, 1976 594
Education, Higher
 demand 599, 603
 problems 597−598
 student politics 601
Education, Secondary
 reform 592
Edward Lear in Greece: journals of a landscape painter in Greece and Albania 49
E.E.C. - European Economic Community
 membership implications 523−528, 539
Egypt
 Greek community 292
 Greek community's contribution to economic development 293

195

Eideneier, H. 325
Eight artists: eight attitudes: eight Greeks. Stephen Antonakos, Vlassis Caniaris, Chryssa, Jannis Kounellis, Pavlos, Lucas Samaras, Takis, Costas Tsoclis 621
Eighteen short songs of the bitter motherland 727
Eighteen texts: writings by contemporary Greek authors 688
E.L.A.S. - National Popular Liberation Army 200
Elections
  1974 470
  1977 467
  statistics 417, 419
Electoral system
  history 419
Electricity 515
Eleftheroudaki synchronos enkyklopaideia, meta plirous lexikou tis ellinikis glossis 790
Elgin marbles 102
Elgin, Thomas Bruce, 7th earl of 102
Elias Venezis 744
Eliot, C. N. E. 214
Eliou, M. 595
Ellines zographoi tou 19ou aiona 612
Ellinika laika mousika organa 639
Ellinikes phoresies 669
Ellinikes phoresies - Greek costumes - Costumes grecs 668
Elliniki vivliographia 1972 793
Elliot, W. R. 79
Ellis, H. S. 529
Elytis, Odysseus 685−687, 699−701
  discographies 829
Embiricos 687
Embroidery 629, 631−633
  Byzantine 630
Emigrants 4
  20th century 257
  remittances' importance in balance of payment 533
Emigrants to Australia 283
  assimilation 284−285
  Sydney, New South Wales 285
Emigrants to Canada
  assimilation 289−291
  Toronto 291
Emigrants to Egypt
  Alexandria 292
  Cairo 292
  contribution to Egypt's economic development 293
Emigrants to Ethiopia 295
  contribution to Ethiopia's economic development 294
Emigrants to Great Britain
  Liverpool 296
  London 296
  Manchester 296
  Oxford 296
Emigrants to Madagascar 382
Emigrants to New Zealand 287
  assimilation 288
Emigrants to the U.S.A. 259
  18th century 265
  20th century repatriates 261
  Anderson, Indiana 273
  assimilation 273, 275−276, 280−281
  Carbon County, Utah 268
  career prospects 272
  Chicago 277
  Denver 278−279
  history 258, 260, 262−265, 269
  life and customs 271
  San Antonio, Texas 274
  Tarpon Springs, Florida 270
Emigration 39−40, 231, 238, 382
  bibliographies 826
  'brain drain' 243−244
  classical period 111
  economic background 240−244
  effects on industry 236
  history 240
  labour opportunities in European countries 235
  political background 244
  short-term migrant workers in West Germany 237
  short-term migrant workers in Western Europe 233, 239, 242
  statistics 223, 226
Employment 542
Encyclopaedias 789−791
England
  literary contacts with Greece 677
English loan words 303
Engonopoulos 687
Enosis movement - union with Greece
  Cyprus 500−502
Enquêtes sociologiques sur les emigrants grecs 239
Entertainment 3

Epirus 55
Epirus 6, 55
  part-cession to Greece, 1881 157
  timber industry 564
Equities
  investment 531−532
Ernest, R. 579
E.S.A. - military police
  torture trial, 1975 459
Essai sur l'émigration grecque: étude démographique, économique et sociale 240
Essai sur la phonétique des parlers de Rhodes: contribution à l'étude des dialectes néogrecs 307
Essays, Modern 734
Essays on the historical geography of the Greek world in the Balkans during the Turkokratia 17
Establishment of the Balkan national states, 1804-1920 104
Ethics
  classical 107
  encyclopaedias 791
Ethiopia
  Greek community 295
  Greek community's contribution to economic development 294
Euboea
  rural life and customs 374
  Venetian rule, 15th century 130
Eudes, D. 188
Eurocommunism 430, 435
Europe, Western
  bibliographies 826
  Greek immigrants 826
European Commission of Human Rights
  report on the Greek case, 1969 455−456
European Economic Community - E.E.C.
  membership implications 523−528, 539
Eustratios Argenti: a study of the Greek church under Turkish rule 335
Evangelinides, M. 509
Evelpidis, C. 362
Events, Greece 1967-1974 465
Evil eye beliefs 398
Exchange of populations
  Greece and Turkey, 1923 246
Exhibition of Greek folk art catalogue 608
Exode rurale et attraction urbaine en Grèce 227
Eyewitness in Greece: the colonels come to power 447

F

Facaros, D. 87
Fair Greece! Sad relic! Literary philhellenism from Shakespeare to Byron 677
Fall of Constantinople 127
Fallmerayer, Jakob Philipp 117
Family and mobility among Greek Americans 276
Family businesses 529
Family law 476
Family life 361, 402
  koumbaros system moral guardian 393
  moral obligations 396
  Sarakatsanoi 375, 380
Famine
  World War II 224
Farewell to Salonica: portrait of an era 254
Farm fragmentation in Greece: the problem and its setting, with eleven village case studies 553
Farming
  Peloponnese 26
Farms
  fragmentation 553
Fate
  folklore 658
Fatouros, D. A. 614, 617
Feasts
  name days 400
Feasts of memory: a journey to a Greek island 9
Federation of Thessaloniki 573
Feinstein, Otto 267
Ferguson, J. 113
Fermor, P. L. 51, 59, 195, 622
Fernau, Friedrich-Wilhelm 343
Fertility rate 223, 225−226
Fertilizers 549
Festivals
  firewalking 667
  Greek islands 86
  Orthodox Church 665

Fielding, X. 67, 195
Films 651
  anthropology 828
Finance 176
Financial history
  World War II 199
Fine arts 100
Finer, L. 7, 739
Finlay, George 118
  catalogue of papers 815
Finlay papers: a catalogue 815
Finley, Moses I. 106, 107
Firewalking festival
  Langada 667
First and second generation Greeks in Chicago 277
First Athenian memories 167
First modern Olympics 674
Fish and fisheries 515
Fixed capital stock and future investment requirements in Greek manufacturing 544
Flaw 731
Fleischer, H. 824
Fleming, A. 464
Fletcher, E. W. 296
Flight of Ikaros: a journey into Greece 60
Flora 93–94
  Greek islands 86
  Rhodes 64
Flowers of Greece and the Aegean 93
Flowers of the Mediterranean 94
Folk art 608
  Macedonia 607
Folk costumes 34
Folk dances 647–649
Folk dances of the Greeks: origins and instructions 647
Folk lore of Chios 662
Folk medicine 410–411
  Rhodes 64
Folk music 640
  discography 641
Folk poetry 682
  modern 681
Folk poetry of modern Greece 681
Folklore 101, 132, 308, 398, 410–411, 655–658, 660, 663–664, 666
  bibliographies 817
  Chios 662
  Dodecanese 659
  Macedonia 661
  Pontos 657
  Thrace 657
Folklore Museum of Northern Greece 607
Folklore Museum, University of Thessaloniki 607
Folktales of Greece 658
Food 406, 672–673
  20th century 519
  history 406, 561
  subsidies from the U.S.A. 519
Food resources 211
Food supply
  statistics 563
Forbes-Boyd, E. 130
Forbes, H. A. 559
Forbes, M. C. 561
Forces politiques en Grèce 417
Foreign aid
  19th century debts 482
  20th century 517–519
  20th century technical assistance 521
  from the U.S.A. 517–519
  investment by Litton Industries 520
Foreign interference in Greek politics: an historical perspective 480
Foreign relations 4, 176
  19th century 124, 156
  20th century 124, 485–489, 491–492, 494–495, 497
  bibliographies 799
  impact of E.E.C. membership on trade 525
  trade 40
  with Greece 487
  with Turkey 489, 495, 497
  with the United Nations 490
  with the U.S.A. 420, 448, 485–486, 488, 491–492, 494
  with the U.S.A., 20th century 493
  with Yugoslavia 489
Foreign skills and technical assistance in Greek development 521
Forests and forestry 40, 515
Forster, E. M. 696
Forty-five stories from the Dodekanese 659
Foss, A. 55, 83

Four Greek poets: C. P. Cavafy, George Seferis, Odysseus Elytis, Nikos Gatsos 685
Fourré, P. 600
France
　short-term migrant workers from Greece 239
　short-term migrant workers returning to Greece 239
Frangopoulos, Th. D. 734
Frankish Greece
　history 131
Fraser, N. 570
Fratricides 703
Frazee, C. A. 330, 337, 342
Frederica. Queen of the Hellenes 210
Freedom and death 704
Freeman, Michael 14
French loan words 304
French travellers' accounts
　bibliographies 808—809
Frescoes, Byzantine 606
Friar, K. 687, 701, 728, 736
Friedl, E. 230, 373, 379, 383—384, 394, 407
Fringe of blue: an autobiography 58
Frischauer, Willi 570
From Mars Hill to Manhattan: the Greek Orthodox in America under Athenagoras I 264
From southern Europe to New Zealand: Greeks and Italians in New Zealand 287
Ftyaras, L. G. 327
Furniture 100

G

Gage, N. 5
Gallipoli memories 166
Gardeners of Salonika: the Macedonian campaign 1915-1918 165
Gardikas, K. 801
Gatsos, Nikos 685—687
Gavras, Costa Z. 651
Gavrielides, N. 400
Gazetteer of Greece 43
Gazetteers 42—43
　Peloponnese 44
Gems 100
Generative interpretation of dialect: a study of modern Greek phonology 298

Genevoix, M. 466
Gennadius, J. 581, 610, 690, 747, 813
Gennadius Library, Athens 747
　catalogues 806—807, 813
Geographic names 42, 103
　Peloponnese 44
Géographie humaine de la Grèce: éléments pour l'étude de l'urbanisation 39
Geography 3, 783
　bibliographies 795, 798
　economic 15
　historical 17—18
　Peloponnese 25—26
　physical 15—16
　Pobia, Crete 33
　Thessaly 23—24
Geography, Political
　Dodecanese islands 37
Georgacas, D. J. 44
Georgakopoulos, T. A. 539
George I, King of Greece 159
George II, King of the Hellenes 178—179
George Theotokas 741
Georges, R. A. 660
Georgiou, P. 286
Germany
　destruction of the Jewish community in Greece 255—256
　invasion of Crete, 1941 187
　invasion of Greece, 1941 179, 185—186
　occupation of Chios, 1941-44 216
　occupation of Greece, World War II 195, 199
　occupation of Greece, World War II, bibliographies 824
　short-term migrant workers in 233
Germany, West
　bibliographies 826
　Greek immigrants 826
　short-term migrant workers from Greece 237, 239
　short-term migrant workers returning to Greece 238—239, 242
Germidis, D. A. 542
Geschichte der griechischen Malerei des 19ten Jahrhunderts 613
Gestures
　insulting 653
Gevetsi, M. 577
Ghika, Nikolas 620, 622
Ghika: paintings, drawing, sculpture 622

199

Giagannos, Ap. 654
Giagannos, Ar. 654
Giannaris, G. 646
Gianos, M. 676
Gibbon, E. 116
Giner, Salvador 360
Glass 100
Glücksberg dynasty 162
Gold sovereigns
 as free-market currency 540
Golisano, F. 616
Gorgopotamos viaduct
 destruction in World War II 192
Gothenburg University, Department of Modern Greek 788
Government 4, 359, 472, 478—479
 1924 period 122
 20th century 437, 442
 bibliographies 795
 Byzantine 114—116
 foreign intervention 480
 history 437, 442
 history, 20th century 438, 440
Grammaire du Grec moderne 318
Grammar of modern Greek on a phonetic basis 317
Granger, C. W. J. 540
Great Britain
 20th century 179
 Greek community 296
 Greek policy, 1940s 197, 203, 208
 Ionian islands protectorate 154
 policy on Greece, 1821-33 141
 policy on Greece, World War II 196
 relations with Greece 179
 south-east Europe policy, 1939-46 189—190
Great Church in captivity: a study of the patriarchate of Constantinople from the eve of the Turkish conquest to the Greek War of Independence 333
Great Island: a study of Crete 66
Great Powers
 19th century 156
 Greek policy 156
Grèce moderne et sa littérature: orientation bibliographique en allemand, anglais, français, italien 820
Greco-Turkish relations
 20th century 171
Greco-Turkish War, 1897 482
Greco-Turkish War, 1921-22 122, 170—173

Greece 15, 76, 177
Greece 1940-1941 185
Greece 1978 70
Greece: a guide to official statistics of agriculture, population, and food supply 563
Greece: a political and economic survey 1939-1953 180
Greece: a political essay 161
Greece: a portrait 4
Greece: a selected list of references 795
Greece: American aid in action, 1947-1956 517
Greece: American dilemma and opportunity 208
Greece and the British connection 1935-1941 179
Greece and Crete 1941 186
Greece and the eastern crisis 1875-1878 157
Greece and the European Community 523
Greece and the European Economic Communities: the first decade of a troubled association 526
Greece and the Great Powers 1863-1875 156
Greece and the Great Powers, 1914-1917 164
Greece and the Great Powers 1944-1947: prelude to the 'Truman Doctrine' 486
Greece and the Greek refugees 175
Greece and its myths 101
Greece in the Bronze Age 96
Greece in transition: essays in the history of modern Greece, 1821-1974 124
Greece of Karamanlis 466
Greece: official standard names approved by the United States Board on Geographic Names 42
Greece: past and present 126
Greece today: the aftermath of the refugee impact 176
Greece under King George 159
Greece under military rule 445
Greece without columns: the making of the modern Greeks 121

Greek agricultural cooperatives within the framework of the Greek social fabric 558
Greek-Albanian frontier commission, 1923 483
Greek alphabet
 use in non-Greek texts 309
Greek-American relations: a critical review 493
Greek Americans: struggle and success 259
Greek architecture 99
Greek book, 1476-1825 746
Greek-Bulgarian frontier incident, 1925 484
Greek calendar customs 665
Greek children in Sydney 285
Greek Civil War 1944-1949 204
Greek cooking 672
Greek dances 648
Greek dilemma: war and aftermath 202
Greek education: reorganization of the administrative structure 582
Greek entanglement 192
Greek experience 110
Greek foreign debt and the Great Powers 1821-1898 482
Greek handicraft 629
Greek industrialists: an economic and social analysis 547
Greek industry in perspective 545
Greek island embroidery 632
Greek island hopping: a handbook for the independent traveller 87
Greek islands 86
Greek language 323
Greek language, Cypriot
 phonology and inflections 299
Greek language, Modern 132, 324, 783, 788
 bibliographies 798
 demotic 311, 313, 316−321, 326, 590
 demotic adoption in educational system 590
 demotic as official language of the state 592
 demotic noun morphology 301
 dialects 298, 308
 dictionaries 310−315
 English idiom 306
 English loan words 303, 306
 French loan words 304
 grammar 316−318
 historical development 297, 313, 323, 675
 Italian loan words 302
 political significance of demotic 712
 Rhodes dialect 307
 textbooks 319−322, 325−326
 translation into English 327
 Turkish influence 308
 verb forms 300
Greek law: three lectures delivered at Cambridge and Oxford in 1946 473
Greek life in town and country 2
Greek loan words 305
Greek loans, 1824 and 1825 482
Greek memories 168
Greek merchant marine 565
Greek monetary developments 1939-1948: a case study of the consequences of World War II for the monetary system of a small nation 534
Greek nation, 1453-1669: the cultural and economic background of modern Greek society 128
Greek Orthodox Church (see Orthodox Church)
Greek peasant 378
Greek peasants, ancient and modern: a comparison of social and moral values 377
Greek penal code 475
Greek political reaction to American and Nato influences 420
Greek portfolio 11
Greek regional development 19
Greek security considerations: a historical perspective 496
Greek socialist movement and the First World War: the road to unity 575
Greek struggle for independence, 1821-1833 140
Greek struggle in Macedonia, 1897-1913 213
Greek studies 818
Greek tragedy 123
Greek trilogy: resistance-liberation-revolution 2-01
Greek War of Independence: its historical setting 142
Greeks: how they live and work 3
Greeks in America: a student's guide to localized history 260

Greeks in Australia 283
Greeks in Canada 289
Greeks in the United States 258
Greeks of to-day 153
Greeks of Vancouver: a study of the preservation of ethnicity 290
Greeks overseas 111
Griechenland und die Europäische Gemeinschaft. Erwartungen und Probleme des Beitritts 528
Griechenland: Volksmusik und neuere Musik 640
Griechische Entwicklungsprobleme: Studien an einem kontinentaleuropäischen Entwicklungsland 512
Griechischen Landschaften: eine Landeskunde 16
Griffin, J. 702
Gritsopoulos, E. 577
Grohmann, Will 617
Grønvald, G. M. 567
Gross, L. 497
Guide books 70, 72, 74−76, 78
  flora 93−94
  islands 87

H

Habenstein, Robert W. 271
Hadjiantoniou, G. A. 334
Hadjimihali, A. 670
Hadjinicolaou, N. 620
Hadzidakis, Manos 646
Haghion Oros 346, 348−350, 352
  bibliographies 354
  history 347, 354
  population 353
  travellers' accounts 351
Halikias, D. J. 536
Halliday, W. R. 308
Hammond, P. 338
Hamson, D. 193
Handbook of Greek art 100
Handbook of the modern Greek vernacular: grammar, texts, glossary 321
Handbuch der Ostkirchenkunde 331
Handicrafts 629
Handweaving 629, 634−635
Haniotis, G. V. 597, 604
Hannay, A. M. 563
Happy day 651
Harlow, M. 465

Harries-Jenkins, Gwyn 429
Harris, K. 326
Hartocollis, P. 413
Hartog, Howard 645
Harvard College Library
  modern Greek collection 814
Harvard University, Widener Library 811
Hasluck, F. W. 347
Health
  mental illness 413
  popular beliefs 410−411
Health and healing in rural Greece: a study of three communities 410
Health services 408
Hellas observed: the American experience of Greece 1775-1865 147
Hellènes dans l'intérieur de l'Égypte: leur apport au relèvement économique et social du pays 293
Hellenic traveller: a guide to the ancient sites of Greece and the Aegean 74
Hellenism and the Balkans 17
Hellenism and the first Greek war of liberation, 1821-1830: continuity and change 143
Hellenism in England: a short history of the Greek people in this country from the earliest times to the present day 296
Hellénisme et l'Égypte moderne 292
Hellenistic civilization 107, 113
Henderson, G. P. 133
Heritage of Hellenism 113
Heurtley, W. A. 15
Hicks, S. M. 494
Higgins, B. 521
High life expectancy on the island of Paros, Greece 411
Higher education
  demand 599, 603
  problems 597−598
Hiking
  guide books 92
Histoire des israelites de Salonique 251
Histoire picturale de la guerre de l'indépendance hellénique par le Général Makriyannis 610
Historical geography 17−18

Historical geography of the Balkans 18
History 10, 15−16, 118−121, 126, 783−784, 787−788
  15th century 128−129
  16th century 128−129
  17th century 128−129
  18th century 129
  19th century 122, 124, 152−153, 155−156, 158−159
  20th century 5, 120−124, 160, 163−164, 178, 180, 208−211, 422, 426, 445−454, 461, 466, 470, 823
  bibliographies 795, 798−799, 802−804, 823
  classical period 108−109
  constitutional 471
  economic 128, 503
  economic, 20th century 504−508
  mediaeval 114−116
  statistics, 19th century 577
  statistics, 20th century 577
History, Modern
  bibliographies 801, 805
  periodicals 801
History of Byzantine music and hymnography 638
History of the Byzantine state 114
History of the decline and fall of the Roman Empire 116
History of Greece from its conquest by the Romans to the present time, B.C. 146 to A.D. 1864 118
History of Greece to the death of Alexander the Great 108
History of Macedonia 1354-1833 212
History of modern Greek literature 675−676
History of the Order of AHEPA 1922-1972, including the Greeks in the New World, and immigration to the United States 281
History of Thessaloniki 219
Hitiris, T. 525
Hoffman, G. W. 22, 516
Holden, D. 121
Hollow legions: Mussolini's blunder, 1940-1941 184
Holst, G. 642
Home book of Greek cookery: a selection of traditional Greek recipes 673
Homeric civilization 106, 110
Homeric society 107
Honour concept 386, 388
  philotimo 389
  Sarakatsanoi 390
Honour, family and patronage: a study of institutions and morals in a Greek mountain community 375
Hopkins, M. 84
Horecky, P. L. 799, 811
Hornby, A. S. 314
Horta - wild greens 561
Horton, George 172
Hösch, E. 805
Hotels 40, 70
Hourmouzios, S. 209
Householder, F. W. 316, 324
Housepian, M. 172
Houses 624, 627
  Chios 628
Housing 29
Howe, J. 188
Howe, R. 672
Human rights
  infringement, 1967 455−459
Humour
  jokes 653
Humphrey, C. R. 280
Hussey, J. M. 114, 115, 815
Huxley, A. 93−94
Hydra
  development plan 580
  paintings by Ghika 622
Hydra: a Greek island town: its growth and form 580
Hymn to liberty 737−738
Hymns, Byzantine 638

I

I was born Greek 463
Iatrides, J. O. 200, 488−489, 493
Iatridis, D. S. 409
Ilinden insurrection, 1903 215
Ill met by moonlight 194
Illiteracy 595
Illustrations 11
Immigration
  short-term migrant workers returning from Western Europe 239, 242

In memoriam: hommage aux victimes juives des Nazis en Grèce 255
In the mountains of Greece 50
Incomes
  distribution 542
  inequality of distribution 538—539
Independence movements 103—104, 122, 125, 137—139
  historical background 105
Industrial capital in Greek development 529
Industrial development 522, 541—542
  20th century 521, 545
  capital investment 529—530, 532
  E.E.C. membership implications 523
  foreign technical assistance 521
  impact on the Greek character 366
Industrialisation, employment and income distribution in Greece: a case study 542
Industrialists 547
Industry 40, 176, 515, 543—544
  20th century 545
  Athens 365
  effects of emigration 236
  history 545
  management 546
  maps and atlases 41
  political attitudes in 20th century 444
Inflation 535
  World War II 534
Influence du français sur le grec. Emprunts lexicaux et calques phraseologiques 304
Inheritance system 384, 396
  Boeotia 383
  Vasilika 373
Inside the Colonels' Greece 446
Institut Français d'Athènes 794
Intellectual history
  19th century 133
Internal migrant 229
Internal migration 227—232, 234, 382
  Boeotia 383
  impact on the dowry system 385
International Financial Commission of Control 482
International labor migration and economic development with special reference to Greece 235
International relations 4

Introducing Greece 6
Introduction à la peinture néo-héllenique 615
Investment, Capital
  in industry 529—530, 544
  in real estate 529—530
Ioannidis, Brigadier 469
Ionian islands 6
  (see also Corfu)
  19th century 154
  guide books 82—83, 89
  history 154
  modern coins 637
Ionian islands to Rhodes: a sea guide 89
Ionian Islands: Zakynthos to Corfu 83
Ionian vision: Greece in Asia Minor, 1919-1922 170
Isaacs, E. 285
Islam 214
Islands, Greek 87
  20th century 63
  bibliographies 795
  folklore 34
  guide books 82—83, 85—86
  life and customs 34, 36
  maps and atlases 31
  population 31
  travellers' accounts 63
Istoria ton ellinikou typou 751
Italian loan words
  bibliographies 302
Italy
  Corfu incident, 1923 483
  invasion of Greece, 1940 179, 184—186
  occupation of Dodecanese islands 15
Izmir
  sacking, 1922 170, 172

J

Jacobson, P. 570
Janowitz, Morris 428
Jecchinis, C. 572
Jelavich, B. 104
Jelavich, C. 104, 818
Jenkins, R. 117, 155, 737
Jewellery 100
Jewish community
  Chios 245
  destruction by the Nazis 255—256
  Salonika 251—255
  Thessaloniki 251—255

Jews
 history 355—356
 relations with the Orthodox Church 355—356
Jioultsis, B. 340
Joachimides, C. M. 621
Johnstone, K. R. 129, 724
Johnstone, P. 630, 632—633
Jokes 658
Jones, H. D. 795
Journals of resistance 462
Judiciary 4

K

Kahane, H. 302
Kahane, R. 302
Kaiser, W. 733
Kalamata
 development plan 578
Kalamotousakis, G. J. 527
Kallifatidou, S. 376, 410
Kalligas, M. 618
Kalymnos 35
 nicknames 401
 sponge divers 36
Kapetanios: partisans and civil war in Greece, 1943-1949 188
Kapheneia
 London 296
 Stavropolis 397
Kapodistrias, Count Ioannis Antonios 150
Karageorgas, D. 538
Karaghiozis 652, 654
Karagouni 249
Karakatsani, A. A. 48
Karamanlis, Constantine 463, 466
 educational reforms 586, 593
 K.K.E. policy 436
Karandonis 687
Karanikas, A. 744
Karanikas, H. 744
Karelli 687
Kariotakis 687
Kartakis, E. A. 541
Kasperson, R. E. 37
Katranides, A. A. 660
Katris, J. A. 447
Katsimbalis, George C. 57, 714, 720
Kavadhias 687
Kavadias, G. B. 380
Kayser, B. 39—40, 227, 370

Kazamias, A. M. 583, 586—587, 593, 601
Kazantzakis and the linguistic revolution in Greek literature 712
Kazantzakis, H. 709—710
Kazantzakis, Nikos 687, 702—713
 bibliographies 714
Kazantzakis: the politics of salvation 710
Kazazis, K. 316
Kedouri, Elie 137
Keeley, E. 685—686, 693—695, 697, 700, 726, 732, 735
Kenna, M. E. 393, 396
Kennedy, Jackie 570
Kerkyra incident, 1923 483
Khouliarakis, M. 577
Kiljunen, Marja-Lüsa 509
King, F. 6
Kinship system
 Sarakatsanoi 391
Kipling, Rudyard 738
Kissinger, Henry
 Cyprus crisis, 1974 492
Kitsikis, D. 419, 433, 436
Kitto, H. D. F. 50
K.K.E. (see also Communism)
K.K.E. - Greek Communist Party 188, 431, 433—436, 764—765, 773
 history 430
Klephtic ballads in relation to Greek history 136
Klephts
 ballads 136
Kofos, E. 156—157, 499
Kokkinis, S. 810
Koliopoulos, J. S. 179
Kolodny, E. Y. 31
Kolokotrones, the klepht and the warrior: sixty years of peril and daring: an autobiography 145
Koloktronis, Theodore 145
Kontoglou, Fotis 620
Korais, Adamantios 137
Korisis, H. 158
Koster, H. 560
Koster, J. B. 635
Kostis Palamas 721
Koty, J. 361
Koumarianou, C. 798
Koumbaros system - moral guardians 393, 396
 Peloponnese 392

Koumoulides, J. T. A. 124, 126, 149, 330, 385
Koundouros, R. 819
Kounellis, Jannis 621
Koupernik, Cyrille 402
Kourvetaris, G. A. 271−272, 277, 372, 425, 427−429
Kousoulas, D. G. 430, 449
Koutsoudas, A. 316
Koutsoukis, K. 437
Koutzovlachs 249
Kraus, D. H. 811
Krautheimer, R. 623
Kreipe, General 194
Krengel, R. 544
Kulukundis, E. 9
Kyparissiotis, Niove 812
Kyriakides, S. P. 660
Kyriakidou-Nestoros, A. 607

L

Labour
  effects of emigration 236
  migration 234
  opportunities in European countries affecting emigration 235
  shortages, 20th century 554−555
  shortages, agriculture 554−555
Labour movements
  20th century 573−574
  World War I 575
Labour shortages in Greek agriculture, 1963-1973 554
Ladino 251
Lambiri-Dimaki, J. 596
Lambiri, I. 367
Laments, Ritual
  history 679
Lancaster, O. 8
Land holdings, Small 553
Land of Nestor: a physical geography of the southwest Peloponnese 25
Landau, Y. H. 557
Landscape of death. The selected poems of Takis Sinopoulos 736
Landscape paintings 49
  Peloponnese 48
Langrod, G. 478
Language and area studies: east central and southeastern Europe: a survey 818
Laras, Loukis 690

Larrabee, S. A. 147
Last temptation 705
Latin America
  bibliographies 826
  Greek immigrants 826
Latin Greece
  history 131
Lauquier, H. C. 274
Lausanne, Treaty of, 1923
  historical background 173
  refugee problems 176
Lauwe, J. Chombart de 552
Law 475
  family 476
  history 473−474
  influence on economic development 477
Lawless, Richard I. 18
Lawrence, A. W. 99
Lawson, J. C. 663
Lea, J. F. 710
League of Nations
  Corfu incident, 1923 483
  Greek-Bulgarian frontier incident, 1925 484
League of Nations and the Great Powers: the Greek-Bulgarian incident, 1925 484
Leake, W. M. 46−47
Lebel, M. 809
Leber, G. J. 281
Lederer, Ivo J. 125
Lee, Arthur S. Gould 162
Lee, D. D. 381
Leeper, R. 197
Legends 658, 661
  survival in modern folklore 663
Legg, K. R. 415, 440
Legislature 4
Lenzer, G. 448
Leon, G. B. 164, 565, 574−575
Levandis, J. A. 482
Levi, P. 73
Levitt, M. P. 713
Leyton, E. 749, 814
Lia
  World War II 5
Lianos, T. P. 236, 242
Liberated Greece and the Morea scientific expedition: the Paytier album in the Stephen Vagliano collection 48
Libraries 813
  directories 810

Libraries, American 812, 814
  directories 811
Liddell, R. 6, 52, 61, 63, 221, 696
Lidderdale, H. A. 144, 611
Life and customs 1—3, 5, 11, 50, 53, 56, 65, 177, 368, 396—397, 401, 517, 666
  19th century 153
  20th century 206
  Boeotia 383
  Chios 662
  dowry system 384
  inheritance system 384
  marriage 387
  Vasilika 373
  women 369
Life in the tomb 715
'Linear B' controversy 95
Linguistics
  bibliographies 817
Literary periodicals
  circulation and policy 777
Literature 783, 788
  20th century 454
  ancient, history 112
  bibliographies 798, 820
  classical 107, 109
  contacts with England 677
  discographies 829
  history, modern 675—677
  modern anthologies 689
  modern chronologies 675
  political 454, 465
Litton Industries
  20th century 520
  investment in Greece 520
Liverpool
  Greek community 296
Livestock 515
Living past of Greece: a time-traveller's tour of historic and prehistoric places 75
Living standards
  Macedonia 21
Loch, J. N. 58
Loch, S. 349
Loizos, P. 500
Lolis, N. B. 475
London
  Greek community 296
Longevity 412
Lord Elgin and the marbles 102
Loucaris, Kyrillos 334
Louis, Helen Brock 280
Loukatos, D. 655

Loukis Laras: reminiscences of a Chiote merchant during the War of Independence 690
Lovinesco, E. 808—809
Loy, W. G. 25
Luard, Evan 207
Lucar, Cyril 334
Lydakis, S. 613

M

McDonald, W. A. 44, 98
McDonald, R. 752
Macedonia 6, 607
  20th century 58, 213, 215
  agricultural development 21
  bibliographies 795
  Bulgarian claims to sovereignty 213
  communism 431
  communist movements 499
  enosis movement 122
  ethnic competition 38
  ethnic problems 215
  folklore 661
  history 212—213, 215, 498
  nationalist movements 498—499
  refugee relief work 58
  World War I 165
Macedonia, East
  migration to the cities 227
Macedonia: its place in Balkan power politics 498
Macedonia: its races and their future 215
Macedonian folklore 661
McGrew, W. W. 520
Mackenzie, C. 166—169
McNall, S. G. 378, 405
McNeill, W. H. 202, 206, 211, 517
Madagascar
  Greek emigrants 382
Maddison, A. 521
Mager, K. 751
Mainland Greece 52
Making of modern Greece: from Byzantium to independence 129
Makris, E. 577
Makriyannis, Ioannis 144, 610—611
Makrynikola, N. 729
Maloney, Clarence 398

207

Mamangakis, Nikos 644
Management 547
  commerce 546
  industry 546
Manchester
  Greek community 296
Mandell, R. D. 674
Mangakis, G. 475
Manganara, J. 238
Mangas 643
Mani peninsula 28, 30, 59
Mani: travels in the southern Peloponnese 59
Maniatis, George C. 531–532
Manos, Constantine 11, 14
Manpower policy and problems in Greece 522
Manpower shortages
  20th century 554–555
  agriculture 554–555
Manpower, Skilled
  emigration 243–244
Mansfield, P. 731
Mantzaridis, G. 353
Manual of modern Greek 322
Manufactures 542–544
  20th century 545
  history 545
  maps and atlases 41
Maps and atlases 16, 40, 70, 72
  Athens 77
  bibliographies 43
  Crete 80
  Greek islands 31
  industry 41
Maps and politics: a review of the ethnographic cartography of Macedonia 38
Marble threshing floor: studies in modern Greek poetry 680
Marder, B. L. 562
Marder, E. J. 178
Margariti
  impact of migration 370
Margariti: village d'Epire 370
Markesinis, B. S. 469–472
Marketing
  producer/merchant relationships 395
Marriage 40, 393
  folklore 661
  infidelity 387
Martens, D. 544
Martindale, D. 372
Maskaleris, T. 721
Massialas, Byron G. 583

Matsas 687
Matthews, K. 205
Matthews, M. 634
Matton, L. 77
Matton, R. 77
Mavrogordato, J. 691
Mavrogordatos, G. 782
Maximos. Metropolitan of Sardis 332
Mead, Margaret 381
Mead, R. 76
Mears, E. G. 176
Mears, Leon 503
Measure of understanding 210
Medals, Modern 637
Media 4, 124
  political influence, 1965-67 439
Medicine, Folk 410–411
  Rhodes 64
Medieval and modern Greek 297
Medieval and modern Greek poetry: an anthology 684
Mega Ellino-Anglikon lexikon 310
Megali elliniki enkyklopaideia 789
Megann, P. 212
Megara
  impact of industrialization 367
Megas, G. A. 658, 665
Meiggs, R. 108
Melissanthi 687
Mémoire sur l'état actuel de la civilization dans la Grèce 137
Memoirs of general Makriyannis 1797-1864 144
Memories of a mountain war: Greece, 1944-1949 205
Men
  regional costumes 669
Mendieta, Emmanuel Amand de 346
Mental illness
  treatment 413
Merchant marine 566, 568–569
  history 565
  Panamanian registrations 566–567
Mercouri, Melina 463, 651
Merlopoulos, P. 417
Mermaid madonna 716
Mesara plain, Crete 33
Messenia
  Bronze Age civilization 98
  life and customs 98
  migration to the cities 227
Metalwork 100, 629
Metamorphosis of Greece since World War II 211
Metaxas, B. N. 566

Metaxas, Ioannis 178−179, 463
Metaxas, Nikodemos 748−749
Meteora monasteries
history 345
Meteora: the rock monasteries of Thessaly 345
Meynaud, J. 417
Michaelides, C. E. 580
Michalakis, A. 519
Migrant workers, short-term
in West Germany 237
in Western Europe 233, 239, 242
returning from West Germany 238
returning from Western Europe 239, 242
Migration, Internal 39−40, 227−232, 234, 382
Boeotia 383
impact on the dowry system 385
impact on villages 370
Mikis Theodorakis: music and social change 646
Military (see also Colonels' regime, 1967-74)
Military academies
recruitment patterns 429
Military-civil relations 161
Military in Greek politics: the 1909 coup d'état 422
Military League
coup d'état, 1909 422
Military police - E.S.A.
torture trial, 1975 459
Le millénaire du Mont Athos, 963-1963: études et mélanges 354
Miller, H. 57
Miller, W. 2, 177
Mims, A. 709, 727
Mindel, Charles H. 271
Mineral resources 40
Mining 515
Minnesota Messenia expedition: reconstructing a Bronze Age regional environment 98
Minoan sites 80−81
Mirambel, A. 318
Mitarachi, P. J. 579
Modern Greece 1
Modern Greece: a short history 119
Modern Greece: facets of underdevelopment 359
Modern Greek and American English in contact 306
Modern Greek coins, 1828-1968 636
Modern Greek culture: a selected bibliography 798
Modern Greek folklore and ancient Greek religion: a study in survivals 663
Modern Greek folktales 656
Modern Greek humor: a collection of jokes and ribald tales 653
Modern Greek in Asia Minor: a study of the dialects of Silli, Cappadocia and Pharasa, with grammar, texts, translations and glossary 308
Modern Greek poetry: translation, introduction, an essay on translation, and notes 687
Modern Greek society: continuity and change: an annotated classification of selected sources 816
Modern Greek Studies Association 786
Modern Greek studies in the West: a critical bibliography of studies on modern Greek linguistics, philology and folklore, in languages other than Greek 817
Modern Greek translation 327
Modern spoken Greek for English-speaking students 320
Mohan, R. P. 372
Moles, I. 128
Moles, P. 128
Molho, M. 253, 255
Monarchy 124, 162, 454, 472
Constantine 167
dynastic table 122
Frederica 210
George I 159
George II 178−179
Otto I 151−152
Paul 209
Monasteries
Meteora 345
Mount Athos 346−353
Monemvasia 79
Monemvasia: the Gibraltar of Greece 79
Monetary equilibrium and economic development, with special reference to the experience of Greece, 1950-1963 535
Monetary policy 535−536
World War II 534

Money and credit in a developing economy: the Greek case 536
Monks of Athos 348
Monuments, Fine Arts and Archives Sub-Commission of the Central Mediterranean Force 609
Moral guardians system - koumbaros 393, 396
  Peloponnese 392
Morals
  mirrored in folklore 664
More Greek folktales 657
Morea 61
Morea (see also Peloponnese)
  17th century 27
  18th century 27
  19th century 27, 47
  20th century 60−61, 707
  guide books 78
  koumbaros system moral guardian 392
  paintings 48
  place names 44
  population movements 232
  travellers' accounts 47, 60−61, 707
Morea Scientific Expedition, 1828 48
Morphology of Greek industry: a study in industrial development 543
Mortality 412
Mosaics 100
Mosaics, Byzantine 606
Moscow Conference, 1944 189
Moskos, Charles C. 259, 371
Moslem minority (see Turkish minority)
Moslem minority in western Thrace 246
Moss, W. Stanley 194
Mossbacher, E. 184
Motoring
  guide books 91
Motoring and camping in Greece 91
Mount Athos 351
Mount Athos 52, 346, 348−350, 352
  bibliographies 354
  history 347, 354
  population 353
  travellers' accounts 351
Mount Athos: the garden of the Panaghia 346
Mountaineering
  guide books 92
Moustaka, C. 229, 588
Mouzelis, N. P. 359−360, 467

Movement for Greek independence 1770-1821: a collection of documents 138
Munkman, C. A. 518
Murderess 722
Museum of Greek Folk Art, Athens 608
Museums
  directories 4, 629
Music 783
  Byzantine 638
  discography, folk 641
  folk 640
  modern 640, 644−646
  settings for poetry 829
Musical instruments
  history 639
Mycenaean civilization 95
Mycenaeans 95
Myers, E. C. W. 192−193
Mykonos
  architecture 579
  history 218
Mykonos: chronique d'une île de l'Égee 218
Myrivilis, S. 715−717
Myrsiades, K. 728
Mythology 101
Mytilini
  novels 716

N

Nagata, J. A. 291
Name days, Personal 400
National anthem 737−738
National bibliography 793−794
National characteristics 51
National Liberation Front - E.A.M. 188, 201
National Library of Greece 793
National Popular Liberation Army - E.L.A.S. 200
National Schism, 1914-17 164, 168−169
National Statistical Service
  Monthly Statistical Bulletin 576
Nationalism 502
  20th century 160

Nationalism and communism in Macedonia 499
Nationalism in Asia and Africa 137
Nationalist movements 103−104, 122, 125, 137−139
　historical background 105
Nationhood 160−161
NATO membership 451
　national attitudes 420
Natsoulas, T. 294
Natural resources 176, 211
Navarino, Naval battle of, 1827 148
Navigation
　Aegean 88−89
　Ionian 89
Nea Dimokratia - New Democracy Party 768, 771
Nea Ionia, Athens
　migrant population 234
　refugee population 234
Near East Foundation 21
Near East Relief 21
Negreponti-Delivanis, M. 514, 542
Nehama, J. 251
Neo-Hellenism
　development in England 135
Neoclassical architecture 625
Neoklassiki arkhitektoniki stin Ellada 625
Neugriechisch für Humanisten 325
New Smyrna: an eighteenth century Greek odyssey 265
New Zealand
　Auckland Greek community 288
　Greek community 287
Newspapers
　circulation and policy 754−765
　history 750
　history, 19th century 751
　history, 20th century 751
　impact of the Colonels' regime, 1967-74 752
Newspapers, Provincial
　policy 766−767
Newton, B. 298−299
Niarchos, N. A. 540
Niarchos, Stavros 570
Nicknames
　Kalymnos 401
　social functions 401
Nicol, D. M. 115, 345
Nicolaou, C. 529
Night sky at Rhodes 65
Nightmare in Athens 461
Nikos Kazantzakis 711

Nikos Kazantzakis: a biography based on his letters 709
No ordinary crown: a biography of King Paul of the Hellenes 209
Nomads 249−250, 375, 380
　honour concept 390
Nomads of the Balkans: an account of life and customs among the Vlachs of northern Pindus 247
Norwich, J. J. 351
Notaras, G. 417
Noun morphology of modern demotic Greek: a descriptive analysis 301
Novels, Modern 690, 702−706, 715−717, 722−724, 730−731, 739−744
　impact of the Asia Minor disaster, 1922 678
Numismatics 636−637

O

O kosmos tou Karaghiozis: figoures 654
O Thiasos 651
O'Ballance, E. 204
Occupation of Chios by the Germans and their administration of the island: described in contemporary documents 216
Odysseus 214
OECD economic surveys: Greece 505
OECD: education and development, country reports: the Mediterranean regional project: Greece 585
Oecumenical Patriarchate
　17th century 334
　18th century 336
　19th century 337
　history 332−334, 336−337
Ohle, E. W. 745
Oikonomikos kai koinonikos atlas tis Ellados: Economic and social atlas of Greece: Atlas économique et sociale de Grèce 40
Old and new Athens 221
Oliver, P. 624
Olson, K. E. 750
Olympics, Modern 674
On Greece and Cyprus: theses index in Britain 819
On the Greek style: selected essays in poetry and Hellenism 734

On the verb in modern Greek 300
Onassis, Aristotle Socrates 570
Oratorios, Modern 700
Oropos
 detention camps 462
Orso, E. G. 653
Orthodox Church 328
Orthodox Church 214, 328—329, 331, 638
 (see also Religion)
 17th century 334
 18th century 335—336
 19th century 124, 337
 20th century 124, 338, 342—343
 festivals and customs 665
 history 264, 328, 332—338, 342—343, 355—356
 impact of the 1975 constitution 344
 monasteries 345—353
 periodicals 357
 political attitudes in 20th century 444
 relations with the Jews 355—356
 relations with the state 330, 337, 342—344
 religious brotherhoods 340
 social aspects 339
 theological trends 341
 U.S.A. 263
Orthodox Church and independent Greece 1821-1852 337
Osborn, J. M. 135
Ostrogorsky, G. 114
Otho I, king of Greece: a biography 151
Otto, King of Greece 151—152, 611
Ottoman rule 17, 134, 214, 333—335
 bibliographies 103
 history 103
 resistance ballads 136
 Thasos 217
 Thessaly 18
 value systems 405
Ottoway, M. 570
Ouranis 687
Ouranopolis 58
Overseas Greeks
 20th century 257
 Australia 283—286, 826
 Canada 289—291, 826
 Egypt 292—293
 England 296
 Ethiopia 294—295
 Federal Republic of Germany 826
 India 295
 Latin America 826
 Madagascar 382
 New Zealand 287—288
 press, U.S.A. 282
 repatriates 261
 South Africa 826
 South America 826
 U.S.A. 258—281, 295, 825—826
Oxford
 Greek community 296
Oxford dictionary of modern Greek 311
Oxford English-Greek learner's dictionary 314
Oxford English picture dictionary: Anglo-elliniko eikonographimeno lexiko 312

P

Paintings 49, 100
 19th century 612—613, 619
 20th century 614—615, 617—622
 Peloponnese 48
 vase 100
 War of Independence, 1821-27 610—611
Palamas, K. 680, 718—720
Palmer, A. 165
Panagopoulos, E. P. 265, 823
Panagoulis, Alexandros 464
Panama
 registrations of shipping companies 566—567
Panama and Greek ships: for shipowners, shipbrokers and everybody in shipping 567
Panathenian stadium 674
Panayotopoulos 687
Panhellenic Socialist Movement - P.A.S.O.K. 460, 467, 769
Pankhurst, R. 295
Papacosma, S. V. 282, 422
Papadiamantis, A. 722
Papadopoullos, T. H. 336
Papadopoulos, Georgios 464, 469
Papadopoulos, S. A. 48, 565, 629
Papageorgiou, C. L. 231, 233
Papaioannou, G. 264
Papaioannou, J. G. 645
Papandreou, Andreas 460, 467, 763
Papandreou, George 200—201, 438, 440, 460
 educational reforms 583, 587, 592

Papandreou, M. 461
Papanikolas, H. Z. 268
Papanoutsos, E. P. 592
Papantoniou, I. 668−669
Papatsonis 687
Pappas 687
Pappas, Irene 651
Parenthood 402
Parliament 415
 dissolution procedure 471
Parnwell, E. C. 312
Paros
 migration to the cities 227, 229
Parthenon 102
P.A.S.O.K. - Panhellenic Socialist
 Movement 460, 467, 769
Passions and ancient days 695
Passport to Greece 7
*'Past' in medieval and modern Greek
 culture* 132
*Pasteurs-nomades méditerranéens: les
 saracatsans de Grèce* 380
Patmos
 architecture 579
Paton, J. M. 45
*Le patriarcat oecumenique dans
 l'église orthodoxe: étude
 historique et canonique* 332
Patronage system 161, 395, 415
Patterson, G. J. 278, 290
Paul, King of the Hellenes 209
Pausanias' guide to Greece 73
Pavlos 621
Payne, Humfry 53−54
Peasant life 358−359, 376, 378, 666
 Euboea 374
 history 377
 Vasilika 373
Pechoux, Pierre-Yves 227, 568
Peloponnese 6, 25−26, 59
 17th century 18, 27
 18th century 27
 19th century 27, 47
 20th century 60−61, 707
 economic factors affecting population
  movements 232
 emigration 232
 guide books 78
 koumbaros system moral
  guardian 392
 migration to the cities 232
 paintings 48
 place names 44
 scientific expedition, 1828 48
 travellers' accounts 47, 60−61, 707

Pelto, P. J. 35
Penal code 475
Pendlebury, J. D. S. 68
Pendzikis 687
Penguin book of Greek verse 683
*Penguin-Hellenews Anglo-Ellinikon
 lexikon* 315
Pentreath, G. 74
Pentzopoulos, D. 174
Pepelasis, A. A. 477, 503, 513, 549,
 554−555
Perachora 53
'Percentages Agreement', 1944 189,
 486
Periodicals
 bibliographies 794
 circulation and policy 768−776
Periodicals, Art
 circulation and policy 778
Periodicals,
 English-language 782−788
 circulation and policy 779−780
Periodicals, Literary 783, 800
 circulation and policy 777
Peristiany, J. G. 230, 371, 382, 388,
 390, 393, 395, 399, 479
Permanent Committee on Geographical
 Names for British Official Use 43
Perodicals, Historical
 bibliographies 801
Persianis, P. K. 591
Personal names 400
Petrides, E. 647
Petrides, T. 647−648
Petropulos, J. A. 132, 143, 152, 480
Petrounias, Evangelos 132
Peytier, Eugène 48
Pharasa
 dialect 308
Philhellenes 146
Philhellenism 146
 bibliographies 821
*Philhellénisme: ouvrages inspirés par
 la guerre de l'indépendence
 grecque 1821-1833* 821
Philip of Macedonia
 legends 661
Philippson, A. 16
Philology
 bibliographies 817
Philosophy, Classical 107, 109
Philotimo - love of honour 389, 664
 influence on politics 443
Photiadis, J. D. 397
Phousouras, G. I. 792

213

Phrantziskakis, E. K. 612
Physical geography 15−16
Pi-Sunyer, Oriel 134
Piece of truth 464
Piket, J. J. C. 26
Pindus, Northern Vlach community 247−248
Pitt-Rivers, Julian 383, 391
Place names 42, 103
Peloponnese 44
Place names of southwest Peloponnesus: register and indexes 44
Planosparaktis 336
Pobia, Crete 33
Pobia: étude géographique d'un village crétois 33
Poems of C. P. Cavafy 691
Poetry
 anthologies 683
 folk 682
 mediaeval anthologies 684
 Poetry, Modern 680, 691−701, 718−721, 725−728, 732−733, 735−738
 20th century 454
 anthologies 684−688
 criticism 734
 discographies 829
 folk 681
 musical settings 829
 political 454, 465
Poet's journal: days of 1945-51 733
Poitevin, J. 552
Political communication in Greece, 1965-1967: the last two years of a parliamentary democracy 439
Political geography
 Dodecanese islands 37
Political parties 415−417
 19th century 158, 418
 20th century 418, 420−421, 441, 460, 462, 467
 history 158, 418−421, 441, 460, 462, 467
 military attitudes in 20th century 429
Political prisoners 462
 torture, 1967 455−456, 458−459, 464
Political system 361, 415−417
 19th century 418
 20th century 418, 421, 439, 441−442
 history 418, 421, 439, 441−442

Politicians 415−417
Politics 3−4, 176
 19th century 124, 152
 20th century 124, 161, 182, 202, 206, 438, 440, 454
 bibliographies 795
 Byzantine 115
 Colonels' regime, 1967-74 450
 development 364
 development, 20th century 180
 foreign intervention 480
 history 182, 454
 influence of philotimo love of honour 443
 military attitudes in 20th century 422−428
 student, history 601
Politics and statecraft in the kingdom of Greece 1833-1843 152
Politics in modern Greece 415
Politis, A. G. 292
Politis, L. 675
Politischen Parteien Griechenlands: ein neuer Staat auf dem Weg zur Demokratie 1821-1910 158
Pollis, A. 443−444
Polunin, O. 94
Polychronopoulou, A. 225
Polydorides, G. K. 598
Polyzos, N. J. 240
Pontos
 folklore 657
Pope Joan 730
Population 39−40
 20th century 222−223, 225−226
 birth rate 223, 225−226
 deaths from famine 224
 Greek islands 31
 history 222−223
 movements 17
 movements, Peloponnese 232
 statistics 563
 World War II 224
La population des îles de la Grèce: essai de geographie insulaire en Méditerranée orientale 31
Population exchanges
 Treaty of Lausanne, 1923 173−175
Portrait of a Greek mountain village 374
Portrait of Greece 5
Ports 515
Postwar growth in Greek agricultural production: a study in sectoral output change 551

Pottery 100, 629
Powell, D. 53−54, 68
Power politics
  20th century 442, 444
Pratt, M. 154
Presidents
  Georgios Papadopoulos 464
  Ioannis Kapodistrias, 1828-31 150
Press
  19th century 751
  20th century 751
  circulation and policy 754−765
  history 750−751
  impact of the Colonels' regime, 1967-74 752
  political influence, 1965-67 439
Press, Provincial
  policy 766−767
Prevelakis, P. 687, 723−724
Price, C. 283
Price stability 535
Prime ministers
  Constantine Karamanlis 463, 466
  Eleftherios Venizelos 163
  Georgios Papadopoulos 464
  Ioannis Metaxas, 1936-41 178
Pring, J. T. 311, 317
Printing
  history 746
Printing press, Greek
  first press in Constantinople 748−749
Problems of development: adult education techniques in developing countries: a Greek case study 600
Problems of development: problems of agricultural co-operation: case study in Greece 552
Proportional representation,
  Electoral 419
Prospero's cell: a guide to the landscape and manners of the island of Corcyra 62
Protestant patriarch: the life of Cyril Lucaris, Patriarch of Constantinople 334
Psacharopoulos, G. 594, 599, 601−602
Psilos, D. D. 511, 519, 529, 531
Psomiades, H. J. 173, 363, 480
Psychiatric treatment 413
Psychoundakis, G. 195
Public administration 478−479
Public health 408
Publishing 745, 800

Puppet theatre, Shadow 652, 654
Pursuit of Greece: an anthology 10
Pym, H. 682

Q

Quatre ans de bibliographie historique en Grèce, avec un supplément pour les années 1965-1969 804
Question of Greek independence: a study of British policy in the Near East, 1821-1833 141
Quinze ans de bibliographie historique en Grèce, avec une annexe pour 1965 802

R

Radio
  daily summaries, 1948 to date 753
Rainbow in the rock: the people of rural Greece 358
Rainfall 40
Raizis, M. B. 738
Rallis, George 593
Rapp, G. R. 98
Rassias, J. 319
Real estate
  capital investment 530
Rebetika 643
  discographies 642
Rebetika: songs from the old Greek underworld 643
Recipes 672−673
Reed, F. A. 707
Reference grammar of literary dhimotiki 316
Reference works 789−791
  bibliographies 799
Reflections on a marine Venus: a companion to the landscape of Rhodes 64
Refugee problems
  Treaty of Lausanne, 1923 174−176
Refugee Settlement Commission 175
Refugees (see Asia Minor Greeks)
Refugees and economic migrants in great Athens: a social survey 234

215

Regional development strategy in southeast Europe: a comparative analysis of Albania, Bulgaria, Greece, Romania and Yugoslavia 516
Regional economic development 19
  Balkan cooperation 516
Regional employment in Greece 231
Regional variation in modern Greece and Cyprus: toward a perspective of the ethnography of Greece 379
Religion 4, 331, 361
  bibliographies 799
  classical 109
  encyclopaedias 791
Religious minorities of Chios: Jews and Roman Catholics 245
Religious tales 658
Reorganisation of public administration in Greece 478
Repatriates
  from the U.S.A. 261
Report on the Greeks: findings of a Twentieth Century Fund team which surveyed conditions in Greece in 1947 206
Report to Greco 708
Research 786
  social science 782
Resettlement problems
  Treaty of Lausanne, 1923 176
Revival of Greek thought 1620-1830 133
Revolt in Athens: the Greek communist 'second round', 1944-1945 200
Revolution and defeat: the story of the Greek communist party 430
Rhodes 64
  dialect 307
  guide books 90
  life and customs 65
Rhodocanakis, Constantine 296
Rice, D. T. 606
Richter, G. M. A. 100
Rick, A. 716
Rinvolucri, M. 329
Risal, P. 220
Ritsos in parentheses 726
Ritsos, Yannis 687, 725−728
  bibliographies 729
  discographies 829
Ritual lament in Greek tradition 679
Ritual laments
  history 679

Road to rebetika: music from a Greek sub-culture: songs of love, sorrow and hashish 642
Roberts, D. F. 404
Roberts, R. J. 748
Rockefeller Foundation
  survey of Crete 32
Rodd, R. 666
Roman Catholic community
  in Chios 245
Romania
  Macedonian claims 215
Romiosyni 51
Rose, Arnold M. 361
Rose, H. J. 662
Rossiter, S. 72, 80
Roufos, R. 446
Roumeli
  20th century 51
  travellers' accounts 51
Roumeli: travels in northern Greece 51
Rousseas, S. 448
Royal family 162
Royal house of Greece 162
Royidis, E. 730
Rozenman, A. 557
Runciman, S. 127, 333
Rural economy 550, 556
Rural reconstruction in Greece: differential social prerequisites and achievements during the development process 556
Rural settlement
  bibliographies 20
Rural society 358, 376, 378, 382
  Boeotia 383
  cultural heritage 394
  drinking practices 414
  Euboea 374
  history 377
  kinship system 391
  Vasilika 373
Russo-Turkish Wars, 1877-78 157
Ryser, W. 564

S

Sabetai, I. D. 244
Safilios-Rothschild, C. 386−387, 403, 664
Sailing
  Aegean 88−89
  Ionian 89

St. Clair, W. 102, 146
Saints
  Rhodes 64
Saints' days 400
Salonica (see Thessaloniki)
Saloutos, T. 258, 260−263
Samarakis, A. 731
Samaras, Lucas 621
Samarina
  Vlach community 247
Sanders, I. T. 249, 358, 366
Sandis, E. E. 234
Sappho
  legends 717
Sarakatsanoi 249−250
  honour concept 390
  kinship system 391
  life and customs 375, 380
Sarandaris 687
Sartre, Jean-Paul 454
Savidis, G. 693, 695, 700
Savings and investment in Greece 530
Savings, Private
  investment 529−532
Scarce, J. 830
Schaffer, Bernard 509
Schein, Muriel Dimen 250, 368−369
Schmidt, S. M. 546
Schneider, S. 643
Schoeder, R. V. 97
School of Hellenic and Roman Studies, University of Birmingham 783
Schoolmistress with the golden eyes 717
Schools 588
Schuster, M. 651
Sciaky, L. 254
Science
  classical 107, 109
  history 65
  official policy 604
Science and development: national reports of the pilot teams, Greece 605
Scientific research 605
Scott-Kilvert, E. D. 743
Scott-Kilvert, Ian 6
Scourge of error, The 336
Scripture of the blind 728
Sculpture 100, 629
  20th century 617
Seaman, P. D. 306
Seasons
  folklore 661
Security
  history 496
Seers, Dudley 509
Seferis, George 680, 685−688, 719, 732−734
  discographies 829
  Selected poems 694, 725
Senior, M. 101
Seraphim, H. J. 512
Serbia
  Macedonian claims 215
Servan-Schreiber, Jean-Jacques 462
Shadow puppet theatre 652, 654
Shapira, M. 556
Shaw, L. H. 551
Sheldon, Peter 6
Shelter in Greece-Oikismoi stin Ellada 624
Shepherding
  history 560
Shepherds 248−250, 376
  honour concept 390
  life and customs 375, 380
Sherrard, P. 1, 10, 352, 680, 685−686, 693−694, 717, 723, 732, 735
Shipping
  history 565
  merchant marine 568−569
  tramp 566
Shlaim, Avi 527
Short history of Greece from early times to 1964 15
Short history of modern Greece 120
Siampos, G. S. 223
Sicilianos, D. 221
Sikelianos, Anghelos 680, 686−687, 735
Silli
  dialects 308
Silverwork 629
Sinopoulos, Takis 736
Sitwell, R. 351
Sivignon, M. 18, 23, 227, 248
Six poets of modern Greece 686
Skalkottas, Nikos 645
Sketch of the history of education in Greece 581
Slonimsky, N. 644
Smith, A. C. 628
Smith, M. L. 66, 170
Smith, P. 198
Smothers, F. 206
Smyrna
  sacking, 1922 170, 172

217

Smyrna 1922: the destruction of a city 172
Social change 359, 362−363, 381−382, 405, 437−438, 440
  20th century 211, 454, 512
  bibliographies 816
  Euboea 374
  history 360
  industrial workers 365−366
  rural areas 358
  villages 368, 370
  women factory workers 367
Social change in a Greek country town: the impact of factory work on the position of women 367
Social planning and policy alternatives in Greece. Income support and aid to families with dependent children 409
Social science 782, 784−785, 787
  bibliographies 782, 816
  research institutions 371
Social Science Centre, Athens 785
Social welfare 4
Socialist movements
  20th century 573−574
  World War I 575
Society 1−3, 160, 177, 206, 211, 359, 361, 381, 784−785, 787
  bibliographies 799, 816
  history 360
  Homeric 106−107
Society, Rural 358, 376, 378, 382, 399
  Boeotia 383
  cultural heritage 394
  drinking practices 414
  Euboea 374
  history 377
  housing 29
  kinship system 391
  Mani peninsula 28
  Vasilika 373
Sociological research 371−372
  fieldwork 407
  honour concept 389
  humour 653
  marital infidelity 387
  village life 368, 370
  village women 369
  women 403
Sociology 230, 372, 379
  history 371
S.O.E. - Special Operations Executive
  World War II 196

Solomos, Dionysios 680, 737−738
Songs, Folk 682
Songs, Modern 642−643, 727
Songs of Greece 682
Sotir - religious brotherhood 340
Sotiropoulos, D. 301
Soumelis, C. 599, 603
South Africa
  bibliographies 826
  Greek immigrants 826
South America
  bibliographies 826
  Greek immigrants 826
Southeastern Europe: a guide to basic publications 799
Southeastern Europe under Ottoman rule 1354-1804 103
Sovereign sun: selected poems 701
Sovereigns, Gold
  as free-market currency 540
Sovereignty
  foreign intervention 480
Special Operations Executive - S.O.E.
  World War II 196
Spells
  folklore 661
Spencer, F. A. 183
Spencer, T. 677
Spender, S. 622
Spiridonakis, B. G. 17
Spirits
  folklore 661
Spiteris, T. 615−616
Sponge diving 36
Sponge fishing 35, 270
Sport 674
Staar, R. F. 434
Stalin, Joseph Vissarionovich 189, 486
Standard of living
  impact of science and technology 605
Stangos, Nikos 725
Starobin, H. 448
State
  bibliographies 799
State and Orthodox Church 330, 337, 342−344
Statistics 4, 40
  20th century 222−223
  agriculture 563
  communism 432
  elections 417, 419
  food supply 563
  mortality 412
  population 222−223, 563

vital 40
yearbooks 576
Statistics, Historical
  19th century 577
  20th century 577
Statistikai meletai 1821-1971. I statistiki kata ta 150 eti apo tis palingenesias tis Ellados 577
Statistiki epiteris tis Ellados 576
Stavrianopoulos, A. 521
Stavrianos, L. S. 208, 256, 481, 823
Stavropolis
  coffee houses 397
Stavropoulos, D. N. 314
Stavrou, N. A. 424
Stavrou, T. G. 727
Stephanides, M. 267
Stephanides, T. Ph. 720
Stern, L. 492
Stewards of the land: the American farm school and modern Greece 562
Stewart, I. McD. G. 187
Stronghold: an account of the four seasons in the White Mountains of Crete 67
Struggle for Crete 20 May-1 June 1941: a story of lost opportunity 187
Struggle for Greece 1941-1949 181
Struggle for Greek independence: essays to mark the 150th anniversary of the Greek War of Independence 139
Stubbs, J. M. 673
Student politics
  history 601
Studies and documents relating to the history of the Greek church and people under Turkish domination 336
Studies in Greek taxation 537
Studies in Latin Greece, A.D. 1205-1715 131
Sugar, Peter F. 103, 125
Sun of death 723
Superstition 376, 410–411, 666
Swanson, D. C. 303, 313, 817
Sweet-Escott, B. 180, 196
Sykianakis, G. N. 557
Symeonidis, C. 305

T

Tachtsis, Kostas 6
Takis 621
Taktsis, C. 739
Talagan, D. P. 269
Tale of a town 724
Tanker fleets
  owned by Onassis 570
Tavuchis, N. 275–276
Tax evasion 537
Taxation 537–539
Taylor, W. 93, 95
Teacher training
  reorganization 590
Technical education 529
  reorganization 590
Technological development 605
Territorial waters
  dispute with Turkey 495, 497
Textbooks
  improvement 590
Textiles 100
Thasos
  history 217
  Ottoman rule, 1453-1912 217
Thasos, son histoire, son administration de 1453 à 1912 217
That Greece might still be free: the philhellenes in the War of Independence 146
Le théâtre grec moderne de 1453 à 1900 650
Theatre, Modern
  history 650
Theatre, Shadow puppet 652, 654
Themelis 687
Theodorakis, Mikis 462, 646, 700
Theodossopoulos, C. 600
Theology 354
Theophilos 619
Theophilos 619–620
Theophilos, Kontoglou, Ghika and Tsarouchis: four painters of 20th century Greece 620
Theory and practice of dissolution of parliament: a comparative study with special reference to the United Kingdom and Greek experience 471
Theotokas, George 678, 740
Theses 782–783, 819
  Great Britain 819

219

La Thessalie: analyse géographique d'une province grecque 23
Thessaloniki 22
  American Farm School 562
  Folklore Museum 607
  history 219−220
  industry 543
  Jewish community 251−255
  workers' federation 573
  World War I 165
Thessaly 6, 18, 23−24
  19th century 18
  20th century 18
  cession to Greece, 1881 157
  migration to the cities 227
They remember America: the story of the repatriated Greek-Americans 261
Thiasos, O 651
Third wedding 739
Thompson, K. 40, 549, 553
Thompson, M. S. 247
Thomson, G. 322−323, 719
Thomson, Sir Basil 168
Thrace 6
  folklore 657
  Langada firewalking festival 667
Thrace, Western
  treatment of Muslim minority 246
Thriskeftiki kai ithiki enkyklopaideia 791
Thumb, A. 321
Topography 10, 16
  bibliographies 795, 799
Topping, P. W. 131, 143
Torture
  political prisoners, 1967 455−456, 458−459, 464
Torture in Greece: the first torturers' trial 1975 459
Toulmin, S. 65
Touraille, J. 332
Tourism 5, 7−9, 13, 70, 72, 74−76, 87, 515
  development 71
Town planning
  Hydra 580
  Kalamata 578
Toynbee, A. J. 171
Tozer, H. F. 118
Trade 176

Trade effects of economic association with the Common Market: the case of Greece 525
Trade, Foreign 40, 515
  impact of E.E.C. membership 525
Trade unionism in Greece: a study in political paternalism 572
Trade unions 572
  Australian Greek attitudes 286
Trading
  producer/merchant relationships 395
Tramp shipping 566
Transport 3, 515
Transport, Internal 571
Travel 7−9, 13, 70, 72, 74−76, 87
  bibliographies 795
Travellers' accounts 135
  14th century 45
  15th century 45
  16th century 45
  19th century 46−47, 153
  20th century 50−55, 57, 59−61, 63, 67, 69
  2nd century 73
  Aegean islands 63
  bibliographies 806−807
  Crete 67, 69
  Epirus 55
  Mani peninsula 59
  Peloponnese 47, 60−61
  Roumeli 51
Travellers' accounts, American
  18th century 147
  19th century 147
Travellers' accounts, French
  bibliographies 808−809
Travellers' guide: Crete 81
Traveller's guide to Corfu and the other Ionian islands 82
Traveller's guide to Rhodes 90
Traveller's history of Greece 109
Traveller's journey is done 54
Travelling players 651
Travels in Greece: journey to the Morea 707
Travels in the Morea 47
Travels in northern Greece 46
Travlos, J. 625
Treaty of Association with the E.E.C., 1962 524−527
Treudley, M. B. 279
Triantis, S. G. 524

Trichopoulos, D. 225
Trombetas, T. P. 418, 438
Truman Doctrine
  background 486—487
Trypanis, C. A. 683—684
Tsarouchis, Yannis 619—620
Tsatsopoulos, A. 740
Tsatsos, C. 466
Tsirkas, Stratis 742
Tsoclis, Costas 621
Tsopanakis, A. G. 307
Tsoucalas, C. 123
Tsouderos, J. E. 558
Tsoukalis, L. 523
Tsounis, M. P. 283
Tsourkas, Cl. 293
Tuckerman, C. K. 153
Turkey
  20th century 489, 495, 497
  Cyprus crisis, 1974 492, 494
  impact on NATO membership 420
  invasion of Cyprus 420
  relations with Greece 489, 495, 497
  treatment of Greek minority 246
Turkey in Europe 214
Turkish language 305
Turkish minority
  in Western Thrace 246
Turkish occupation 17, 214
  history 103
  Thasos 217
  Thessaly 18
Turkish War, 1921-22 170—173
Turvey, R. 537
Twelve lays of the Gipsy 721
Twelve lays of the gypsy 719
Twelve words of the gypsy 718, 720
Twentieth Century Fund
  report on conditions in Greece, 1947 206
Two studies on modern Greek folklore 660
Tyciak, J. 331

U

Underdevelopment, Economic 509, 513
Unification of Greece 1770-1923 122
United Nations
  Cyprus dispute 490
  policy concerning Greek Civil War, 1946-49 207
  relations with Greece 490

Universities 599
  problems 597—598
Urbanization 39, 211, 227—230, 232, 234, 366
  (see also Migration, Internal)
  economic impact of 510
  impact on the dowry system 385
  Megara 367
U.S. foreign policy toward Greece and Cyprus: the clash of principle and pragmatism 494
U.S.A.
  20th century 485—488, 491—492, 494, 517—519
  20th century Greek repatriates 261
  aid to Greece 517—519
  assimilation of Greeks 275, 276
  bibliographies 825—826
  career prospects 272
  Greek community 259, 271—272, 275—276, 280—281, 825
  Greek emigrants 258, 260, 262—264, 269, 826
  Greek language in 306
  Greek policy, 1940-49 208
  Greek press 282
  Greek studies 818
  history 258, 260, 262
  involvement in Greek Civil War, 1946-49 487—488
  life and customs 271
  relations with Cyprus 494
  relations with Greece 147, 420, 448, 460—461, 485—488, 491—492, 494
  relations with Greece, 20th century 493
  Wyoming Greek community 269
U.S.A., Anderson, Indiana
  Greek community 273
U.S.A., Carbon County, Utah
  Greek community 268
U.S.A., Chicago
  Greek community 266, 277
  political affiliations 277
U.S.A., Denver
  Greek community 278—279
U.S.A., Detroit
  Greek community 267
U.S.A., New Smyrna, Florida
  Greek community, 18th century 265
U.S.A., San Antonio, Texas
  Greek community 274

U.S.A., Tarpon Springs, Florida
  Greek community 270
*Usos y costumbres de los Sefardies de
  Salonica* 253
U.S.S.R.
  relations with Greece 189, 486

V

Vacalopoulos, A. E. 128, 212, 219
Vafopoulos, G. Th. 687
Vagliano, Stephen 48
Valaoras, V. G. 222, 224−225, 412
Valkaniki vivliographia 796
Valsa, M. 650
Value-added tax - V.A.T. 539
Value systems
  Ottoman rule 405
van Doorn, Jacques 428−429
Varnalis 687
  discographies 829
Vase painting 100
*Vasileion tis Ellados. Ypourgeion
  syntonismou. Rhythmistiki meleti
  anaptyxeos poleos kai periokhis
  Kalamatas* 578
Vasilika 384, 407
  life and customs 373
*Vasilika: a village in modern
  Greece* 373
Vasiliou, Spiros 7
Vassilakis, Maria 6
Vassiliou, G. 389, 402
Vassiliou, V. G. 389, 402
V.A.T. - value-added tax 539
Vaternelle, R. 40
Vatikiotis, P. J. 161
Vegetables
  history 561
Veloukhiotis, Ares 188
Venetian rule 130
Venezis, Ilias 743, 744
Venice
  conquest of the Peloponnese,
    1684-87 27
  rule over Aegean islands, 15th
    century 130
Venizelos, Eleftherios 66, 163−164,
    167, 169, 422
*Venizelos: patriot, statesman,
  revolutionary* 163
Veremis, T. 423, 496
Vermeule, E. 96

*Victoria and Albert Museum: a guide
  to Greek island embroidery* 633
Views of Attica 56
Villa Ariadne 68
Village communities 211
Village life 5
La ville convoitée: Salonique 220
*Villes et paysages de Grèce: Athènes et
  ses monuments du xviie siècle à
  nos jours* 77
*Viomikhanikos atlas tis Ellados:
  apographia 1963. Industrial atlas
  of Greece: census of 1963. Atlas
  industriel de la Grèce:
  recensement de 1963* 41
Visiting patterns 400
Visvizi-Dontas, D. 124
Vital statistics 40
  20th century 222−223
  history 222−223
*Vivliographia ton ellinikon
  vivliographion 1791-1947* 792
Vivliographiki Etaireia tis Ellados 793
*Vivliothikes kai arkheia stin Ellada:
  symvoli sti meleti tis pnevmatikis
  istorias tou neou Ellinismou* 810
Vlachos, Evangelos C. 239, 273, 510,
    816, 826
Vlachos, Helen 758
Vlachs 249−250
  architecture 247
  folklore 247
  history 247
  language 247
  life and customs 247−248
Vlassis, G. D. 289
*Vocabulary of modern spoken
  Greek* 313
Vocational education
  reorganization 590
Vodoz, J. 564
*Vokalismus der griechischen
  Lehnwörter im Türkischen* 305
von Ivanka, E. 331
Vooys, A. C. de 24, 26
Voros, F. K. 590
Voulgaris, Pandelis 651
Vouras, P. P. 515
*Le voyage de Grèce: bibliographie des
  voyageurs français en Grèce au
  XXe siècle, 1900-1968* 809
Voyages
  bibliographies 806−807

Voyages and travels in Greece, the Near East and adjacent regions made previous to the year 1801, being part of a larger catalogue of works on geography, cartography, voyages and travels, in the Gennadius Library in Athens 806
Voyages and travels in the Near East made during the XIX century. Being a part of a larger catalogue of works on geography, cartography, voyages and travels, in the Gennadius Library in Athens 807
Voyageurs français en Grèce au XIXe siècle 808
Vrettakos 687
Vryonis, S. 132

W

Wace, A. J. B. 247, 631
Wages
 20th century 555
 agricultural labourers 555
Wagstaff, J. M. 18, 20, 27−30, 627
Walcot, P. 377
Walker, E. 198
Walton, F. R. 746−747
War and post-war Greece: an analysis based on Greek writings 183
War in the Aegean 198
War of Independence, 1821-27 27
 bibliographies 143, 821
 British policy 141
 cultural background 133
 foreign loans 482
 historical background 139, 143
 history 140, 142
 impact on Cyprus 149
 impact on the Orthodox Church 337
 literature 821
 novels 690
 paintings commissioned by General Makriyannis 610−611
 personal accounts 144−145

War of Independence in pictures: copies by Demetrios Zographos from originals by his father Panayiotis Zographos commissioned by General Makriyannis and presented to Her Majesty Queen Victoria through her minister at Athens Sir Edmund Lyons 1839 611
Warburton, I. P. 300
Ward, B. 19
Ware, T. 328, 335
Warner, R. 56, 691, 734
Waters of Marah: the present state of the Greek church 338
We fell among Greeks 193
Weaving 629, 634−635
Web of modern Greek politics 416
Webb, Graham 462
Weber, S. H. 806−807
Weintraub, D. 556
Weitz, Raanan 557
Welfare services 4, 408−409
Wellesz, E. 638
Westebbe, R. M. 519, 529−530
Western question in Greece and Turkey: a study in the contact of civilisations 171
Wheeler, M. 450
When Greek meets Greek 197
Widener Library, Harvard University 811
Wiertz, P. 331
Wild greens - horta 561
Wildman, C. 706
Wilkinson, H. R. 38
Will, F. 718
Wilson, Andrew 495, 497
Wilson, Henry Maitland, baron 198
Winds of Crete 69
Windsor Castle
 paintings of the War of Independence, 1821-27 611
Witchcraft 398
Women
 educational reform, 1976-77 595
 feminism 403
 illiteracy 595
 industrialization 367
 regional costumes 668
 village life 369
Wood-Ritsatakis, A. 408
Woodcarving 629
Woodhouse, C. M. 15, 119, 142, 146, 148, 150, 181−182

223

Workers' federations 572
Works of art in Greece, the Greek islands and the Dodecanese: losses and survivals in the war 609
World of Odysseus 106
World War I
  bibliographies 795
  Gallipoli campaign 166
  Greek policy 164
  intelligence activities 166−169
  labour movements 575
  Macedonian campaign, 1915-18 165
  novels 715
  personal accounts 166−169
  Salonika front, 1915-18 165
  socialist movements 575
World War II 201
  art losses and survivals 609
  Axis occupation 182−183
  bibliographies 795, 823−824
  British policy 189−190, 197
  Crete 195
  Crete campaign, 1941 186−187
  destruction of the Jewish community 255−256
  Dodecanese campaign, 1943 198
  famine 224
  German occupation 199
  German occupation of Chios, 1941-44 216
  Greek resistance 181, 188, 190−193, 195−196
  inflation 534
  Italian and German invasions, 1940-41 179, 184−186
  kidnapping of General Kreipe 194
  monetary policy 534
  novels 742
  Special Operations Executive S.O.E. 196
  village life 5
Wrong horse: the politics of intervention and the failure of American diplomacy 492

X

Xanthakis, N. 519
Xanthopoulides, G. 722
Xenakis, Yannis 644
Xydis, S. G. 125, 199, 453, 486−487

Y

Yachting
  Aegean 88−89
  Ionian 89
Yannakakis, I. 435
Yannaras, C. 341
Yannina
  urbanization 229
Yannopoulos, G. N. 445, 526−527
Yeracaris, C. A. 364
Yithion 30
Young, M. 82
Yugoslavia
  20th century 489
  claims to Macedonia 498−499
  relations with Greece 489

Z

Zagori
  migration to the cities 229
Zakhos-Papazahariou, E. 309
Zakynthos
  guide books 83
Zakythinos, D. A. 129
Zante
  guide books 83
Zepos, P. J. 473−474
Zervos, C. 622
Zographos, Demetrios 611
Zographos, Panayiotis 611
Zoi - religious brotherhood 340
Zolotas, X. 235, 535
Zora, P. 608
Zorba the Greek 651, 706
Zwischen Konstantinopel und Moskau: orthodoxe Kirchenpolitik im Nahen Osten 1967-1975 343

Map of Greece
This map shows the more important towns and other features.

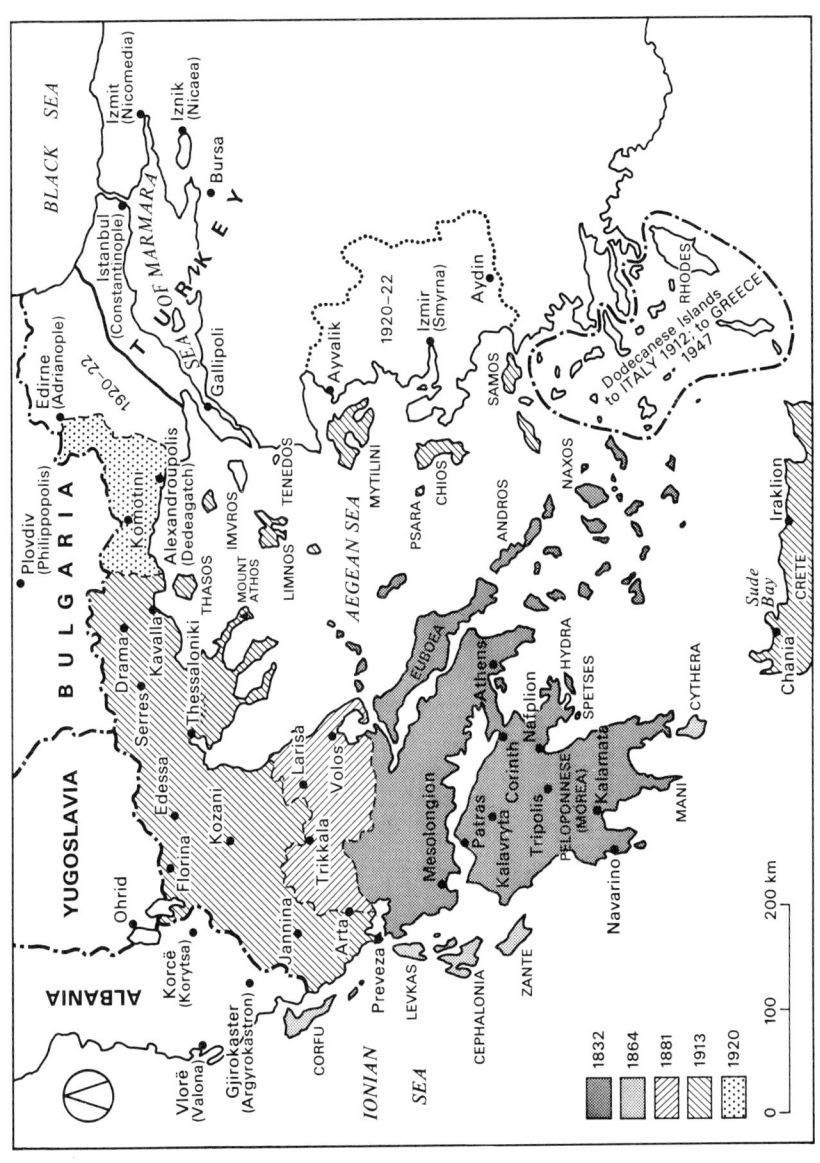

Ref Z 2281 .C58 1980
Clogg, Mary Jo.
Greece

APR 1 9 1985